HELLENISTIC

POETRY

HELLENISTIC

POETRY

An Anthology

Selected and translated by

BARBARA HUGHES FOWLER

THE UNIVERSITY OF WISCONSIN PRESS

The University of Wisconsin Press
114 North Murray Street
Madison, Wisconsin 53715

3 Henrietta Street
London WC2E 8LU, England

Library of Congress Cataloging-in-Publication Data
Hellenistic poetry: an anthology / selected and translated by Barbara
    Hughes Fowler.
    378 pp.   cm.
        1. Greek poetry, Hellenistic—Translations into English.
    2. English poetry—Translations from Greek (Hellenistic)
    I. Fowler, Barbara Hughes, 1926–
    PA3622.F69   1990
    881'.0108 — dc20   90-50087
    ISBN 0-299-12530-0   CIP
    ISBN 0-299-12534-3 (pbk.)

To B.J.H.
for her faith

CONTENTS

HERODAS

ARATUS

MOSCHUS

BION

PSEUDO-MOSCHUS

FROM *THE GREEK ANTHOLOGY*

CONTENTS

A Technopaignion

PREFACE

I HAVE CHOSEN to include in this volume works that are reasonably complete and self-contained enough in content to be readily comprehensible to the Greekless undergraduate and general public, for whom this book is intended. I have not, therefore, included fragments from Powell's *Collectanea Alexandrina,* Page's *Select Papyri III: Poetry,* or Lloyd-Jones' and Parsons' *Supplementum Hellenisticum,* nor have I included those poems or pieces of poems that deal with the obscure and even disputed literary influences and quarrels of their time. I assume that serious scholars concerned with such matters will not need translations of those works and will know where to go for commentary upon them. I intend my Glossary of Proper Names, which contains the names of the poets included in this volume, to serve as minimal notes upon the poems I present.

By Hellenistic I mean in general the period of time between the death of Alexander in 323 B.C. and the death of Augustus in A.D. 14. A few of the epigrammatists in this volume are probably later in date than that, but I thought them Hellenistic enough in spirit to be included in this collection.

I should like particularly to thank my research assistant, Jennifer Smith, who prepared the glossary entries for the *Argonautica* and who checked all my translations against the texts and so saved me from several errors; Kathryn Chapin, who, meticulously, prepared the maps for the *Argonautica;* Ruth Melville, who with sensitivity and discretion edited the manuscript; Norma Maynard, our departmental secretary, who with infinite patience prepared on her word processor version after version of this manuscript; and, above all, Barbara Hanrahan of the University of Wisconsin Press, who, beneficently, believed from the beginning in this project.

Madison, 1989

INTRODUCTION

I

HELLENISTIC POETRY is distinguished by variety of genre, range of mood, novelty of subject, and display of technique. Its inspiration was manifold. The campaigns of Alexander brought the Greeks, never insular, into contact with ever more exotic peoples, with unfamiliar flora and fauna, with the philosophies and science of southeast Asia. Just as Greek goldsmiths took their techniques from Macedonia east to the Crimea and west to the Pillars of Hercules, so these same artists used new animal motifs from Persia and India—antelopes and elephants—to fashion the elegant jewelry of their day. Indeed, these rings, bracelets, necklaces, pendants, earrings, breast and hair ornaments might well be taken as symbols of the delicacy of workmanship and intricacy of influences in Hellenistic poetry.[1]

Pella, Alexander's capital in Macedonia, had even before his time become an important cultural center. After his death and the division of his empire into the Antigonid, Seleucid, Attalid, and Ptolemaic kingdoms, Delos, Cos, Rhodes, Cyprus, Pergamum, Magnesia, Ephesus, and particularly Alexandria became new centers of art and learning.

No longer secure in the comparatively self-contained city-state, the educated people of the Hellenistic metropolis turned away from the absolute values of Plato and Aristotle and comforted themselves in their more fluid society with the individualistic philosophies of Stoicism and Epicureanism. Drama, epic, and rhetoric continued to flourish, but what has, perhaps not entirely accidentally, come down to us are not tragedies of universal man or comedies and orations of political import but pastoral, an entirely new and fanciful genre; epyllia and hymns that are in large part burlesque; aitiological poems of quaint and antiquarian interest; a short epic of an entirely new romantic cast; an astronomical poem with a meteorological appendix;

---

1. I have given elsewhere a fuller account of the Hellenistic sensibility: *The Hellenistic Aesthetic* (Madison, 1989).

and hundreds of highly polished epigrams, funereal, amatory, and dedicatory in content, witty or pathetic in mood.

Just as the philosophers turned to systems that would provide intelligent people a means of achieving a worthwhile and satisfactory life in this present world, so artists turned from the expression of universal truths to that of the particular passions. Quite new in the history of Western literature are the sensitive descriptions of heterosexual love; the sense of sinning; the pathos of the death of young women before marriage or in childbirth, of children dead in infancy, of young men dead before their parents, of the very old. New too, accordingly, is the sympathetic treatment of women, children, babies, and pets, of cities and the ordinary people who inhabit them; the delight in what is tiny—butterflies, mosquitoes, mice—and what is enormous—the Cyclopes and other giants; the increased attraction of faraway peoples and places.

At Alexandria the Museum provided poets with access not only to the great library and all its antiquarian lore but to a medical school that specialized in anatomy, apparently discovered the nervous system, and made significant advances in ophthalmology. The new science of optics, which was almost entirely geometric in method, influenced architects and architectural and landscape painters and, directly or indirectly, the poets of the period as well. A zoo and processions of exotic animals inspired poets and artists alike. Geographers, mapmakers, and astronomers all contributed to the new poetic. We see the influence of all three in the *Argonautica* of Apollonius of Rhodes, and Aratus' *Phaenomena* is really a textbook of astronomy. Magic, heretofore a submerged aspect of Greek culture, plays a significant role in the works of Theocritus and Apollonius. Astrology too may have helped to shape Apollonius' epic.[2]

The visual arts—jewelry, mosaics, sculpture, and painting—seem also to have had a profound influence upon Hellenistic poetry, although the influence must have been in part mutual. We see the mark of sculpture in the description of giants in the first book of the *Argonautica* and of Jason's contest with the bulls and the earth-born in Book III, and the effect of painting in the marvelous land- and seascapes throughout the poem. Besides the magnificence of the baroque, we find in Hellenistic poetry a taste for the rococo in the emphasis on children and pets. Closely allied with both the baroque and the rococo is a new predilection for the grotesque and the burlesque.

---

2. P. L. P. Bogue, "Astronomy in the *Argonautica* of Apollonius Rhodius" (Ph.D. diss., University of Illinois, Urbana, 1977).

Just as the artists of the period refined their techniques in sculpture, paint-
ing, mosaics, and jewelry, so the poets refined their versification and made the
musicality of their lines a mark of Hellenistic poetry. They made artificial use
of the Doric dialect, attracted apparently by its broad echoing vowels. They
wrought a number of subtle changes in the dactylic hexameter, the meter of
Homer, and Apollonius made such sophisticated use of polysyllabic words that
he could compose a six-foot line with only four words. One can compare this
technical virtuosity with the ability of the artists of the period to portray with
ever increasing success a third dimension in sculpture and painting, with the
delicate enameling and filigree work of the jewelers, with the sparkling tech-
nique of the mosaicists.

II

I have chosen to translate for this collection those Hellenistic poems that
I think especially appealing and at the same time most representative of the va-
riety of genres, moods, themes, and styles of the period.

Theocritus' *Idyll I* established the convention of the pastoral as a mask
for grief and inspired certain of Virgil's *Eclogues,* Milton's "Lycidas," Shelley's
"Adonais," Yeats' "Shepherd and Goatherd," and initiated the whole of the
Western pastoral tradition. *Idyll II* gives us an astonishing glimpse of a sub-
culture: the rites Simaetha performs to win back — or to destroy — her faithless
lover are attested in the magic papyri of the period. *Idylls VI* and *XI,* which
tell of the Cyclops in love, are delightful examples of the Hellenistic fascina-
tion with both the burlesque and the grotesque. *Idyll VII* is remarkable for its
sensuous description of the late summer and *XIII* for the tenderness of Heracles'
love for Hylas. *Idyll XXIV* begins with a humorous mock-heroic account of
the baby Heracles' strangling of the snakes and ends with a detailed descrip-
tion of his *paideia,* his education — always a favorite subject of the Greeks. *Idyll
XV* gives us a shrewd and comical view of two young matrons who, after
complaining about their husbands, venture forth into the noisy streets of Alex-
andria to attend at King Ptolemy's palace a festival of the Dying Adonis. It is
our only contemporary description of that city in the third century B.C. and
one of the few accounts of city life in Hellenistic literature. The poets may have
lived in the city, but they preferred to write, fancifully or realistically, about
the country.

From Callimachus I have chosen the four *Hymns* that I think will most appeal to a modern audience. The *Hymn to Artemis* contains a charming burlesque of the goddess as a little girl and so represents also the Alexandrian taste for the rococo. We do not know whether these poems were written for actual occasions, but the *Hymn to Apollo* and *On the Bath of Pallas* are musically marked by ritual refrains, and the latter is entertaining too for the story it tells. The *Hymn to Demeter* is another sophisticated example of the burlesque. The epigrams and the fragments from the *Hecale* and the *Galatea* that I have included are simply those that I like best. The fragments do, however, exemplify the ability of the Alexandrians to evoke the sweetness of nature. *The Mousetrap,* a fragment of a longer work, perhaps the *Victoria Berenices,* reflects the Alexandrian taste for the tiny and the commonplace.

I have included the whole of the *Argonautica* because I think that it will in its entirety appeal to a modern audience. The subtle psychological analyses of Medea in love and remorse, of Jason as a leader given to temporary bouts of doubt and despair: the anthropological observation of exotic peoples; the cartographer's description of sea courses and coastlines; the accounts of real magic; the presentation of iridescent landscapes; the thematic use of color: the red-gold glow of the fleece, the scarlet of woven garments, the rosy blushes of Eros and Medea; the burlesque of goddesses; the baroque descriptions of giants, writhing serpents, and perils at sea; the surreal atmosphere of the visit to the Syrtes—all this as well as the narrative itself will, I believe, surprise and enchant the contemporary reader.

Aratus' Weather Signs from his *Phaenomena* were the inspiration for certain passages of Virgil's *Georgics,* and his Proem is deliberately reminiscent of Hesiod's *Works and Days* but is important also because of its Stoic overtones. I have translated Aratus, however, chiefly for his own sake. His sometimes awkward Greek and his particularized observation of creatures and meteorological phenomena contribute to a naive charm that I find irresistible. The *Mimes* of Herodas give us an entertaining glimpse of middle- or lower-class life in a city, perhaps Cos, which has its parallel in Theocritus' *Idyll XV.*

Moschus' *Europa* is another mock-epic which combines deliberately clumsy grotesquerie with true Alexandrian prettiness. Bion's *Lament for Adonis* and Pseudo-Moschus' *Lament for Bion* are later versions of the pastoral; they have gone beyond Theocritean sensuousness to a startling sensuality.

From *The Greek Anthology* I have selected epigrams from the three major Hellenistic categories: the epitaphs, real or imaginary, for the dead; the dedicatory epigrams, which give us such a revealing view of the work and play of the men, women, and children of the era; and the amatory epigrams, which, for obvious reasons, charm us all.

Finally, I have included one of the *technopaignia,* the puzzle-poems of the period. These, like the emblematic poems of the English metaphysical poets of the seventeenth century, took on the page the shape of the subject of the poem: an axe, an egg, altars, shepherd's pipes. One of them has to be read in alternate lines, from the top down and from the bottom up. Another is so filled with wordplay that it is impossible really to translate. The one I have chosen, *Wings,* is less complicated. It is written about Eros and is in the shape of his wings; it was perhaps inscribed upon a votive statue representing him as a bearded child.

III

I have for the most part translated the dactylic hexameter, the meter of the great majority of these poems, with a six-beat basically iambic line, but to prevent that line from breaking in two, to add variety, and often to make sound match sense I have used a heavy admixture of anapests, trochees, tribrachs, and syncopated feet. In a very few instances involving proper names (e.g., Telephaasa) I have allowed a hypermetric syllable. In some cases, particularly where the content seemed lighter, I have used a five-beat line, and I have done the elegiac couplets of Callimachus' *Bath of Pallas* and the "limping" iambics of Herodas in the same meter. I did the fragments and epigrams of Callimachus in whatever meter came to mind. The other epigrams from the *Greek Anthology* I did in alternating six- and five-beat lines to give the effect on the page of the elegiac couplet.

I have not been consistent in my transliteration of Greek names—I can bring myself to write neither Core nor Lykians—but my general principle has been to use the conventional Latinized-Anglicized version of familiar names and sometimes to preserve the Greek spelling for more obscure or fictional persons, as in the names of some of the characters in Herodas' *Mimes.*

I have used the following texts: A. S. F. Gow, *Theocritus,* 2 vols. (Cambridge, 1965); R. Pfeiffer, *Callimachus,* 2 vols. (Oxford 1949, reprinted 1965); H. Fraenkel, *Apollonii Rhodii Argonautica* (Oxford, 1961, reprinted 1964, 1967); A. S. F. Gow, *Bucolici Graeci* (Oxford, 1952, reprinted 1962, 1966); I. C. Cunningham, *Herodas Mimiambi* (Oxford, 1971); J. Martin, *Arati Phaenomena* (Florence, 1956); A. S. F. Gow and D. L. Page, *The Greek Anthology: Hellenistic Epigrams,* 2 vols. (Cambridge, 1965); A. S. F. Gow and D. L. Page, *The Garland of Philip,* 2 vols. (Cambridge, 1968). For Rufinus, I used W. R. Paton, *The Greek Anthology* (London and Cambridge, Mass., 1960).

THEOCRITUS

Idyll 1

Thyrsis

TITYRUS: Sweet is the whispering of that pine tree, goatherd,
    making music beside the spring, and sweet too
    is the sound of your piping. After Pan you will take
    the second prize. If he takes the horned goat,
    you will get the she-goat. If he takes
    the she-goat for his prize, the kid will fall to you.
    The flesh of a kid is very nice before she's milked.

GOATHERD: More sweet, O shepherd, is your song than the water that
            tumbles
    and splashes there from the rock above. If the Muses take
    the ewe, you shall have the stall-fed lamb for your prize.
    If they choose the lamb, you'll later get the ewe.

TITYRUS: Please, in the name of the nymphs, O goatherd, please, sit here
    beside this sloping knoll and shrubs of tamarisk
    and pipe, and I shall meanwhile pasture your goats.

GOATHERD: O shepherd, we may not at noon, we may not pipe for fear
    of Pan, for he is resting then and weary from
    the hunt. His temper is bitter, and acrid wrath sits ever
    at his nostril. But you, Thyrsis, often sing
    the sorrows of Daphnis, and you have mastered the pastoral
            song.

    Come let us sit beneath this elm, facing Priapus
    and the springs, the shepherds' seat, and the oaks, and if you
            sing
    as once you sang, contesting with Chromis of Libya,
    I'll give you to milk three times a goat that has just borne
            twins,
    who though she has two kids, gives two pails besides,
    and a deep cup washed over to coat with sweet wax,

two-handled, freshly carved, and fragrant yet from the knife.
Ivy winds around above its lip, ivy
dusted with clusters of gold. Along it trails the tendril,
all aglow with its yellow fruit. Inside a woman
like a wondrous creation of gods is carved. She wears a headband
and cloak. Beside her two men with fair long hair
contend with one another from either side with words,
but this doesn't touch her heart, for now she looks at one
and smiles, and now she casts her thought to the other, while they,
long hollow-eyed from love, struggle to no avail.
Next to them is carved an old fisherman
and a rugged rock upon which the ancient man
struggles to draw up a great net to make
a cast. He is like a man who labors mightily.
You would say that he was fishing with all the force
of his limbs. So do the sinews swell all about
his neck, though his hair is white; he has the strength of youth.
Not far from the ancient sea-worn man there is a vineyard,
beautifully weighted with darkening clusters. A little boy
sits on a dry-stone wall and guards it. Two foxes
skulk about. One roams up and down the rows
and plunders the vines of the ripe grapes. The other plots
against his purse and says she'll never let him go
until she's got his breakfast bread. But the boy plaits
a pretty cricket cage with rush and asphodel
and cares less for his pouch or for the vine rows
than he takes joy in his plaiting. Everywhere
about the cup the pliant acanthus spreads, a marvel
to goatherds and a wonder to strike your heart too.
I paid the ferryman of Calydna a goat for it
and a big cheese of white milk, but never yet
has it touched my lips. It lies immaculate still. I'll give
you gladly the pleasure of it, my friend, if you will sing
that lovely song, nor do I mock you at all. Come,
my good man, for surely you never can keep your song
down there in Hades that brings oblivion of all.

Thyrsis: Begin, dear Muses, now begin the pastoral song.

Thyrsis of Aetna am I, and the voice of Thyrsis is sweet.
Where were you when Daphnis was wasting, where were you,
    Nymphs?
In the lovely valleys of Pindus or of Peneius? For surely
you did not keep the mighty stream of the river Anapus
nor the rocky peak of Aetna nor Acis' sacred water.

Begin, dear Muses, now begin the pastoral song.

For him the jackals howled, for him the wolves, for him
when he died even the lion came out of the forest and wept.

Begin, dear Muses, now begin the pastoral song.

Many cows about his feet and many bulls,
many heifers and many calves lamented him.

Begin, dear Muses, now begin the pastoral song.

Hermes, first, came from the mountain and said, "Daphnis,
who tortures you? With whom, my friend, are you so in love?"

Begin, dear Muses, now begin the pastoral song.

The cowherds came, the shepherds came, and the goatherds.
All asked what his sorrow was. Priapus came and said,
"Pitiable Daphnis, why do you pine? For you the girl
roams past all the fountains, wanders through every grove—

Begin, dear Muses, now begin the pastoral song.

"searching. Unlucky in love and truly distraught are you.
You were called a cowherd, but now you resemble the goatherd,
for the goatherd, when he sees how the nannies are mounted, cries
his eyes out that he was not born a billy goat.

Begin, dear Muses, now begin the pastoral song.

"And you, when you see the girls and how they laugh, then you
cry your eyes out that you're not dancing with them."

To these the cowherd made no reply but bore
his bitter love, bore it until his fated end.

Begin, dear Muses, now begin the pastoral song.

Even Cypris came with a sweet smile, a secret smile,
and holding back her heavy wrath, she spoke and said,
"Surely, Daphnis, you vowed that you'd give Love a fall,
but now haven't you yourself been thrown by heartless Love?"

Begin, dear Muses, now begin the pastoral song.

Daphnis at last made answer to her. "Angry Cypris,
vindictive Cypris, Cypris hateful to mortal men,
do you think, then, that my every sun is already set?
Even in Hades Daphnis will be a grief to Love.

Begin, dear Muses, now begin the pastoral song.

"Do they not say of Cypris the 'cowherd . . .'? Go
to Anchises, to Ida. There are oaks there and galingale
and there the bees are humming sweetly about the hives.

Begin, dear Muses, now begin the pastoral song.

"Even Adonis is in his bloom. He pastures sheep,
he shoots hares, and chases beasts of every kind.

Begin, O Muses, begin again the pastoral song.

"Go take your stand again before Diomedes and say,
'I vanquish Daphnis the cowherd: now fight with me.'

Begin, O Muses, begin again the pastoral song.

"O wolves, O jackals, O bears that dwell in your mountain caves,
good-bye. Daphnis the cowherd will no longer come
to your woods, your oak thickets, your groves. Good-bye,
    Arethusa,
and all you rivers that pour down Thybris your lovely waters.

Begin, O Muses, begin again the pastoral song.

"I am that Daphnis who pastured here his herds of cows.
Daphnis am I who watered here his bulls and his calves.

Begin, O Muses, begin again the pastoral song.

"O Pan, Pan, whether you roam the Lycaean range
or walk on mighty Maenalus, come to Sicily's isle,
leaving Helice's peak and the steep tomb of the son
of Lycaon that brings delight to even the Blessed Ones.

O Muses, cease, come cease from the pastoral song.

"Come, O lord, and take this pipe, fragrant from honey's
compacted wax and bound about its lovely lip,
for I am drawn down to Hades now by Love.

"Bear violets now, O brambles, bear violets, thorns, and let
the lovely narcissus bloom on juniper trees. Let all
be opposite of all, and let the pine bear pears
since Daphnis is dying. Let the stag drag the hounds.
From mountain tops let owls sing to nightingales."

O Muses, cease, come cease from the pastoral song.

So much he said and stopped, and Aphrodite wanted
to raise him up again, but all the thread from the Fates
was run, and Daphnis went to the stream. The eddies washed
        over
him whom the Muses loved and the Nymphs did not dislike.

O Muses, cease, come cease from the pastoral song.

Now you must give me the goat and the bowl that I may milk
        her
and make libation to the Muses. Good-bye, Muses,
Good-bye. Another time I'll sing you a sweeter song.

GOATHERD: May your lovely mouth be filled with honey, Thyrsis, filled
with the honeycomb. May you eat the sweet figs of Aegilus,
for you surpass the cicada in song. Here is the cup.
See how sweetly it smells. You'll think that it's been washed
at the Springs of the Hours. Come here, Cissaetha. Now milk
        her. Nannies,
don't be so skittish — the billy goat will be aroused.

7

Idyll II
The Sorceress

Where is my bay? Bring it, Thestylis. Where are my charms?
Wreathe the bowl with a sheep's fine crimson fleece that I
may bind that man, my love who is so cruel to me.
This is the twelfth day since the wretch has come to me.
He doesn't know whether I live or if I'm dead,
nor has he knocked at my door—he is so hard. Surely
Aphrodite and Love have taken elsewhere his fickle wits.
I'll go to see him at Timagetus' wrestling school
tomorrow and scold him for treating me so. But now I'll bind
him with fire-spells. Shine brightly, Moon, for I shall sing
softly to you, goddess, and to Hecate
of the world below. Even dogs shudder when she
comes over the black blood and the tombs of the dead. Hail,
O horrid Hecate, and attend me to the end.
Make these drugs of mine more dire than those of Circe,
or even than those of Medea or those of blond Perimede.

Draw to my house, my magic wheel, that man of mine.

First, barley melts in the fire. Strew it on,
Thestylis. You fool, where have your wits flown?
Am I a jest, you abominable girl, even to you?
Strew it on and say, "The bones of Delphis I strew."

Draw to my house, my magic wheel, that man of mine.

Delphis pained me, and I for Delphis burn this bay.
As these leaves crackle loud in the fire and suddenly catch,
and we can see not even the ashes of them, so
may the flesh of Delphis too diminish and melt in the flame.

Draw to my house, my magic wheel, that man of mine.

Now I shall burn the bran. Artemis, you who could move
Hades' adamant and anything else as strong—
Thestylis, the dogs are howling throughout the town.
The goddess is at the crossroads. Quick! Sound the bronze!

Draw to my house, my magic wheel, that man of mine.

Look, the sea is still, and the breezes too are still,
but the pain within my breast is not at all still,
for I am all aflame for him who has made me
not a wife but a miserable thing—no virgin now.

Draw to my house, my magic wheel, that man of mine.

Now just as I with the goddess's help melt this wax,
so straightway may Delphis of Myndus melt with love,
and just as Aphrodite turns this brazen rhomb,
so may Delphis also turn about my door.

Draw to my house, my magic wheel, that man of mine.

Three times I make libation, Lady, and three times
I cry, "Whether a woman lies with him now or a man
may he forget them as once they say Theseus
in Dia forgot Ariadne of the lovely hair."

Draw to my house, my magic wheel, that man of mine.

Coltsfoot's a weed that grows in Arcadia. For it all
the foals run mad on the hills and all the swift mares,
and so may I see Delphis, and may he come to this house,
like a creature gone mad, from that sleek and splendid wrestling school.

Draw to my house, my magic wheel, that man of mine.

Delphis lost this fringe from his cloak. I pluck it now.
I cast it into the savage flame. O tormenting Love,
why do you drink all the black blood from my flesh,
clinging fast to me like some sucking leech from the swamp?

Draw to my house, my magic wheel, that man of mine.

I'll powder a lizard and bring him tomorrow an evil brew.
Now, Thestylis, take these magic herbs and knead them upon
his doorstep during the dark of night, and, whispering, say,
"These are the bones of Delphis. The bones of Delphis I knead."

Now that I am alone, how shall I lament
my love? Where shall I begin? Who brought this trouble
on me? Our Anaxo, Eubulus' daughter, carried a basket
to Artemis' grove. For the goddess that day many wild beasts
paraded about her. Among them went a lioness.

Tell me, my Lady Moon, from where did my love come?

Theumaridas' Thracian nurse, now dead, who lived next door,
begged and beseeched me to go and see the Procession. And I,
unhappily, went. I wore a lovely linen dress
with Clearista's delicate cloak thrown over it.

Tell me, my Lady Moon, from where did my love come?

When I had come halfway along the road, at Lycon's,
I saw Delphis and Eudamippus walking together.
Their beards were more golden than helichryse to see
and their breasts more gleaming by far than even you, O Moon,
for they had just left the lovely toil of the wrestling school.

Tell me, my Lady Moon, from where did my love come?

When I saw them both, I went mad. My wretched heart
was set on fire. My beauty wasted away. No longer
could I bear to look at that show. Nor do I know how I
got home again. Some scorching fever shook me,
and I lay on my bed for ten days and ten nights.

Tell me, my Lady Moon, from where did my love come?

Often my skin turned as yellow as fustic dye,
all my hair was falling out of my head, and only
bones were left of me and skin. To whose house,
what hag, mumbling her magic charms, did I not go?
For it was no light matter and time was running out.

Tell me, my Lady Moon, from where did my love come?

And so I told my slave the truth. "Thestylis,
find me some cure for this painful disease. That Myndian boy
completely possesses me. Go and keep watch
at Timagetus' wrestling school, for he is always
going there and that is where he loves to sit.

Tell me, my Lady Moon, from where did my love come?

"And when you know he's alone, nod to him silently
and say, 'Simaetha summons you,' and bring him here."
So I spoke and she went and brought back to my house
Delphis, his skin still so sleekly oiled, and I
the moment I saw him crossing my threshold with nimble foot—

Tell me, my Lady Moon, from where did my love come?

turned colder all over than winter snow and from my brow
the sweat, just like the damp dews, kept streaming down,
nor could I say a word, not even so much as babes
when they whimper in sleep and call out for their dear mothers,
but all my lovely flesh became as stiff as a doll's.

Tell me, my Lady Moon, from where did my love come?

With a glance at me the heartless boy fixed his eyes
upon the ground. He sat on the couch and, sitting, he said,
"Truly, Simaetha, you outran my arrival by only
as much as recently I outran the charming Philinus
when you sent a summons to me to come here to your house.

Tell me, my Lady Moon, from where did my love come?

"For I would have come, yes, by sweet Love, I would
have come, with two friends, or three, just at dark
carrying in my cloak the apples of Dionysus
and on my brow the white poplar, holy plant
of Heracles, twined around with crimson bands.

Tell me, my Lady Moon, from where did my love come?

"And if you had welcomed me, that would have been sweet,
for I am called agile and comely among all
the young men, and I'd have slept if only I'd kissed
your lips. But if you'd thrust me out and bolted the door,
truly torches and axes had come against you.

Tell me, my Lady Moon, from where did my love come?

"But I owe thanks, I swear, to Cypris first of all
and after Cypris you, secondly, rescued me
from the flame, my girl, calling me here to this house of yours,
half-burned like this. Love often kindles a flame more blazing
than that Hephaestus lights on the isle of Lipara.

Tell me, my Lady Moon, from where did my love come?

"With black madness he frightens the virgin girl from her room
and the bride to leave her husband's bed before it's cold."
That is what he said, and I, too easily won,
took his hand and drew him down to the soft couch.
And soon flesh ripened to flesh and both our faces
were warmer than before and we were whispering sweetly
and—not to babble on, dear Moon—soon
all was done and we two fulfilled our desire.
He had no fault to find with me till yesterday
nor I with him. But today there came to me the mother
of Philista our flute-girl and Melixo, when her steeds
were bringing rosy Dawn from ocean up to sky.
She told me many other things and how Delphis
was in love. Whether his desire was for a man
or woman she said she could not say but only this:
he toasted Love in unmixed wine and at last he went
tearing off, swearing he'd bury that house in wreaths.
Such were the things my visitor told me and she is right,
for truly at other times he'd come to me three
and four times and often he'd leave his Dorian leather
oil flask with me. But this is the twelfth day
that I've not seen him. Mustn't he have some other joy

and have forgotten me? Now I shall bind him with spells,
but if he pains me still, by the Fates, he shall rattle
Hades' gates—such wicked drugs I keep for him
in my box, learned, my Mistress, from an Assyrian man.
But good-bye, my Lady, turn your steeds again toward Ocean.
I shall bear my longing just as I have before.
Good-bye, Moon of the gleaming throne, and now good-bye
you other stars that follow the car of quiet night.

Damoetas and Daphnis

Damoetas and Daphnis the cowherd once drove
their flocks to a single place, Aratus. The beard
of one was red, the other's half-grown. Beside
a spring on a summer's day at noon they sat
and sang. Daphnis began since his was the challenge:

DAPHNIS

"Polyphemus, Galatea with apples pelts your flocks
and calls you cursed in love and a goatherd man,
and you don't look at her, you wretch, but sit
and sweetly pipe. But, see, again she pelts
the bitch that guards your sheep and looks to sea
and barks—the lovely waves that splash upon
the sands reflect her as she runs along
the beach. Don't let her lunge at the girl's legs
as she comes from the sea or tear her lovely flesh.
From there she flirts with you. As from the thorn
the thistledown in parching summertime,
she flees who loves and loves who loves her not
and moves her counter from the line. Often,
Polyphemus, foul to a lover seems very fair."

Damoetas began to play to him and sang.

DAMOETAS

"I saw her, by Pan, when she was pelting my flock.
With my one sweet eye I saw her, my only eye,
with which may I see forever to the end.

(May Telemus the seer who sings of evil for me
keep it for his house, his children, his own!)
I don't look at her. I'm teasing her.
I say I've got another girl. She hears.
She's jealous, she wastes away, and from the sea
she peeps, stung by love, at my flocks and caves.
I hiss at my dog to bark at her, for when
I fell in love it nuzzled her and whined.
Perhaps when she sees me doing this she'll send
a messenger. But I'll lock the doors until
she swears she'll spread her bed on this isle with me,
because I'm not so ugly as they say.
Lately I looked in the sea — there was a calm —
and my beard was fair and so was my single eye,
or so it seemed to me, and my teeth shone
with beams whiter than those of the Parian stone.
Lest I be bewitched, three times I've spat
inside my cloak as the hag Cotyttaris taught."

Damoetas kissed Daphnis after this song
and gave him a pipe. He got a pretty flute.
Damoetas played the flute and Daphnis his pipe.
On the soft grass the heifers began to dance.
Neither won the match — unconquered the two.

Idyll VII
Harvest Home

There was a time when Eucritus and I were going
from the town to the Haleis, and Amyntas made a third with us,
for to Deo, Phrasidamus and Antigenes were presenting
first fruits, the two sons of Lycopeus, noble
if any were from goodly forebears, from Clytia
and from Calchon himself, who made the spring of Bourina
gush forth from his foot when he pressed his knee to the rock. And just
beside the spring, poplars and elms with canopies
of foliage high overhead wove with their green leaves
shadows for the grove. We'd not gone even half
our way nor seen Brasilas' tomb when, with the Muses,
we met a traveler, a worthy Cydonian man,
Lycidas by name. A goatherd was he, nor could one mistake
the fact, for he was exceedingly like a goatherd to see.
On his shoulders he wore the tawny hide of a shaggy goat
smelling of fresh rennet. And on his chest he'd girt
an ancient tunic with a broad belt, and in his hand
he held a crooked club of wild olive wood.
He grinned silently with smiling eyes and spoke,
but all the while laughter played about his lips.
"Simichidas, where at noon do you take your way when even
the lizard sleeps in the dry-stone wall and not even
the tomb-crested larks flutter about? Do you hasten unasked
to a feast or some citizen's vat? So each stone sings as it springs
from your boot." I said, "Lycidas, friend, all men say
that you are the best piper by far among reapers
and herdsmen, and this certainly cheers my heart, and yet
I rather think that I am equally skilled. But this
is the road to the harvest home. Companions of mine prepare
for fair-robed Demeter a feast, first fruits of their wealth,

for the goddess has filled their threshing floors with a rich measure
of barleycorn. But come, common the road, common
also the dawn, so let us make our country song.
Perhaps one will profit the other, for I too have
the Muses' clear voice. I'm called the best of bards, but this
I'm slow to believe, for never do I suppose that I
prevail against noble Sicelidas of Samos
nor Philetas, but like a frog with cicadas do I contend."
Cunningly I spoke, and the goatherd smiled sweetly
and said, "I'll make you a gift of this olive club since you
are a shoot fashioned all for truth by father Zeus,
for I hate the builder who seeks to make his house as high
as Mount Oromedon's peak and all the Muses' cocks
who crow, all in vain, against the Chian bard.
But come, let us begin straightway the bucolic song,
Simichidas—but see if it pleases you, this song
which I composed on the mountainside but yesterday.

"Ageanax shall have fair voyage to Mitylene
when the Kids stand in the west and the south wind speeds the waves
and when Orion's feet are low upon Ocean
if he saves Lycidas from the ovens of Aphrodite,
for hot is my love of him, and it burns me all to ash.
The halcyons shall lay to rest the waves and the sea,
the south wind and the east which stirs the seaweed
from its depths—the halcyons, most beloved of birds
to the green-eyed Nymphs and those whose prey is from the sea.
For Ageanax as he seeks passage to Mitylene
may all the weather be fair, good sailing to harbor's end,
and I on that day will wreathe my brow with crown
of anise or rose or blossoms of white violet
and I will draw from the bowl the wine of Ptelea
as I lie beside the hearth and someone roasts the bean
in the fire, and my couch shall be covered-over full cubit high
with fleabane and asphodel and curling celery,
and I will drink remembering Ageanax,

in my very cups as I press my voluptuous lip to the dregs.
Two shepherds shall pipe for me, one from Acharnae and one
from Lycope, and Tityrus nearby shall sing
how once Daphnis the cowherd loved Xenea,
and the hill grieved for him and the oaks that grow upon
the banks of the river Himera kept a dirge for him
when he was wasting like snow beneath high Haemus
or Athos or Rhodope or the furthest Caucasus,
and he shall sing how once the wide coffer enclosed
the goatherd alive by the wicked shamelessness of a king,
and how the snub-nosed bees came from the meadows
to the sweet cedar chest and fed him on soft flowers,
for the Muse had shed honey-sweet nectar upon his lips.
O blessed Comatas, you had the very same joys.
You too were closed within a chest and you too
fed on honeycomb, enduring the spring of the year.
Would that you were counted among the living with me
that I might have pastured your pretty goats on the hills and heard
your voice as you lay beneath the oaks or the pines and played
and sang so sweetly your song, O heavenly Comatas."
So much he sang and ceased and after him I said,
"Lycidas, my friend, many other things
the Nymphs have taught me while I tended my herds on the hills —
good songs; their fame had reached the throne of Zeus.
But this is by far the best of all of those with which
I shall begin to honor you, O Muses' friend.

"For Simichidas the Loves did sneeze, but he, poor man,
loves Myrto as much as goats do love the season of spring.
But Aratus, dearest friend in everything to me,
keeps beneath his heart passion for a boy.
Aristis knows, a noble man, the best by far,
whom Phoebus himself wouldn't grudge to sing with his lyre beside
his tripods, how because of a boy Aratus is burned
by love to the bone. O Pan, whose lot is the lovely plain
of Homole, may you lay him unasked in the arms of my friend,

whether he be tender Philinus or some other lad,
and if you do this, O dear Pan, may Arcadian boys
not flog you then with squills about your shoulders and back
when scant meat is ready for them. But should you nod
otherwise, may all your flesh be bitten and scratched
with nails and may you sleep in beds of nettle and be
in winter's midst on the Edonian hills hard by
the Bear turned to the river Hebrus, and herd in summer
your flocks among the nethermost Ethiopians
beneath the Blemyes' rock from where the Nile is no longer seen.
But leave the sweet stream of Hyetis and Byblis,
and Oecus, the steep seat of fair-haired Dione,
O Loves, rosy as blushing apples, and wound for me
with your arrows and bows the charming Philinus, wound him, I ask,
for he has no pity, the wretch, for my host and guest, for my friend.
And truly more ripe than a pear is he and the women cry,
'Alas, Philinus, your lovely bloom is falling from you.'
We ought no longer to keep our guard at his porch, Aratus,
nor wear out our feet. But let the cock of dawn give up
another to numbing pain with his early clarion call.
And may one alone from this wrestling school, Molon, be strangled,
my friend. May peace be our concern, and may a crone
come to spit and so prevent evil from us."

So much I said, and he laughed as sweetly as before
and offered me his shepherd's staff, friendship's gift
from the Muses. He took the road to Pyxa, inclined to the left.
But Eucritus and I and the fair Amyntas turned
toward Phrasidamus' farm and lay, taking delight
in deep beds of sweet rush and new-cut vine leaves,
and above our heads many poplars and many elms
made murmuring sound, and sacred water close at hand
from the rocky cave of the Nymphs came trickling and splashing down,
while on the shadowy boughs the swarthy cicadas kept up
their chattering song, and far off the tree frog
called in dense thorns of the wild raspberry brake.

The larks and the finches sang and the turtledove mourned,
and the tawny bees flitted and hummed about the springs,
and everything smelled of rich summer, of harvest time.
Wild pears rolled at our feet, and at our sides
apples in plenty, and saplings hung low to the ground,
their branches weighted down with their burden of wild plums,
and the four-year seal was loosed from the head of the wine jars.
O Nymphs of Castalia who keep the steep of Mount Parnassus,
was it such a bowl as this that old Cheiron set
before Heracles in Pholus' rocky cave?
Was it nectar such as this that long ago inspired
that shepherd beside the Anapus, the mighty Polyphemus,
who pelted ships with mountains, to dance among his folds,
a draft such as this you mixed, O Nymphs, beside
the altar of Demeter of the Threshing Floor?
On her heap may I plant again the great winnowing fan,
and may she smile with poppies and sheaves in either hand.

Idyll XI

Cyclops

For love there is no other drug, Nicias,
it seems to me, neither unguent nor salve,
than the Muses. This remedy is delicate
and sweet for mortal men, but not easy to find.
5 You know this well, of course, as a doctor and one
whom the nine Muses love exceedingly well.
So at least the Cyclops, my countryman,
Polyphemus of old, got along quite well when he loved
Galatea and the down was just showing
10 on his temples and chin. He didn't woo her
with apples or roses or ringlets, but with sheer madness.
He counted everything else beside the point.
Often his sheep would come back to the fold themselves
from the green pastures while he, alone, would sing
15 from dawn of Galatea, wasting away
upon the shore where the seaweed lay. He had
beneath his heart a most angry wound, where
the mighty Cyprian goddess had fixed her shaft.
But he found the cure. He'd sit upon a cliff
20 and gaze out to sea while he sang songs like these:
O white Galatea, why do you spurn your lover?
Galatea — whiter than curd to see, more tender
than the lamb, more skittish than the calf,
more glistening than the unripe grape. Why
25 do you come when sweet sleep embraces me
and go when sweet sleep releases me —
as the ewe goes when she glimpses the gray wolf?
I fell in love with you, girl, when first
you came with your mother to pick the hyacinths
30 that grow upon the hill and I showed you the path.

—Once I'd seen you, I couldn't stop—not then
— or later or even now. But you don't care.
— No, by Zeus, no, you don't care at all.
— I know, my charming girl, why you shun me.
35 It's because a single shaggy eyebrow stretches
— from ear to ear across my whole forehead.
— There is just one eye beneath and the nose
— is broad above my lip. But still, such
— that I am, I tend a thousand head of cattle.
40 From them I draw and drink the best of milk.
— I never lack for cheese, neither in summer
— nor autumn nor in the worst of winter. My racks
— are always weighted down. No other Cyclops
— can pipe as I can, singing of me and you,
45 my darling sweet apple, many times
— in the depths of night. I raise eleven fawns
— with collars for you and four bear cubs.
— Come to me and you'll have no less than these.
— Leave the gray sea to gasp on the shore.
50 You'll sleep more sweetly here in my cave with me.
— There are bays there and slender cypresses.
— There is dark ivy and the vine with its sweet fruit.
— There is cool water, which heavily wooded Aetna
— sheds from her white snows, an ambrosial drink
55 for me. (Who would choose the waves of the sea
— rather than these?) But if I myself seem
— too shaggy to you, I have logs of oak and beneath
— the ash an everlasting fire. With these
— you may burn my soul and even my single eye—
60 for there is nothing sweeter than that to me.
— O dear, I wish that my mother had borne me with gills—
— I could have dived down to you and kissed
— your hand if you won't allow me to kiss your mouth.
— I'd have brought you white lilies or soft poppies
65 with petals of scarlet. But one grows in summer,
— the other in winter. I couldn't have brought them both

together. Now, my girl, I'll learn straightway
at least to swim, if only some stranger would come,
sailing here in his ship, so that I could know
70 what pleasure you find to dwell there in the depths.
Come out, Galatea, and when you've come out,
forget, as I do, to go home again.
Shepherd with me and milk and set the cheese
with acid drops of rennet. My mother alone
75 does me wrong and I blame her. For never
once has she said a kind word for me
to you, though she sees that I grow thinner
day by day. I shall tell her that my head
throbs and my feet throb so that she may suffer—
80 since I suffer. O Cyclops, Cyclops, where
have your wits flown? You'd show much better sense
if you'd go out and weave crates for your cheese
and gather and bring fresh green shoots for your lambs.
Milk the ewe that's here. Why chase the one
85 that's gone? Perhaps you'll find another Galatea
lovelier than this. Many girls ask me
to play by night and giggle too when I listen.
It's obvious that on land I am someone.

So did the Cyclops shepherd his love with song
90 and fared better than if he'd spent gold.

Idyll XIII
Hylas

Not for us alone did the god, Nicias,
as once we thought, beget that child Love,
not for us did the fair first seem fair,
for we are mortal and do not see tomorrow.
But even Amphityron's son of brazen heart
who survived the savage lion loved a boy,
the charming Hylas who wore his hair long.
He taught him all, as a father his own son,
that had made him noble and worthy of song.
He never parted from him, not even at noon,
nor when Dawn drove her white steeds to the sky,
nor when the twittering chicks looked to their roost
and their mother ruffled her wings on her sooty perch.
He wanted the boy to be shaped to his taste, and become
in his companionship a true man.
But when Jason sailed in search of the golden fleece,
Aeson's son, and the nobles joined his crew,
chosen from all the cities that could be of use,
there came to rich Iolcus the laboring man,
son of Alcmena, heroine of Midea.
With him Hylas embarked on the well-benched Argo.
The ship kept free of the clashing dark blue rocks
and at running speed rushed into Phasis' deep—
like an eagle—a great gulf. Since then the rocks
stand well apart. But when the Pleiades rose
and the farthest fields pastured the young lambs,
in spring, the godlike band remembered their trip,
and the heroes sat down in Argo, the hollow ship,
and anchored the third day of a south wind
at the Hellespont within Propontis where Cian

oxen made wide the furrows with worn plow.
Stepping upon the shore, in pairs, they dined
at evening, and many made a single couch,
for the meadow supplied a great bed of leaves,
and they cut deep galingale and flowering rush,
and blond Hylas set off with brazen pail
to fetch water for dinner for Heracles
and sturdy Telamon, those comrades who feasted
always at one table. He soon found a spring
in low-lying ground. Rushes grew around
and dark swallowwort, green maidenhair,
pliant parsley, and creeping dog's tooth.
Amid the water the nymphs were beginning their dance—
they never sleep, are dread to countryfolk—
Eunice and Malis and Nycheia with glances of spring.
The boy held forth his wide-mouthed pail for drink,
reaching to dip. The nymphs all grasped at his hand,
for love had fluttered the wits of all of them
for the Argive boy. Into the black water
he fell headlong, as when a fiery star
falls into the sea and a sailor cries,
"Make your tackle tight, my boys—it's a sailing wind!"
The nymphs held the lad upon their knees and tried
with tender words to comfort him while he wept.
But Amphitryon's son, frantic at loss of the boy,
was gone with his bow bent in the Scythian way
and his club, which he always kept in his right hand.
Three times "Hylas" he called from the depths of his throat.
Three times the boy replied, but his voice came faint
from the spring. Though very near, he seemed far,
as when a carnivorous lion hears the voice
of a fawn and speeds from his lair for a ready meal,
so Heracles amid the untrodden thorns
was wracked by his love for the boy. He covered much ground—
lovers are wretched—wandering over hills
and oak groves, and Jason he quite forgot.

The ship had its rig aloft, its crew on hand,
but at midnight the heroes took down the sails again
awaiting him who went where his feet led,
crazed, for a god had cruelly torn his heart.
And so the lovely Hylas is counted among
the blest, and the heroes mocked Heracles
because he deserted the Argo of sixty oars
and went to Colchis and unfriendly Phasis on foot.

Idyll xv
Gorgo and Praxinoa

GORGO: Praxinoa at home?

PRAXINOA: Gorgo dear! It's been an age!
She *is* at home. I'm amazed that even now you're here.
Eunoa, see to a chair for her and a cushion too.

GORGO: It does beautifully just as it is.   PRAXINOA: Do sit down.

GORGO: I was out of my mind to come! What with the crowd and the
      horses
I scarcely got here to your place alive, Praxinoa.
Soldiers' boots and men in military cloaks
everywhere you looked! And the road went on forever.
And your house was always further and further along.

PRAXINOA: That's that moron of mine! He comes to the ends of the earth
and takes a hovel, not a house, so that we can't be neighbors.
Sheer spite! The jealous brute. He's always the same.

GORGO: Don't talk about your husband, Dinon, like that, my dear,
before the little one. See how he's staring at you?
Never mind, Zoppie, my sweet. She doesn't mean Daddy.

PRAXINOA: Good heavens, the baby understands.

GORGO: Lovely Daddy!

PRAXINOA: Yes, well, that daddy of his the other day,
it was just the other day, I said to him, I did,
Papa, go buy me some soap and some rouge from the shop.
He came back with salt, the big six-foot lummox!

GORGO: Mine's the same. Money means nothing to Diocleidas.
Yesterday for the price of seven drachmas he got
five fleeces, just dog's hair, only the pluckings
of old purses, all filth, endless work for me.

But come, put on your cloak and your gown. Let's go to see
the *Adonis* at rich King Ptolemy's palace. I hear that the queen
is arranging a lovely spectacle.   PRAXINOA: All's rich with the
   rich.

GORGO: What you've seen you can talk about afterward to someone
   who hasn't.
   It's time to get going.   PRAXINOA: For the lazy it's always a
   holiday.
   Eunoa, scarface, pick up that spinning and put it back
   with the rest. Cats like to sleep soft. Get a move on. Quick,
   bring me some water. First I need water—she brings soap.
   Never mind, just give it here. Not so much!
   Pour the water. Idiot, you've splashed my dress.
   Enough! With the gods' help I've got myself washed!
   Now where's the key to the big chest? Bring it here.

GORGO: Praxinoa, that dress with the long pleats becomes you.
   Tell me, what did the cloth cost you off the loom?

PRAXINOA: Don't remind me, Gorgo! More than two minas
   of hard cash—and my very soul into the work.

GORGO: It's turned out very well. You can certainly say that.

PRAXINOA: Bring me my coat and my straw hat. Put them on
   properly. I'm not going to take you, baby. Boo,
   horsey bite! Cry all you like. No need for you
   to be maimed. Let's go, Phrygia, take the little one
   and play with him. Call in the dog and lock the door.
   My god, what a crowd! How are we going to get through
   this mob? Ants—you can't count or measure them.
   I will say, you've done us many a favor, Ptolemy,
   since your father joined the immortals. Nowadays
   no criminal sneaks up to attack you on the street,
   Egyptian-style. The wicked tricks those bands of crooks
   used to play—demons, every last one of them!
   Dear Gorgo, what's to become of us? The royal chargers!
   My good man, don't trample me. That bay is rearing!

Look how wild it is! Get out of the way, Eunoa,
you reckless girl! He'll kill the groom that's leading him.
How glad I am that I left the baby safe at home!

GORGO: It's all right, Praxinoa. We've got behind them now.
They've gone where they belong.   PRAXINOA: And I've
collected my wits.
Since childhood a horse and a cold snake have frightened me
most
of all. Let's get on. This mob is swamping us.

GORGO: From the palace, mother?   OLD WOMAN: I am, my dears.
GORGO: Easy to
get in?   OLD WOMAN: The Achaeans got into Troy by trying,
my pretties.
They always say, where there's a will, there is a way.

GORGO: The old lady gave her oracles and left.

PRAXINOA: Women know all—even how Zeus seduced Hera.

GORGO: Praxinoa, look, what a crowd around the doors!

PRAXINOA: Fearsome! Gorgo, give me your hand, and you, Eunoa,
take Eutychis's, and mind, you don't wander off.
We'll all go in together. Stick close to us, Eunoa.
Oh dear, oh dear, already, Gorgo, my summer wrap
is ripped in two. For heaven's sake, my good sir,
as you hope for god's blessing, watch out for my summer cloak.

STRANGER: It's not my fault, but I'll try.   PRAXINOA: It really is a mob.
They shove like pigs.   STRANGER: There now, ma'am, we're all
right.

PRAXINOA: May you be all right, kind sir, to the very end of your days
for taking care of us. A kind, considerate man!
Our Eunoa's being squeezed. Come on, you coward, shove!
That's fine. "All inside," as he said when he locked in the bride.

GORGO: Praxinoa, come here. Look at these tapestries—
how delicate, how charming—garments for the gods!

PRAXINOA: Lady Athena! What weavers they were to make them —
what artists to draw the lines so accurately! The figures
stand and turn so realistically in it —
they're alive, not woven. Oh, the skill of human beings!
And look how marvelously he lies on his silver couch,
the fine down just showing on his temples and cheeks,
thrice-loved Adonis, even in Acheron loved.

SECOND STRANGER: For goodness' sake, ladies, do stop that ceaseless prattle!
Turtledoves! Those broad alphas will wear me out!

PRAXINOA: Dear me, where's this gentleman from? What's it to you
if we do coo? Order your slaves. It's Syracusans
you're bossing about. We're Corinthians, I'd have
you know, by descent, just like Bellerophon. We talk
Peloponnesian. Dorians, I assume, are allowed
to speak Dorian. Persephone, no more masters, please!
One's enough. It's nothing to me. You're wasting your breath!

GORGO: Quiet, Praxinoa. She's going to sing the Adonis, the daughter
of the Argive woman, the accomplished singer who did the
best
in last year's dirge. She'll give us something lovely, I know.
Listen, she's just clearing her throat — about to begin.

SINGER

Lady, you who love Golgi and Idalium,
and sheer Eryx, Aphrodite of golden toys,
see how in the twelfth month the dear Hours,
soft of foot and slowest of the Blessed, have brought
Adonis to you from ever-flowing Acheron.
Longed for, they come, bringing a gift to every mortal.
Cyprian child of Dione, you, men say, have made
Berenice immortal from mortal state, distilling ambrosia
into her woman's breast. To please you, O goddess
of many names and many shrines, Berenice's daughter,

Arsinoa, fair as Helen, favors Adonis with every
lovely thing: in season all that fruit trees bear
and delicate gardens kept in little silver baskets
and golden flasks of Syrian scent and all the cakes
that women make on the kneading tray, mixing colors
of every kind with white wheat flour and those they make
from sweet honey and also those from moist oil.
Every creature of earth and air is there as well,
and green arbors are built, twined with tender dill,
and little boy Loves flutter above like baby
nightingales that flit from branch to branch to try
their fledgling wings. O ebony, O gold, O eagles
of shining ivory bearing to Zeus, the son of Cronus,
a boy to pour his wine. And crimson coverlets,
more soft than sleep. Miletus will say and the shepherd of Samos,
"It's we who have strewn the couch with wools for the lovely
      Adonis."
The Cyprian lies in Adonis' rosy arms and he
in hers. Of eighteen or nineteen years is the bridegroom.
His kisses do not prick. The reddish down is still
upon his lip. And now good-bye to Cypris as she
embraces the groom. All together at dawn with the dew
we shall bear him out to the waves that splash upon the beach,
and there, letting down our hair and baring our breasts
and letting our dresses fall to the ankle we shall begin
our shrill lament. O dear Adonis, you alone,
as they say, of demigods came here and to Acheron.
This happened not to Agamemnon nor mighty Ajax,
that hero of heavy wrath, nor Hector, the eldest of Hecuba's
twenty sons, nor to Patroclus or Pyrrhus, returning
from Troy, nor the earlier Lapiths and Deucalion's kind,
nor to the Pelopidae and Pelasgian kings of Argos.
Be propitious, O dear Adonis, another year.
You have found us happy now in your coming, Adonis, and when
you come back again, you will come to us as one beloved.

GORGO: Praxinoa, that woman is the cleverest thing, blessed
in all that she knows, totally blessed to sing so sweetly.
Still, it's time to get home. Diocleidas hasn't been fed.
The man's all vinegar. Don't, when he's hungry, even go near!
Good-bye, beloved Adon, come back to find us content.

Idyll XXIV

Little Heracles

Once, when Heracles was ten months old, Alcmena,
woman of Midea, bathed both him and Iphicles,
younger by a night, gave them their fill of milk,
and put them to bed in the brazen shield, that beautiful weapon
Amphitryon had stripped away from Pterelaus
when he fell. Stroking the boys' heads, the woman sang,
"Sleep, my babies, sweetly sleep and wake again.
Safely sleep, my children, my twins, my very soul.
Happily slumber and happily come again to the dawn."
So she sang and spun the mighty shield and sleep
overtook them. But when the Bear at midnight wheels to the west
against Orion himself, who shows his enormous shoulder,
then devious Hera sped two horrible monstrous snakes,
with undulating coils of midnight blue, against
the broad threshold of the house's timbered doors
and commanded them to devour the infant Heracles.
They uncoiled and writhed their blood-devouring bellies
upon the earth and from their eyes a wicked fire
flickered as slithering they spat forth their fatal venom.
But when with licking tongues they crept close to the boys,
then there awoke—for Zeus knew all—the dear babes
of lady Alcmena, and there was light throughout the house.
Iphicles, as soon as he spied the evil beasts
above the hollow shield and saw their savage teeth,
screamed aloud and kicked aside his woolly blanket,
struggling to escape. But Heracles attacked
head on and held them with his hands in a heavy grip,
grasping them by the throat where deadly serpents hold
their baneful venom that even immortal gods abhor.
So then the snakes coiled their spires about the boy,

33

that unweaned nursling child who never cried, and then
again relaxed their spines as they suffered, struggling to find
a slack of that compelling grasp. Alcmena heard
them scream and she was first to wake. "Amphitryon,
get up! For I am paralyzed with fear. Get up,
and do not wait to put your sandals on your feet!
Do you not hear how the younger child shrieks? Nor know
that though it is the dead of night, the walls are all
as clear to see as though it were the shining dawn?
Something strange is going on throughout the house,
my dear husband; yes, there is." So she spoke.
Amphitryon obeyed his wife, got out of bed,
and rushed for his gorgeous sword, which always hung above
his cedarwood couch upon its peg. He reached out for
his baldric, freshly spun, and with the other hand
lifted the sheath, a mighty work of lotus wood,
and then the spacious room was filled again with dark.
Next he shouted to his slaves, who slumbered deeply,
"Bring fire! Quick as you can! Take it from the hearth,
my slaves! And shove back the sturdy bolts of the doors."
"Get up, you stout-hearted thralls, himself is calling out!"
Thus a Phoenician woman who slept beside the mills.
Straightway with the kindling of their lamps the slaves came forth,
and the house was filled with folk rushing all about.
When then they saw the suckling Heracles clutching tight
in his tender hands the two beasts, they cried out
in wonder, but he kept brandishing the snakes before
Amphitryon and jumped up high, delighting in
his baby-prime, and laughed and laid at his father's feet
those terrible monsters asleep in the swoon of death. And then
Alcmena caught to her breast Iphicles, rigid with fright,
in spasms of terror, but their father Amphitryon laid
the other babe beneath his blanket of lamb's wool,
and going back to bed, he put his mind to sleep.
The cocks were just for the third time trumpeting
the break of dawn when Alcmena called Teiresias

34

and told him of this strange affair, commanding him
to say in reply what the consequence would be.
"Nor, even if the gods intend some wickedness,
conceal it in respect for me. Not even so
can mortal men escape what Fate speeds from the spindle.
Seer, son of Everes, I teach you what you know."
So spoke the queen, and he replied with words like these:
"Courage, woman, bearer of the best of children,
blood of Perseus, courage. Put in your heart the better
of things to come. By the sweet light that long ago
left these eyes of mine, many Achaean women
will rub with their hands the soft yarn over their knees
and sing late in the evening of Alcmena by name,
and you shall have honor among all the women of Argos,
such a man shall ascend to the star-bedecked heaven,
your son, a hero, broad in the chest. All other
men and wild beasts too will be less than he.
He is destined to complete twelve labors and then
to dwell in the house of his father Zeus. A pyre at Trachis
shall consume his mortal remains. In time he shall be called
son-in-law of immortal gods, of even those
who urged the lurking monsters to tear apart the babe.
[The day will come when the jagged-tooth wolf finding the fawn
in its lair will not care to do the creature harm.]
But, woman, let there be fire prepared beneath the ash
and make ready dry wood of camel's thorn or of
the jujube or bramble or wild pear, beaten and parched
by the wind, and on that wild cleft wood at midnight burn
the serpents, the hour when they intended to kill your child.
At dawn let one of your handmaids gather up the ash
from the fire and carry it all across the river and to
the rugged rocks and cast it beyond the boundaries,
and let her return again without a single glance
behind. And first, with pure sulphur fumigate
the house, and then, as custom decrees, sprinkle there
from a wool-bound branch clear water mixed with salt,

35

and sacrifice to Zeus on high a young male pig
that you may always be superior to your foes."
So spoke Teiresias, and leaving his ivory chair,
he went away, though bowed by the weight of his many years.
Heracles was nurtured by his mother's love
as though he were a young sapling that grows in an orchard
and called the son of Amphitryon, the Argive man.
Letters old Linus taught the boy—Apollo's son,
a hero, and ever wakeful guardian to Heracles;
to stretch the bow and shoot an arrow at the mark,
Eurytus, rich in broad ancestral plowlands.
But Eumolpus, Philammon's son, made him a bard and molded
both his hands upon the boxwood lyre. And all
the tricks with which the hip-twisting men of Argos trip
each other, wrestling, with their legs, and all the skills
that boxers, clever with their leather thongs, and all
that pancratiasts, who fall to the ground, have found devices
to aid their art—all this he learned from Hermes' son,
Harpalycus of Panopeus. No one seeing him
even from afar would with courage await
him as contestant in the lists, such was his brow
that scowled and overshot the ferocious cast of his face.
To drive his horses and chariot and protect the nave
of the wheel as he safely steered about the turning post,
Amphitryon himself fondly taught his son,
for many prizes had he brought back from the swift races
in horse-rearing Argos. Unbroken were the chariots
he mounted and only time slackened their leather thongs.
How with leveled spear to hold his shoulder beneath
his shield and aim at his man, withstanding the stroke of swords,
to arrange the phalanx and take the measure of enemy troops
coming on, to command the cavalry, Castor taught,
the son of Hippalus, a fugitive from Argos,
for Tydeus once received from Adrastus his whole estate
and his spreading vineyard and dwelt in the land of horse-driving Argos.
None among the demigods was Castor's equal

as warrior until old age wore away his youth.
This was how his dear mother had Heracles schooled.
The child's bed was a lion's skin, set next to his father,
and this gave him great delight. His dinner was roast flesh
and a big Dorian loaf of bread in a basket, enough
to satisfy, you may be sure, a gardening man.
During the day he took a little uncooked lunch.
He wore simple clothes to just above his shins . . .

. . . .

CALLIMACHUS

Hymn to Apollo

How Apollo's laurel sapling shakes,
how all his temple trembles! Far away
be he who sins. Now surely Apollo knocks
with lovely foot at the door. Do you not see?
Sweetly nods the Delian palm of a sudden
and beautifully sings the swan in the misty air.
Now bolts, push yourselves back from the gates,
now bars, for the god is no longer far away.
Prepare yourselves, O youths, for the song and the dance.
Not to everyone does Apollo appear,
but to him who is good. Who sees Apollo is great;
who sees him not is humble. We shall see,
Far-Archer, and be not ever humble.
Let boys not keep silent their lyre nor soundless
their step when Apollo is present if they wish to marry
and cut their hoary locks and if the wall
is to stand secure upon its ancient foundations.
I am pleased with the boys since the shell is no longer still.
Hush when you hear the song to Apollo. Hushed
is even the sea when the bards glorify
the lyre or the bow, the gear of Lycoreian Apollo.
Nor does Thetis his mother keen for Achilles
when she hears "Hië Paeëon, Hië Paeëon."
Even the weeping rock puts off its pain,
the wet stone set in Phrygia, marble
like a woman, openmouthed in woe.
Cry Hië, Hië. It is evil to vie
with the Blessed. He who fights with the Blessed would fight
with my king too, would fight with even Apollo.
Apollo will honor the chorus because it sings

to please his heart. For he has power since
he sits at the right of Zeus. Nor will the chorus
sing of Phoebus for one day alone, for he
is often sung. Who would not easily sing
of Phoebus? Golden is the garment of
Apollo; of gold his cloak and his lyre, his quiver
and Lyctian bow. Of gold are his sandals too.
For Apollo is rich in gold, and many possessions
has he: at Pytho you could witness this.
Always beautiful, forever young,
never has the slightest down come
upon the girlish cheeks of Phoebus Apollo.
His hair distills fragrant oils upon
the ground. Not tallow do his locks exude
but Panaceia itself. In whatever city
those drops of dew fall to the ground, all
is free from doom. There is none so endowed with skill
as Apollo. His is the archer, his the bard.
To Phoebus is given in trust the bow and song.
His are the pebbles of divination and prophets.
From Phoebus physicians learn deferral of death.
We call him Phoebus and Nomius ever since
beside Amphrysus he reared the yoked mares,
burnt with love for the young king, Admetus.
Easily would the cattle herd increase,
nor would the she-goats be in want of young,
if upon them while they fed Apollo
cast his eye. Nor would the ewes lack milk
nor fail to conceive, but all would have lambs beneath,
and the mother of one would soon be mother of two.
Men measure out cities following Phoebus, for Phoebus
forever takes delight in the founding of cities,
and Phoebus himself weaves their foundations.
Four years old was Phoebus when first he fixed
foundations in lovely Ortygia near Circular Lake.
Artemis from the hunt kept bringing the heads

of Cynthian goats, and Apollo braided an altar.
From horns he built the base, he made the altar
from horns, and built of horns the walls around.
So he learned to raise first foundations.
Phoebus too told Battus of my city
deep in soil and, as a raven, auspicious
to our founder, led his people to Libya,
and swore that he would grant the walls of cities
to our kings. Apollo is forever
faithful to his oath. O Apollo,
many call you Boedromius,
many Clarius—everywhere your name
is frequent—but I, Carneius, for so my fathers.
Sparta, Carneius, was your first foundation,
the second, Thera; the third was the city Cyrene.
From Sparta the sixth generation of Oedipus
brought you to Thera's colony. From Thera
Battus set you beside the Asbystian land
and built for you a most beautiful shrine. In the city
he set an annual festival in which
many a bull, O lord, falls to his haunches
for the very last time. Hië, Hië, Carneïus,
approached with many prayers. Your altars wear
flowers in spring, all the pied blossoms
that the hours bring forth when the west wind breathes dew;
in winter, the sweet crocus. Forever and always
is your fire, nor does the ash ever feed
on yesterday's coals. Greatly did Phoebus rejoice
when the belted warrior-men of Enyo danced
with the tawny-haired women of Libya as the hours
of the fixed Carnean feast came round for them.
Not yet could the Dorians approach the streams of Cyre
but lived in Azilis, dense with wooded glens.
These the lord himself beheld and showed
them to his bride as he stood upon the horned
Myrtle-hill when Hypseus' daughter slew

the lion that savaged the kin of Eurypylus.
No dance more divine than this has Apollo seen,
nor has he given to any city so many
blessings as to Cyrene, remembering
that earlier rape. Nor have the sons of Battus
honored any god more than Apollo.
Hië, Hië, Paeëon we hear since when
the Delphians first discovered this refrain,
when you displayed the shot of your golden bow.
Going down to Pytho, you met a beast,
a dread supernatural snake, which you slew,
shooting one swift shaft after another,
and the people shouted, Hië, Hië, Paeëon,
shoot an arrow!" Your mother bore you to be
a helper, and still from that comes your song of praise.
Envy spoke to Apollo's ear in secret.
"I do not admire the bard who does not sing
as many things as does the sea." Apollo
shoved Envy with his foot and said this:
"Mighty is the flow of Assyria's river,
but much dirt of earth and much rubbish
it carries on its water. Not to Deo
from every water do the Melissae carry
but from the tiny stream that trickles from
a sacred spring, a blossom bright and pure."
Hail, my lord, Apollo. As for Blame —
let him depart and go where Envy is!

III

Hymn to Artemis

We sing a hymn to Artemis, for it is
no trifling matter to pass her by, whose delight
is the bow and hunting of hares, the spacious dance
and play upon the mountain tops, and we
begin from when, still a little girl,
she sat upon her father's knees and said,
"Give me, papa, my virginity
to keep forever, and give me many names
that Phoebus Apollo not contend with me.
Give me a bow and arrows—wait, father,
I don't ask for a quiver or a big bow.
The Cyclopes will make me arrows soon
and a bow beautifully bent. Just let me be
a Bringer of Light and wear a dress with a border
of color that comes to the knee so that I can slay
wild beasts. And give me for my chorus sixty
daughters of Ocean, all nine years old, all
children still without a woman's sash.
And give me for serving maids twenty nymphs
of Amnisus to care for my buskins well and when
I no longer shoot lynxes and deer to care
for my fleet hounds. And give me all the mountains.
Allot to me whatever city you please,
for seldom does Artemis go down to the town.
On the mountains I'll live and visit the cities of men
only when women tortured by childbirth pangs
summon me. The Fates decreed at the hour
of my birth that I be helper to them, because
my mother had no pain when she carried me
nor when she gave me birth. With no distress

she put me from her limbs." So she spoke
and wanted to touch her father's beard and stretched
many a little hand in vain to reach it.
Her father laughed and nodded assent and said,
caressing her, "When goddesses bear me children
like this, little do I care for Hera's
jealous wrath. Take everything, my child,
that you ask—and welcome—and still bigger things
your father will give to you. Three times ten cities
and more than one towered bastion I'll grant.
Three times ten cities that will not know
how to exalt any other goddess but you,
but you alone to exalt and be called a city
of Artemis. And many cities to share,
inland and on the islands. In all of them
will be altars and groves of Artemis,
and you will be a guardian of harbors and ways."
So he spoke and nodded decree of his words.
The maiden went to the snowy mountain of Crete,
forested in leaves, and from there to Ocean.
She chose many nymphs, all nine years old,
all children still without a woman's sash.
The river Caeratus rejoiced greatly,
and Tethys rejoiced, because they sent their daughters
to be attendants to the daughter of Leto.
She went straightway to visit the Cyclopes,
whom she came upon on the island of Lipara
(Lipara now but then Meligunis by name)
standing at the anvils of Hephaestus
around a molten mass of red-hot iron,
for a mighty work was being hurried on.
They were forging for Poseidon a horse trough.
The nymphs were afraid when they saw the awful monsters.
They were like the jutting crags of Ossa, and each
had a single gleaming eye beneath his brow,
like a shield of four ox hides for size, and glowered

frightfully from beneath. And they were afraid
when they heard the thud of the anvil echoing loud
and the mighty blast of the bellows and deep groan
of the Cyclopes themselves. For Aetna moaned,
Trinacia moaned, the Sicanians' seat, their neighbor
Italy. Cyrnus too moaned out loud
when they raised their hammers high above their shoulders
and with alternate strokes labored mightily,
and from the furnace or iron the bronze seethed.
And so the daughters of Ocean could not bear
with calm to look upon them face to face,
nor could they withstand the din in their ears. No wonder!
Not even the daughters of the Blessed can look
at them without a shudder and they are certainly
no longer little girls. But when any
little girl disobeys her mother, the mother
calls the Cyclopes to her child, Arges
or Steropes, and from the innermost room
of the house comes Hermes, smeared with burnt ash.
At once he spooks the little girl, and she
hides in her mother's lap and covers her eyes
with her hands. But you, maiden, even sooner,
while still only three years old, when Leto came
carrying you in her arms at Hephaestus' call
that he might give you birth gifts, and Brontes
sat you on his sturdy knees, you tore
the shaggy hair from his big chest and pulled
it out by force. And even now the middle
of his chest is bare, just as when mange
attacks the temples and eats away the hair.
Quite boldly then you addressed them and said,
"Cyclopes, make for me too a bow,
arrows, and hollow quiver for my shafts,
for I am Leto's child, as is Apollo,
and if I slay with my bow some savage beast
or wild monster, the Cyclopes will feast."

You spoke, and they fulfilled your wish. At once
you armed and quickly went again in search
of hounds. You came to Pan's Arcadian stable.
He was hacking up the flesh of a Maenalian lynx
so that his breeding bitches could eat it for food.
To you the Bearded One gave two dogs
black and white, three that were red, and one
spotted all over. These dragged lions down
when they got them by the throat and hauled them alive
to the fold. He gave you seven Arcadian bitches
quicker than the winds. These are swiftest
to pursue fawns and unblinking hare and to find
the lair of the stag and where the porcupine
beds and to follow upon the track of gazelles.
Going from there (and your hounds rushed with you),
you found at the foot of Parnassus gamboling deer,
a big herd. They always grazed on the banks
of black-pebbled Anaurus. Larger than bulls,
gold gleamed from their horns. Suddenly
you were amazed and said to your own heart,
"This would be a first catch to do
Artemis proud!" There were five in all. Four
you took with swift foot, without the chase
of hounds, to draw your hasty chariot.
One escaped over the river Celadon
at Hera's device to be in later time
a labor for Heracles, and that one reached
the Ceryneian hill. Artemis, goddess
of maidenhood, slayer of Tityos,
golden was your armor and your belt,
and you yoked a golden chariot. Of gold
were the bridles you put upon your young deer.
Where first did your horned team transport you?
To Thracian Haemus. From there the blast of Boreas
brings ice and chilling cold to unclad men.
Where did you cut the pine? From what flame

48

did you kindle it? On Mysian Olympus, and you
put into it the breath of unquenchable fire,
which your father's thunderbolts distill.
How often did you test your silver bow?
You shot first at the elm, then at an oak,
and then at a wild beast. The fourth time,
and it was not long after, you shot at the city
of unjust men, those who sinned against
themselves and those who sinned against strangers.
Poor wretches! On them you will inflict
your harsh wrath. Plague feeds on their flocks;
and frost, their cultivated fields. For sons
old men will cut their hair in grief. Their wives
are stricken and die in childbirth, or if they escape,
they bear children not one of whom can stand
on straight legs. But for those you gaze upon
with grace and smiles, the plowland bears abundant sheaves,
and their breed of four-footed beasts increases, and so
there increases too prosperity. Nor do
they visit the tomb except to carry there
the very old. Nor does dissension wound
their race, though it ravages even well-established
and stable homes, but in-laws place their chairs
about a single table. May my true friend,
my Lady, be one of those, and may I myself
be one of them, O Queen, and song forever
be my care. In my songs will be the marriage
of Leto, and often you, and Apollo too,
and all your contests, your hounds, your bow, your chariots,
which carry you, wondrous to see, with ease
when you drive to the house of Zeus. At the entrance there
as they greet you, gracious Hermes takes your weapons
and Apollo whatever wild beast you bring, at least
before mighty Heracles came, but now
Phoebus no longer has this task, for so
does the Anvil of Tiryns stand always before

the gates, waiting to see if you will bring
him when you come some fat meat, and all
the gods laugh at him—they cannot stop—
especially his own mother-in-law,
when from his car he lugs a huge bull
or a wild boar by the hind foot, gasping.
With this wily word he admonishes you, goddess:
"Shoot at the bad beasts that mortals may call
you, like me, their helper. Leave deer and hare
to feed on the mountainsides. What harm could deer,
what harm could hare do? It is boars that ravage
the plowed fields, the planted crops, and oxen
are great trouble to men. Shoot also at them."
So he spoke and quickly set to work
about the big beast. For though beneath
a Phrygian oak his limbs were deified,
he has not given up his gluttony.
He has that belly still with which once
he encountered poor Theiodamas at the plow.
For you the Amnisian nymphs loose the deer
from the yoke and curry them, and from the meadow
of Hera they cull and bring for them to feed
in abundance the quick-springing clover, which also
feeds the horses of Zeus. And golden troughs
they fill with water to be a pleasing drink
for the hind. You yourself go to the house
of your father, where all alike invite you to sit,
but you sit next to Apollo. But when the nymphs
circle you in the dance near the springs of Inopus
or in Pitane—for Pitane too is yours—
or in Limnae, or where, goddess, you came to live
from Scythia, in Alae Araphenides,
renouncing the Taurian rites, then may my oxen
not cleave a four-acre fallow for wages beneath
the hand of a plowman from another land,
for surely they would come to the barnyard

lame of foot and galled of neck, even
though they were Stymphaean, nine years old,
and drawing by the horns. These are far
the best for cutting a furrow deep. For Helios
never passes by that lovely dance
but stops his car to gaze, and the days lengthen.
What islands now, what hills, please you most?
What harbor? What city? Whom of nymphs do you love
especially? What heroines have you taken
as your companions? Tell me, goddess, and I
shall sing to others. Of islands Doliche,
of cities Perge pleases you, of mountains
Taygeton, of harbors Euripus. Beyond
others you love the Gortynian nymph, slayer
of stags, the good marksman, Britomartis.
For frantic love of her Minos once
ran up and down the Cretan hills. The nymph
would hide now beneath the shaggy oaks
and now in the marshy meadow. For nine months
he wandered over steeps and crags and kept
pursuing until, almost caught, she leapt
into the sea from the height of a scarp and fell
into a fisherman's net and so was saved.
Since then the Cydonians call the nymph Dictyna
and the mountain from which the nymph leapt Dictaeon,
and they set up altars and sacrifice. The garland
that day is mastic or pine. Myrtle goes
untouched, for then when she fled, a myrtle bough
got caught in the maiden's clothes, and she therefore
was furious with the myrtle. Upis, Queen,
beautiful Bringer of Light, you also the Cretans
call by the name of that nymph. And Cyrene you made
your companion too. Once to her you gave
two hunting hounds with which the daughter of Hypseus
beside the Iolcian tomb took the prize.
And the blond wife of Cephalus, son of Deioneus,

my lady, you made your partner in the chase,
and lovely Anticleia you loved as you loved
your own eyes. These were the first to wear
the swift bow and quivers on their shoulders.
Their right shoulders bore the quiver-baldric,
and the breast showed always bare. You praised too
Atalanta, the girl with quick feet, slayer
of boars, the daughter of Arcadian Iasius,
and taught her to hunt with hounds and marksmanship.
Those summoned to hunt the Calydonian boar
find no fault with her, for victory's tokens
came to Arcadia, which keeps the teeth of the boar.
Nor do I suppose that Hylaeus and witless Rhoecus
for all their hate find fault with her bowmanship
in Hades. For their flanks with whose gore the crown
of Maenalus flowed will not assent to the lie.
Lady of many halls, of many cities,
rejoice, Goddess of the Tunic, who live
in Miletus, for Neleus made you his guide when he
put his ships to sea from Cecrops' land.
Chesian, Imbrasian, foremost throned, to you
Agamemnon put up in your shrine his ship's rudder,
a charm against the calm, when you bound the winds
for him when Achaean ships set sail to vex
the Teucrian towns, angered for Helen of Rhamnus.
For you Proetus established two temples,
one of the Maiden, because you collected for him
his virgin daughters who roamed the Azanian hills,
the other in Lusa to the Gentle, because
you took away from his daughters their savage spirit.
For you the Amazons, desirous of war,
once in seaside Ephesus set up
an image of wood beneath a trunk of oak,
and Hippo performed a sacrifice for you,
and they themselves, Upis, Queen, danced
a war dance, first in shields and arms,

and then in a circle arranged a broad chorus.
The shrill pipes made fine accompaniment
that they might beat with their feet the ground together,
for not yet had they pierced the bones of the fawn,
Artemis' work and a mischief to deer. The echo
reached to Sardis and the Berecynthian range.
They with their feet beat quick and their quivers rattled.
Afterward around that image of wood
was built a broad foundation. Dawn will see
nothing more divine, more opulent.
With ease would it surpass the shrine of Pytho.
Therefore arrogant Lygdamis threatened in madness
to plunder it and led against it a host
of Cimmerians who milk mares and were in number
equal to the sands. They live close by
the Straits of the Cow, Inachus' daughter, Io.
Oh, wretched of kings, how much he sinned!
Neither was he himself to return again
to Scythia, nor any other of those
whose wagons stood in Cayster's marshy plain.
For your bow forever defends Ephesus.
Lady of Munychia, Protector of Harbors,
rejoice, Lady of Pherae. Let none dishonor
Artemis — for when Oeneus dishonored her altar
ugly struggles came upon his city —
nor any strive with her in the shooting of stags
or contend in archery. For the son of Atreus
did not boast of slight requital. And let
not any court the maiden, for neither Otus
nor Orion was suitor to his advantage.
Nor let any avoid the annual dance,
for not without tears did Hippo refuse to circle
in dance about the altar. Rejoice, my Queen,
and graciously, please, receive my song to you.

V

On the Bath of Pallas

All of you that pour the bath for Pallas,
come out, come out! I heard just now the neigh
of the sacred steeds, and the goddess is ready to go.
Hurry now, Pelasgus' tawny-haired daughters,
hurry! For never did Athena wash
her magnificent arms before brushing the dust
from her horses' flanks, not even when she came
from the savage giants, her armor all spattered with gore,
but first by far she loosed her horses' necks
from the chariot and in Ocean's streams she washed
away the specks of sweat and from their mouths
that champed the bit she wiped the clotted foam.
Achaean daughters come! Bring not scent
nor alabaster boxes (I hear the noise
of the axle naves), who pour the bath for Pallas,
bring not scent nor alabaster boxes
(for mixed unguents do not please Athena),
and bring not a mirror, her face is always fair.
Not even when the Phrygian judged the contest
on Ida did the mighty goddess look
into the orichalc or translucent swirl
of Simois, nor did Hera. But Cypris took
the gleaming bronze and often rearranged
the same lock. But Pallas, after running
twice sixty double laps, like the twin stars
of Lacedaemon beside the river Eurotas,
taking simple oils, anointed herself
with skill — the ultimate fruit of her own tree.
O maidens, the blush ran up her like the color
of the morning rose or pomegranate seed.

So now bring only the manly olive oil
with which Castor and Heracles anoint
themselves. And bring her a comb made all of gold
that she may arrange her hair once she has
cleansed with oil her glistening locks. Come out,
Athena! A company dear to your heart is here,
the virgin daughters of the mighty sons
of Arestor. O Athena, Diomedes' shield
is carried too, since this is Argive custom.
Eumedes taught them so in earlier times.
He was a priest who had learned to please you. Once,
when he learned that the people were plotting death for him,
he took your holy image and fled and dwelt
on the Creion hill, the Creion hill. You
he established there, goddess, on jagged rocks.
Therefore their name now is the Pallatid Rocks.
Come out, Athena, Sacker of Cities, with helmet
of gold, taking delight in the clatter of horses
and shields. Water-bearers, do not dip
today. Today, Argos, drink from the springs
and not from the rivers. Today, serving maids,
take your pitchers to Physadeia or to
Amymone, the daughter of Danaus. For mixing
his waters with flowers and gold, Inachus will come
from the pasturing hills, bringing a beautiful bath
for Athena. But Pelasgian, take care
lest even unwillingly you see the queen.
Who sees Pallas, the city-protector, nude,
shall look upon Argos for this, the very last time.
Lady Athena, come out. Meanwhile I
shall tell to these a story not mine but others'.
Children, once in Thebes Athena loved
beyond her other companions a single nymph,
Teiresias' mother, and she was never apart
from her. But when she drove her horses toward
ancient Thespiae or toward Coroneia

or into Haliartus, going through
Boeotia's cultivated fields, or toward
Coroneia, where the fragrant grove and altar
stand beside the river Curalius,
many times did the goddess mount the nymph
upon her car. There was no chatter of nymphs
or sweet arrangement of dance where Chariclo
did not take the lead, but many tears
awaited even her in time to come,
although she was a companion dear to the heart
of Athena. Once, undoing the pins of their robes
beside the beautifully flowing Spring of the Horse
on Helicon, they bathed. The quiet of noon
lay on the mountain. Both of them were bathing.
It was the hour of noon, and a deep quiet
lay on the mountain. Teiresias alone whose cheeks
were just darkening with down still roamed
with his hounds the sacred spot. With unspeakable thirst
he came to the flowing spring, poor wretch,
and unwittingly saw the things unlawful to see.
Though angered, still Athena said to him,
"What god, O son of Everes, led you to take
this harsh road so that never again will you
take back your eyes?" She spoke and night took away
the eyes of the boy. He stood speechless, for pain
stiffened his knees and distress checked his voice.
The nymph called out, "What have you done to my boy?
Is this the kind of friends you goddesses are?
You've taken away the eyes of my child. Poor boy,
you've seen Athena's breast and flanks, but you'll not
see the sun again. O wretched me! O mountains,
O Helicon, where I can no longer come,
much have you exacted for small offense!
You lost a few gazelles and deer and took
the eyes of my child!" At the same time, the mother
embraced her dear boy child and, keening like

the grieving nightingales, she led him away.
The goddess Athena pitied her companion
and spoke this word to her, "Lovely lady,
reject all that you have said in anger.
It was not I who made your child blind.
Athena does not find it sweet to snatch
the eyes of children. The law of Cronus is:
He who gazes upon an immortal when
the god himself has not made that choice,
gazes at this for an enormous price.
Lovely lady, one can't undo the deed,
since thus allotted the flaxen threads of the fates
when first you gave him birth. But now, accept,
O son of Everes, your dire recompense.
How many victims will Cadmus' daughter burn
in aftertime, how many Aristaeus,
praying to see their only son blind,
the young Actaeon. He will join in the chase
with mighty Artemis, but neither the chase
nor their companionship in archery
upon the hills will save him then, when
unwittingly he sees the charming bath
of the goddess. His own hounds will then devour
their former lord. His mother will gather the bones
of her son, roaming all the oak thickets.
She will call you fortunate and blessed,
because you received your son from the mountains blind.
O companion, do not mourn. For your son
there await many other honors from me
for your sake. I will make him a prophet, sung
by men to come, surpassing all others by far.
He shall know the birds, which is auspicious,
of all the number that fly, and which of those
is of evil augury. He shall utter
many prophecies to Boeotians, many
to Cadmus, and later to the mighty sons

of Labdacus. I will give him a large staff
to guide his feet as need demands, and I
will give him too a very long span of life.
He alone, when he dies, shall walk among
the dead with consciousness, honored by
the great Agesilaus." She spoke and nodded,
and Pallas' nod assures accomplishment,
since to Athena alone of his daughters has Zeus
granted that she acquire her father's rights,
you who pour the bath, and no mother
bore the goddess, but the head of Zeus.
The head of Zeus nods not to lies, nor does
the daughter [of Zeus countenance lies . . .]

Now surely Athena comes. Receive the goddess,
maidens whose charge this is, with praise, with prayers,
and with joyous cries. Rejoice, goddess, and care
for Inachian Argos. Rejoice as you drive forth
your steeds—and may you drive them back again
with joy, and preserve all the Danaans' lot.

VI

Hymn to Demeter

As the basket comes in procession, greet it, women:
"Hail Demeter, bountiful of food,
generous with many measures of grain."
When the basket comes, view it from the ground,
uninitiates. Do not gaze from the roof
or from above, neither child nor wife
nor virgin girl who still lets down her hair,
nor when spitting from dry mouths we fast.
From the clouds Hesperus watches for its approach,
Hesperus who alone persuaded Demeter
to drink when she pursued the invisible tracks
of her raped daughter. Lady, how could your feet
carry you to the setting sun, to where
the black men and the golden apples are?
You did not drink, you did not eat, nor did
you bathe in that time. Thrice you crossed
Achelous, swirling with silver, and just as often
you crossed each of the eternal rivers.
Thrice beside the well Callichorus you sat
on the ground, and though you thirsted, you did not drink,
nor did you eat, nor did you bathe. But no,
let us not speak of what brought tears
to Deo. Better to tell how she gave to cities
pleasant customs. Better how she was first
to cut the stalk and sacred sheaves of wheat
and then drove oxen to stomp them, and when she taught
Triptolemus that noble art. And better
[that a man avoid transgression . . .]
. . . . to see.
Not yet did Pelasgians dwell in Cnidus, but still

in holy Dotium, and there for you they made
a lovely grove, copious with trees,
Scarcely could an arrow have passed through.
In it were pine and huge elms, and in it
were pear trees and the lovely sweet-apple,
and water, as though it were amber, rushed up from the ditches.
The goddess was mad for that place, as much as she was
for Eleusis, as much as she was for Triopum or Enna.
When their propitious spirit was angered with
the Triopidae, the worse counsel took hold
of Erysichthon. He rushed with twenty attendants,
all in the prime of youth, all giant men,
strong enough to lift a whole city,
arming them with double axes and hatchets,
and they ran shamelessly into the grove
of Demeter. There was a poplar, a tall tree
that touched the sky, and there at noon the nymphs
liked to play. This tree, struck first, shrieked out
an ill-omened call to the rest. Demeter heard
that her holy tree was suffering. Angered, she said,
"Who is chopping down my lovely trees?"
At once she put on the disguise of Nicippe, whom
the city had made her public priestess. She held
in her hand her wreaths and blossom of poppy; her key
hung from her shoulder. She spoke, admonishing
the shameless and wicked mortal man, "My child,
who chop down trees dedicated to gods,
cease, my child of your parents' many desires,
stop, turn back your attendants, lest you anger
the lady Demeter, whose sanctuary you sack."
Glowering at her far more fiercely than does
a lioness, newly delivered of cubs, at a hunter
on the mountain Tmarus—her eye, they say, is wildest—
he said, "Give way, lest I fix my mighty ax
in your flesh! These trees will make my roofed house,
where I shall always give pleasant feasts enough

for my companions." So the boy spoke,
and Nemesis wrote down his wicked words.
Demeter was angered unspeakably and became
again a goddess. Her footsteps touched the earth,
but her head rose up to Olympus, and they, half-dead
when they saw the lady, rushed suddenly off,
abandoning their bronze axes in trees.
The others she let go, for by compulsion
they followed beneath their master's hand, but she
replied to their angry lord, "Yes, yes,
build your house, dog, dog, in which
you'll have your dinner parties. For frequent will be
your future feasts." So much she said and fashioned
wickedness for Erysichthon. Straightway
she put in him a harsh and savage hunger,
burning and strong, and he was tortured by
a mighty disease. Poor wretch, as much as he ate,
so much again was his desire. Twenty
prepared his dinner and twelve drew off the wine.
Whatever annoys Demeter, annoys also
Dionysus, who shares his anger with Demeter.
His embarrassed parents sent him not to feasts
or common banquets. Every excuse was found.
The Ormenidae came to invite him to the games
of Itone's Athena. His mother declined for him.
"He's not at home. Yesterday he went
to Crannon, demanding a debt of a hundred oxen."
Polyxo came, Actorion's mother, for she
was preparing a marriage for her child, inviting
both Triopas and his son. But the woman,
heavy at heart, shed a tear and said,
"Triopas will come, but a boar struck Erysichthon
on Pindus of sweet glades. He's been in bed
for nine days." Poor doting mother, what lie
didn't you tell? Someone was giving a feast.
"Erysichthon is out of the country." Someone brought home

a bride. "Erysichthon was struck by a quoit," or
"He fell from his chariot," or "He's counting his flocks
on Othrys." Meanwhile, he within the house,
an all-day banqueter, ate things by the thousands.
His wicked belly leapt the more as he ate.
All the edibles flowed, thanklessly,
in vain, into the depths, as it were, of the sea.
Like the snow on Mimas, a wax doll in the sun,
and even more than these he melted right down
to the sinews. Sinews and bones were all that were left
of the wretched man. His mother wept, and both
his sisters groaned heavily and the breast
that gave him suck and the ten serving maids,
again and again. Triopas himself clutched
at his grizzled locks and called upon Poseidon,
who did not listen, speaking words like these,
"False father, see this third generation
of yours, if indeed I am the son of you
and Canace, the daughter of Aeolus,
and this wretched child is mine. Would that he
had been shot by Apollo and I had buried him
with my own hands. But now he sits before
my eyes, a wickedly ravenous appetite.
Either relieve him of his cruel affliction
or take him off and feed him yourself.
My tables have given out. My byres are bereft,
my stables empty of quadrupeds. Already
my cooks have told me, 'No, enough is enough!'"
They loosed even the mules from the great wagons.
He ate the heifer his mother was rearing for Hestia,
he ate the racehorse, he ate the war-horse, he ate
the cat at which the little vermin trembled.
As long as there were stores in Triopas' house,
only the household rooms were aware of the curse,
but when his teeth exhausted the deep house,
then the prince sat at the crossroads,

begging for crumbs and garbage thrown from the feast.
Demeter, may that man not be my friend
who is hateful to you, nor may he be my neighbor.
Evil neighbors are enemies to me.
Sing, maidens, and mothers, greet with them,
"Hail Demeter, bountiful of food,
generous with many measures of grain."
And as the four white horses bring the basket,
so the goddess of broad dominion will bring
to us shining spring and shining summer
and winter and autumn too and save us for
another year. And as without sandals
or hair bands we pace the city, so
shall we have feet and heads forever unharmed.
As the basket bearers bear baskets full
of gold, so may we acquire gold
ungrudged. Allow the uninitiate
to follow as far as the Prytaneia, but
the initiates to the goddess herself, those who
are less than sixty years old. For those who are heavy
with age or stretch their hand to Eileithyia
or are in pain, it is enough for them
to go as far as their knees are able. To them
Deo shall give all things in full measure
just as though they had come as far as her temple.
Hail goddess, and save this city in concord
and in prosperity, and bring to the fields
produce of every kind. Pasture cattle,
bring us flocks, bring us sheaves, and bring
the harvest. Nourish also peace that he
who sows may also reap. Be propitious,
thrice invoked, foremost of goddesses.

Epigrams

II (2)

Someone told me, Heracleitus,
that you were dead and brought me
close to tears, for I remembered
how often in our talk we put
the sun to bed. You, I suppose,
my Halicarnassian friend,
are ashes four times long ago,
but your nightingales still live.
On them Hades who snatches all
away shall not cast his hand.

IV (5)

Timon, for you exist no more,
which do you hate more,
the darkness or the light?
"The dark, for the Great Majority
of you reside in Hades."

XIX (21)

Here Philip the father buried
his twelve-year-old son
Nicoteles, his great hope.

XX (22)

At dawn we buried Melanippus. At sunset
his sister Basilo died by her own hand.
She could not bear to place her brother upon

the pyre and live. The house of Aristippus,
their father, saw a double catastrophe,
and all Cyrene bowed her head when she saw
the house, once blessed in its children, thus bereft.

XVII (19)

Would that there had never been swift ships!
We would not be mourning Sopolis, Diocleides' son.
But now his corpse floats in the sea somewhere, and we
pass by, instead of him, a name and an empty tomb.

III (4)

Do not say "Godspeed" to me, wicked heart,
but pass on by. It will be Godspeed to me
if only you do not laugh.

XXXI (33)

On the mountain, Epicydes the hunter seeks
every hare and the track of the roe deer, though chilled
by frost and snow. But if someone says, "Here,
this wild beast is shot," he refuses it.
Such is my love. It can follow all that flees,
but passes by what lies at its very side.

XXVIII (30)

I hate the cyclic poem, nor do I rejoice
in the path that takes the many to and fro.
I loathe the roaming lover, nor do I drink
from every spring. I detest all common things.
Lysanius, you are comely, yes, comely. Before
Echo repeats, someone says, "Another's."

XXVII (29)

Hesiod's is the theme and his the style,
but I think that the poet of Soli copied off
not the whole of the song but only the most
honey-sweet of his lines. Delicate verse,
hail, the coin of Aratus' sleeplessness!

XXXV (23, ll. 7–8)

You pass by the tomb of Battus' son, well skilled
in song, and also in season to laugh in his cups.

XXXVIII (39)

These gifts to Aphrodite
did the fickle Simon
dedicate: a portrait
of herself, the band
that kissed her breasts,
her torch, and the wands
that the wretched girl
used to carry about.

XXI (23, ll. 1–6)

Whoever passes by my tomb, know
that I am son and sire of Callimachus
of Cyrene. You would know them both, for once
the one led his fatherland in arms. The other
composed songs surpassing the strength of envy.
No wonder, for whom the Muses look upon
as children, not askance, they do not put
aside as friends, once their locks are white.

XXIII (25)

"Goodbye, O sun," said Cleombrotus of Ambracia
and jumped from a high wall into Hades. He'd seen
no evil worthy of death but had read one work
of Plato, that dialogue on the immortal soul.

Fragments from *Hecale* and *Galatea*

Hecale, fr. 238, ll. 15–17

As long as it was still noon and the earth
was warm, so long was the glittering sky more
translucent than glass, nor did a hint of mist
appear but the heaven spread cloudless . . . .

Hecale, fr. 260, ll. 63–69

They fell asleep but not for long, for soon
there came that frosty hour before dawn
when the hands of thieves no longer look for prey,
for the lamps of dawn already shine. And somewhere
a water-drawing man sings his song of the well,
and the axles creaking beneath the wagons wake
the man who has his house beside the highway,
while the smithy's slaves, deafened themselves, torment
with frequent . . . .

Hecale, fr. 260, ll. 11–14

The south wind does not shed so great a cast
of leaves, nor does the north, not even when
the month of falling leaves comes round as those
the rustics then tossed over and about Theseus . . . .

Galataea, fr. 378

or rather the sacred fish with the golden faces
or perch or all things else the ineffable depth
of the salt sea bears . . . .

The Mousetrap

And when the star that comes at the set of the sun
and brings the flocks to the folds was about to loose
the leather straps from the oxens' necks, . . . and he
shines on Ophion's race, the older gods . . . .
the door. But when he heard the squeak, like the deer
to whose ears . . . . softly he spoke,
"Obnoxious neighbors, whyever have you come
again to scrape our house clean, since it's sure
you bring nothing along. God made you a torment to hosts."
He said this and cast down the work he had
in his hands, for he was fashioning a secret to trick
the mice. In the two traps he set the deadly bait,
taking barley mixed . . . .
. . . . he summoned them to their death.
Often from the lamp they licked the fat oil
drawing it off with their tails when the lid was not
in place . . . .
. . . . sometimes from another
. . . .
               the work of a poor man
                           they danced
on his head and drove sleep away from his eyes,
but this was the most outrageous thing that the thieves
did in the brief night and that angered him most:
the rogues gnawed through his pauper's clothes and his cloak
of goat's hair and his purse, but he prepared for them
a double death, a mousetrap with a catch
that was fashioned to make an especially long leap.

APOLLONIUS OF RHODES

THE ARGONAUTICA

Book I

Beginning from you, Phoebus, I shall tell the glory
of men born long ago who down the mouth of Pontus
between the Cyanean rocks at King Peleus' command
in search of the golden fleece sailed the well-benched Argo.
Such was the oracle Peleus heard, that a grim fate
awaited him to be slain at command of the man he should see
stepping forth from the people and wearing a single sandal.
And not long after in accord with that prophecy Jason,
crossing the streams of stormy Anaurus on foot, saved
one shoe from the mud; the other he left behind,
caught there below and held back by the floods. He came
to Peleus, face to face, to share the feast which he
prepared for Poseidon his father and all the other gods,
though he paid no heed to Pelasgian Hera. As soon as the king
saw him, he took thought and contrived for him the trial
of a troubled sailing so that he upon the sea
or among foreign men should lose his voyage home.

The ship then, as bards who lived before make known,
Argus built with Athena's direction. But now I shall
relate the names and lineage of heroes, the paths
of the long salt sea, and all that in their wanderings
they did. May the Muses be inspiration for my song.

Let us first then mention Orpheus, whom once Calliope
herself, they say, lying with Thracian Oeagrus bore
near the Pimpleian peak. Men say that he enchanted
resisting rocks on the hills with the sound of his songs and also
the river streams. The wild oaks, tokens still
of that magical strain, that flourish upon the Thracian coast
at Zone grow close-thronged, all in a row. He led
them down, charmed with the song of his lyre, from Pieria.

Such was Orpheus, whom Jason at Cheiron's command chose
to share his toils, the king of Bistonian Pieria.

　　Straightway there came Asterion, whom Cometes begot
beside the waters of swirling Apidanus. He dwelt
at Peiresiae hard by the Phylleian mountain where
the mighty Apidanus and shining Enipeus join,
both together, flowing from afar into one.

　　Leaving Larisa there came to them Polyphemus, son
of Eilatus, who in earlier times among the Lapiths
of exceeding strength, when they armed against the Centaurs, fought
in his younger years, but now his limbs were heavier,
although his spirit of war remained as ever before.

　　Nor was Iphiclus left long behind in Phylace.
He was uncle to Aeson's son, for Aeson had married his sister
Alcimede, the daughter of Phylacus. His kinship
with her demanded that he be counted among the host.

　　Nor did Admetus, king of Pherae, rich in sheep,
remain behind beneath the Chalcodonian peak.

　　Nor at Alope did Hermes' sons, rich
in fields of wheat and trained in trickery, Erytus
and Echion, stay behind. As third with them there went
Aethalides, their kinsman, whom Eupolemeia bore
beside Amphrysus' stream, the daughter of Myrmidon
from Phthia; the others, Menetes' Antianeira bore.

　　Leaving rich Gyrton there came Coronus, the son
of Caeneus, brave, but not more brave than his own father,
for bards celebrate that Caeneus, though still alive,
perished by hand of the Centaurs when he apart and alone
bested them in contest, and though they rallied, they had
the strength neither to rout nor to slay him, but he
unbroken, unbent, descended deep beneath the earth,
struck down by the rushing fall of massed and sturdy pines.

　　Titaresian Mopsus came, whom beyond all men
the son of Leto taught augury from birds.
There came Eurydamas, the son of Ctimenus.
He lived at Dolopian Ctimene near the Xynian lake.

Actor sent his son Menoetius from Opus
that he might go in company with chiefs of men.

*I. 69
–104*

Eurytion followed and Eribotes, who was very strong,
the son of Teleon, the one; the other of Irus,
Actor's son. Of Teleon, famed Eribotes;
of Irus, Eurytion. A third with them was Oileus,
exceptional in courage and well trained to assail
the foe from the rear when its battle line is in disarray.

But from Euboea came Canthus, whom Canethus sent,
the son of Abas, and he was eager but destined not
to voyage home to Cerinthus again. It was his fate
and that of Mopsus too, though skilled in prophecy,
to wander and be slain in remotest Libya.
No evil passes belief for men to touch upon
since they buried them in Libya as far away
from the Colchians as is the space that lies between
the setting and the rising of the sun to see.

With him were clustered Clytius and Iphitus,
guardians of Oechalia, sons of the cruel Eurytus,
to whom Apollo had given his bow, but he had no joy
of the gift since he strove of his own will with the donor himself.

After them there came the sons of Aeacus,
not both from the same place for they had wandered and settled
far from Aegina when they had slain their brother Phocus,
senselessly. Telamon dwelt in the Attic isle,
but Peleus stole off to live in Phthia, rich in soil.

After these there came from Cecropia warlike Butes,
son of noble Teleon, and Phalerus who bore
the fine ashen spear. His father Alcon had sent him.
Though he had no other sons to care for his old age
and livelihood, he sent his only beloved son
to be conspicuous among the bold heroes.
But Theseus, who excelled all the sons of Erechtheus,
an invisible bond restrained beneath the Taenarian earth,
for with Peirithous he had followed a common road.
The two would have made for all an easier end of their toil.

Tiphys, son of Hagnias, left the Siphaean people
of the Thespians. He was skilled to predict the rising wave
of the wide sea and to detect from sun and star
stormy blasts of wind and favorable breeze for sailing.
Tritonian Athena herself urged him to join the host
of chiefs, and he came as one they welcomed heartily.
She herself constructed the swift ship and Argus,
son of Arestor, built it with her at her suggestion.
And so it was the most superior of all ships
that ever have made trial of sea by means of oars.

Phlias then after these came from Araethyrea,
where he dwelt in opulence by grace of Dionysus,
his father, beside his hearth at the springs of the river Asopus.

From Argos came Areius and Talaus, sons of Bias,
and strong Leodocus, whom Pero, daughter of Neleus,
bore. Because of her the Aeolid Melampus
suffered serious woe in the stables of Iphiclus.

Nor do we learn that Heracles of stout heart
made light of the son of Aeson's passionate command,
but when he heard report of the heroes' congregation,
and had left Arcadia for the fallow of Lyrceian Argos
by the road on which he carried live the boar that fed
in the glens of Lampeia near the great Erymanthian marsh,
at the entrance of Mycenae's marketplace he shook
from his enormous back the boar bundled with ropes,
and he himself of his own will against Eurystheus'
wish set forth and with him Hylas, a noble companion,
in prime of youth to carry his arrows and guard his bow.

Next there came a descendant of godly Danaus,
Nauplius, son of Clytonaeus, Naubolus' son;
of Lernus was Naubolus son, and Lernus we know was son
of Proetus, son of Nauplius, and to Poseidon once
his wife Amymone, daughter of Danaus, bore Nauplius,
who excelled beyond all men in skill of sailing ships.

Idmon was last to come of all those that dwelt
in Argos. Though knowing his own death by augury,

he came lest the people begrudge him glorious renown.
He was not the son of Abas in truth, but Leto's son
begat him that he be counted among the Aeolids
of fame and taught him himself the art of prophecy,
how to observe the birds and see the signs in the fire.

*I. 141
–176*

From Sparta Aetolian Leda sent powerful Polydeuces
and Castor well trained to drive steeds of swift foot.
These in the house of Tyndareus she bore, her darling sons,
in a single labor, nor did she reject their petition to go,
for she had resolution worthy of Zeus' bed.

The sons of Aphareus, Lynceus and haughty Idas, came
from Arene, excessively confident in their great strength,
the two of them. Lynceus also excelled in sharpest
sight, if true at least is the tale that that hero
could easily cast his gaze even beneath the earth.

With them Neleian Periclymenus started to come,
eldest of all the sons born at Pylos to godly Neleus.
Poseidon had granted to him strength without bounds
and the gift that whatever shape he should choose to assume in the fight
should be his to have in conflict and clash of battle in war.

Amphidamas and Cepheus came from Arcadia.
They dwelt in Tegea and Apheidas' estate, the two sons
of Aleus. There followed, a third with them as they went,
Ancaeus, whom his father Lycurgus sent, a brother
born before both of them. But he was left
behind in the city to care for Aleus now growing old,
and so he gave his son to go along with his brothers.
Ancaeus went wearing a Maenalian bear's hide
and brandishing in his right hand a double-edged ax,
for his grandfather Aleus had hidden his weapons deep within
the house in the hope that he might somehow delay his departure.

There also came Augeias. Rumor had it that he
was Helios' son. He was king of the Elean men and exulted
much in his wealth. He longed passionately to see
the Colchian land and Aeetes himself, the Colchian king.

There came Asterius and Amphion, the sons

of Hyperasius, from Achaean Pellene, which once
their grandfather Pelles built on the brows of Aegialus.
      After them, leaving Taenarus, there came
Euphemus, whom Europa bore, most swift of foot,
to Poseidon. She was the daughter of Tityos, great in strength.
He used to run upon the swell of the gray-green sea,
nor did he dip his quick feet, but just wetting
no more than the tips of his toes would go his watery way.
      And two other sons of Poseidon came. The one,
departing from the bastion of brilliant Miletus, Erginus.
The other left from Parthenia, seat of Imbrasian Hera,
haughty Ancaeus. Both boasted skill in sailing and war.
      After them the son of Oeneus, setting out
from Calydon, came, Meleager the strong, and Laocoon —
Laocoon, the brother of Oeneus, not of the same
mother, for a hireling woman bore him, whom, now old,
Oeneus dispatched to guard and care for his own son.
So Meleager, though young, joined the exceedingly bold
band of heroes. No other better than he, I think,
apart from Heracles, had come had he lingered yet
another year and been reared among the Aetolians.
      His uncle, well trained to fight with the javelin and in
the hand to hand, Iphiclus, son of Thestius, followed
by the same road to accompany him as he went on his way,
and with him Palaemonius, son of Olenian Lernus,
of Lernus by common report, but in fact by birth of Hephaestus,
and therefore lame in both feet, but no one would dare
reproach his manliness or his hands, and he was counted
among all the chiefs increasing glory for Jason.
      Now from the Phocians came Iphitus, sprung from Naubolus,
Ornytus' son. He had been Jason's host when once
he went to Pytho to ask for oracles about
his voyage, for there he welcomed him in his own house.
      Then came Zetes and Calais, the sons of Boreas,
whom once Oreithyia bore, the daughter of Erechtheus,
in the farthest reach of frigid Thrace. It was from there

78

that Thracian Boreas carried her off from Cecropia
while she was whirling in the dance beside Ilissus.
He took her from there to the place they call Sarpedon's rock
beside the stream of the river Erginus, and wrapping her
around with shadowy clouds, he had his way with her.
They were fluttering their dusky wings at either side
of their ankle bones as they rose, a marvel great to see,
pinions that glittered with golden scales. Around their backs
from the top of the head and neck, on this side and that,
their blue-black locks were constantly shaken and tossed by the winds.

Nor did Acastus, mighty Pelias' son, desire
to linger behind in the halls of his stalwart father, nor
did Argus, who rendered service to goddess Athena, but
they too were going to be counted among the host.

So many were the counselors that gathered to join
the son of Aeson, all the princes that the dwellers around
called the Minyae, for the most and the best would boast
that they were born of the blood of the daughters of Minyas,
and so his mother Alcimede, born of Clymene, daughter
of Minyas, gave birth to Jason, son of Aeson.

Now when the slaves had made ready all the gear
with which well-equipped ships are fitted out
within, when need drives men to sail upon the sea,
then they went to the ship through the city where on the shore
Magnesian Pagasae lies, and all around a crowd
of people ran, in haste together, and the heroes shone
like stars gleaming between the clouds. So each man
would say as he saw them there dashing about in arms,
"Zeus lord, what is Pelias' mind? Where
does he send such a host of heroes out of all Achaea?
On one day with fatal fire they would destroy
Aeetes' palace should he not give to them of his own
free will the golden fleece. One cannot shun the path.
The task is difficult for those who venture on."

So they talked here and there throughout the town,
and often the women raised their hands to the gods in heaven

and prayed that they grant return, the absolute wish of their hearts.
One of them wailed to another as she shed her tears and said,
    "Poor Alcimede, evil has come to you, though late,
nor have you completed your life in glory. Aeson too
is a man of wretched fate. It would surely be better for him
if already he lay wrapped about in his shroud beneath
the earth and knew nothing yet of bitter tasks.
Would that the black wave when virgin Helle perished
had washed over Phrixus too with the ram, but the evil monster
emitted a human voice that he might cause Alcimede
sorrows in aftertime and also myriad woes."
    So the women spoke at the going forth of the heroes.
Within, many slaves, both men and women, were gathered,
and his mother, stricken with speechlessness. A sharp pang
afflicted each, and with them his father in grim old age,
wrapped closely around upon his bed, would lie and groan.
But Jason then would assuage their grief, giving them heart,
and commanded the slaves to take up his weapons of war, and they
in silence, with eyes downcast, lifted his armor up.
And just as his mother had at the first embraced her son,
so she clung and wept, unstintingly, as a young girl,
all alone, falls gladly upon her grizzled nurse
and weeps — there are no others now to care for her,
but she beneath a stepmother leads a burdensome life,
for the woman misuses her with many a fresh reproach,
and her heart within as she grieves is bound by wretchedness,
nor can she sob forth all the sorrow that struggles to speak —
so Alcimede wept, unstintingly, holding her son
in her arms and spoke a word like this in her yearning concern:
    "Would that on that day, miserable that I am,
when I heard King Pelias speak forth his evil command, I had
abandoned my life and had oblivion of cares
so that you yourself might have buried me with your own hands,
my child. For this was my only remaining wish from you.
All other reward for rearing you I have long enjoyed.
Now I, admired among Achaean women before,

shall be abandoned like a thrall in my empty halls,
wasting away, ill-starred, in longing for you, by whom
I had much honor and glory before. For you alone
I loosed my sash, first and last, for especially
to me Eileithyia begrudged abundant progeny.
How foolish I was! Not so much as in a dream
did I suppose that Phrixus' escape would bring me bane."

Groaning like this, she grieved, and her serving women stood by,
and wailed, but Jason spoke to her with soothing words:
"Do not for me, my mother, harbor gloom and anguish
excessively, since you will not with your tears ward off
the evil from me but only add sorrow yet to sorrow.
For unforeseen is the pain that gods allot to mortals.
Have the courage to bear your portion of them although
anguished at soul. Take heart from Athena's covenants
and the oracles, since Phoebus has given propitious responses,
and then after that from the aid of the princes. But now do you
remain quietly here in your halls with your serving maids
and be not a bird of evil augury to the ship.
My kinsmen and slaves will follow me as I go there."

He spoke and then rose up to start forth from the house.
And as Apollo goes from his fragrant temple forth
to sacred Delos or Claros or Pytho or broad Lycia
beside the streams of Xanthus, so did Jason go
through the thronging crowd of his people. A cry rose up
as they shouted all together. There met him ancient Iphias,
the priestess of Artemis who guards the city, and she
kissed his right hand but could not speak a word
to him, eager though she was, for the crowd pushed on,
and she was left there, shoved aside, as the old are
by the young, and he slipped by and soon was far away.

But when he had left the city's well-built streets, he came
to Pagasae's beach, and there his companions welcomed him
where they had waited, all in crowds, beside the Argo.
He approached and stood and they gathered about to face him.
They noticed Acastus and Argus coming down from the city,

and they were amazed to see them rushing speedily,
despite the will of Pelias. Argus, the son of Arestor,
had cast about his back the hide of a bull, black
with hair, that came right down to his feet. The other wore
a lovely cloak of double fold which Pelopeia
his sister had given him. Jason, nevertheless,
refrained from asking every single thing but ordered
the men to sit all together in conference.
And there upon the rolled sails and the mast that lay
on the ground beside them they all sat down in rows,
and the son of Aeson with good intent addressed them:
     "All the gear that a ship needs to be fitted out
is ready for our departure, all in perfect order.
We shall not for this cause make long delay of sailing,
once only the breezes blow, but friends — for common the voyage
home to Hellas again and common our way to Aeetes —
choose therefore ungrudgingly the bravest man
to be our leader. He shall take on everything,
concern for our quarrels and covenants we make with strangers."
     So he spoke, and the young heroes turned their gaze
to bold Heracles, who sat in their midst, and they all
with a single shout entreated him to take command.
But he, from where he sat, stretched forth his hand and said,
"Let no one offer this glory to me, for I shall not
accept, and I shall prevent another from standing up.
Let him who gathered us together command this throng."
     He spoke, magnanimously, and they approved of what
Heracles bade. Then warlike Jason himself rose up,
rejoicing, and spoke like this to the fervent band of men:
     "If, indeed, you entrust your glory to my protection,
no longer, as even before, let our journey be delayed,
but now, propitiating Phoebus with sacrifices,
let us prepare a feast immediately. Until
my slaves arrive, the stewards of my steadings, whose
concern it is to choose well and drive here
oxen from my herd, let us draw the ship into

the sea. Store all the tackle aboard and draw lots
for rowing benches. Meanwhile let us build
upon the beach an altar to Apollo of Embarkation,
who by oracular response promised to signal
and show to me the courses of the sea, if I
with sacrifice to him began my feat for the king."
     He spoke and was first to turn to the task, and they stood up,
obeying him. They piled their clothes, thick and high,
upon a smooth ledge of rock which the sea missed
with its waves but the stormy brine had washed long before.
At Argus' instruction they first of all girt the ship
powerfully with a rope twisted well within,
straining it tight on either side that the planks be fitted
fast with the bolts and have the force to meet the surge.
Quickly they dug a ditch as wide as the ship's space
and at the prow into the sea as far as the ship
would run when they dragged it down there by hand. They dug
forever deeper in front of the keel and laid in the trench
polished logs and slanted the ship down upon
the first logs that she might slide and slip along
on them. Above, on this side and that, they reversed the oars
and bound them, projecting a cubit's length, to the thole pins,
and the men themselves stood, one at each on either side,
and shoved with chests and hands together. Then Tiphys leapt
aboard to spur the youths to push at the proper moment.
With a mighty shout he gave the order. At once, the youths,
groaning, with a single powerful shove, thrust the ship
from her seat and forced her forward, bracing themselves with their feet,
and Pelian Argo went smoothly with them. On either side
they shouted out as they sped along. Beneath the keel
the sturdy logs groaned with the friction. A black smoke
fumed about them because of the weight, and the ship slipped
into the brine. But the men reined her back as she rushed
ahead. They fitted the oars around the thole pins,
and put on board the mast, the well-made sails, and the stores.
     Now, when they had prepared everything with care,

then, first of all, they apportioned the rowing benches by lot,
two men taking one place. The middle bench they chose
for Heracles apart from the other heroes and for
Ancaeus who dwelt in the city of Tegea. For them alone
they left the middle bench just as it was and not
to be chosen by lot. Approvingly they trusted to Tiphys
to guide and care for the helm of the beautifully keeled ship.
Then, piling up pebbles beside the sea, they built
an altar there upon the beach to Apollo named
God of the Shore and God of Embarkation, and quickly
they placed above it logs of parched olive wood.
Meanwhile cowherds of Jason, Aeson's son, had driven
before them from the herd two oxen. These the younger
companions hauled close to the altar and others proffered
water basins and barley groats, and Jason prayed,
calling out upon Apollo, god of his fathers,

"Hear me, lord, who dwell in Pagasae and the city
Aesonis, named for my sire, you promised me when I
consulted at Pytho that you would reveal my journey's issue
and end, for you yourself are cause of my adventures.
Now steer the ship yourself together with my companions,
safe and sound, there and back again to Hellas.
Afterward, as many as make the voyage home
will lay on your altar again shining sacrifice
of bulls, but at Pytho and at Ortygia I will bring
countless gifts. But come now, Archer from Afar,
accept this sacrifice we make as first grace
for this ship on embarkation. And may I loose,
O lord, with prospering fate, the hawsers by your advice,
and may the breeze blow gently as it speeds us upon
the deep of the sea beneath a sky of fair-weather calm."

He spoke and with his prayer cast the barley groats.
Heracles and haughty Ancaeus girt themselves
to slay the bulls. The former struck one mid-brow with his club,
and it collapsed in a heap and sank right there to the ground.
Ancaeus slashed the broad neck of the other with ax
of bronze and cut through the powerful tendons and the bull fell,

doubled over, face forward, on both its horns.
The comrades quickly slit the throats and flayed the hides.
They hacked and carved and cut out the sacred thigh bones
and covered them all closely wrapped together with fat
and burned them upon the split wood. And Aeson's son
poured out unmixed libations. Idmon rejoiced, seeing
the flame as it blazed from sacrifices on every side
and the dark smoke spiraling up in swirling billows
of purplish black, propitiously, and straightway
he spoke bluntly about the intent of Leto's son:

"For you it is the god's desire and destiny
to travel here again together with the fleece,
but countless trials lie in wait for you between
departure and return. For me it is decreed
by loathsome lot of god to die far away
somewhere upon the Asian continent. Thus
though I knew even before from birds my destiny,
I have departed my fatherland to board the ship
that glory be left for me in my halls from embarkation."

So he spoke, and the youths, hearing his divination,
rejoiced for their return. But anguish took them for Idmon's
lot. Now when the sun passes by the halt of noon
and the rocky crags just shadow the plowed fields as the sun
slips down beneath the evening dusk, then at last
they all piled upon the sands a deep bed
of leaves close beside the break of the gray surge
upon the beach and lay down, all in a row.
Beside them were spread countless stores of edibles
and sweet wine which cupbearers had drawn off in jugs.
Afterward, taking turns, they told tales
to one another as youths often do, when
at feast and cup they take joyous delight and then
insatiate violence is far away from their thoughts.
But there the son of Aeson, distracted, brooded over
every single thing, mute and with eyes downcast.
Idas observed and railed at him with loud voice:

"Son of Aeson, what scheme is this you turn at heart?

Speak your mind in our midst. Does terror come upon
and conquer you as it confounds cowardly men?
Now let know my furious spear, with which in wars
I win renown surpassing others—nor does Zeus
help me so much as does my own spear—no pain
will now be fatal, no mission unfulfilled, so long
as Idas follows along, even though god opposes,
such an accomplice you bring in me from Arene."

 He spoke, and holding a full cup with both hands,
he drained the sweet wine, unmixed, and his lips and cheeks,
blue-black with his beard, were soaked with it, and all
the men thundered together, but Idmon spoke bluntly:
 "What is the matter with you? Do you devise your doom
before your day? Or does the straight wine embolden
your heart to swell in your chest to your destruction and urge
that you insult the gods? There are other words
to console and hearten a comrade. But you have spoken with all
arrogance. Such boasts, they say, Aloeus' sons
once sputtered to the blessed ones. In bravery
you are not the equal of them, and yet they were both shot down
by the arrows of Leto's son even though they were very strong."

 So he spoke, and Aphareian Idas laughed
out loud and, sneering, answered him with cutting words:
 "Come now and tell me this in prophecy, whether
for me as well the gods will bring to fulfillment a doom
such as your own father assured the sons of Aleus.
Consider how you will escape safe from my hands if you
are caught making prophecies empty as the winds."

 So in anger he railed. The quarrel would have gone on
had not the companions and son of Aeson himself restrained
with single upbraiding shout the wrangling men and Orpheus
lifted his lyre in his left hand and attempted song.

 He sang how earth and heaven and sea, in former time
fitted together with one another in single form,
by destructive strife were shorn, one apart from the other,
and how always secure in the sky the stars keep

86

their place and the paths of the moon and also those of the sun,
and how the mountains rose and how the sounding rivers
and their nymphs and all the creeping creatures came to be.
He sang how first Ophion and Eurynome, daughter
of Ocean, held the sovereignty of snowy Olympus
and how by force of hands Ophion yielded to Cronus
his privilege, Eurynome hers to Rhea, and fell,
both of them into the waves of Ocean's stream.
The others meanwhile ruled the blessed Titan gods
till Zeus, still a child, with childish thoughts at heart,
dwelt in the Dictaean cave, for not yet
had the earth-born Cyclopes empowered him with the bolt
of thunder and lightning flash, for these give glory to Zeus.

He sang and stayed his lyre and his ambrosial voice,
but though he stopped, they all, insatiate, inclined
their heads, quietly, to catch in listening ears
enchantment still. Such charm of song he left in them.
And not long after this they mixed libations for Zeus,
as it is right to do, and, standing, they poured them upon
burning tongues and bethought them of sleep in the murky dark.

But when shining dawn with sparkling eyes beheld
the steep peaks of Pelion and from the wind
the ruffled sea washed upon the clear points,
then Tiphys awoke and at once roused his companions to go
on board the ship, preparing to fit the oars in place.

Uncannily, the harbor of Pagasae and also
Pelian Argo herself cried out, urging departure.
For inside her a divine beam had been driven, which
from Dodona's oak Athena had fitted mid-keel.
The men went to their benches. One followed another,
just as they had apportioned before, to row. In place,
in perfect order, they sat, each one beside his gear.
In the middle sat Ancaeus and powerful Heracles,
who laid his club close beside him. Beneath his feet
the ship's keel was washed from below. Already the cables
were being slipped, and they poured wine upon the waves,

but Jason, in tears, turned his eyes from his fatherland.
And they, just as youths set up a dance to Phoebus
either in Pytho or in Ortygia somewhere beside
Ismenian waters, and all together around the altar
to the tune of the lyre beat with quick feet the ground,
So they to Orpheus' lyre beat with their blades the voracious
deep and the surge slapped their oars. On this side and that
the black brine was frothed with foam and frightfully boiled
at the might of the powerful men. Their armor beneath the sun
flashed like flame as the ship raced on, and their long wake
shone white behind like a path one sees on a green plain.
From heaven all the gods looked down on that day
at the ship and the band of men, half-divine, who then
were the noblest of those that sailed the seas. On the highest peaks
the Pelion nymphs gazed in wonder, seeing the work
of Athena and the heroes themselves plying the oars.
And from the mountain top there came down to the sea
Cheiron, Philyra's son, and where the surf breaks white
he dipped his toes, and with many a wave of his big hand
he wished them well as they set out and bade them
safe return. His wife was there too and carried Achilles,
Peleus' son, in her arms to show to his dear father.

But when they had left the harbor's circled shore with the wit
and skill of Tiphys, Hagnias' son, who in his hands
tended the polished rudder to steer them straight and true,
then they stood the tall mast in the mast box
and lashed it with forestays, which they stretched taut at the sides
and, hauling it up to the mast top, let down the sail,
and there fell upon it a piping breeze. On the deck they cast
the ropes, one by one, around the polished pins
and skimmed smoothly past the long Tisaean headland.
For them Orpheus struck his lyre, Oeagrus' son,
and sang a rhythmic song of Artemis, savior of ships,
nobly sired, who guards the watches of the deep
and keeps the Iolcian land. Fish darted over
the deep sea, mammoth mixed with small, and gamboled

in their wake, as when in the steps of the shepherd myriad sheep
follow, sated with grass, to the fold—he goes before,
playing prettily upon his shrill pipe
a shepherd's melody—so the fish followed
and a breeze from aft bore the ship forever on.

    Straightway the Pelasgians' misty land of many fields
of grain sank from view and they passed by Pelion's scar,
speeding always on, and the Sepian point sank,
and there appeared on the sea Sciathos and afar
Peiresiae and the clear point of mainland Magnesia
and Dolops' tomb. Here then at evening they beached as the winds
blew against. Doing honor to Dolops at dusk, they burned
victims of sheep as the sea surged with the swell and lingered
for two days on the shore. On the third day they put forth
the ship, spreading out on high its enormous sail.
Still men call that beach the Argo's Setting Forth.

    Sailing forward from there they ran past Meliboea,
looking upon a headland and beach ill-used by the winds.
At dawn they saw Homole hard by, reclining
on the sea, and skirted it. Not long afterward
they were to put behind the Amyrus river's outfall.
From there they looked upon Eurymenae and ravines,
so often flooded, of Ossa and Olympus, but then
they reached Pallene's slopes beyond Canastra's beach,
running all night with the breath of the wind. At dawn as they went
Athos rose up, the Thracian mountain, which, though it lies
as far away as a well-trimmed merchantman could sail
by noon, shadows Lemnos with its highest peak
even as far as Myrine. For them that day till dusk
the breeze was very fresh, and the ship's sails were stretched.
But with the rays of the setting sun the wind left off,
and it was with oars that they reached the rocky Sintian isle.

    Here all the male population together through the womens'
transgression had without pity been slain in the previous year.
For the men in loathing had denied their wedded wives
and had conceived a savage passion for captive women,

whom they themselves had brought from over the sea from their raids
on Thrace, for the terrible rage of Cypris pursued them,
because for a long time they had deprived her of gifts.
Oh, wretches sadly insatiate of jealousy!
Not only their own husbands did they slaughter together
with the captives because of the marriage bed but all the males
at once that afterward they pay no recompense
for the grim gore. Of all the women Hypsipyle
alone spared her ancient father, Thoas, who ruled
the people. Him she sent in a hollow chest to float
over the sea in the hope that he might escape. At the island
of Oenoe fishermen hauled him ashore (Oenoe,
before, but afterward Sicinus, from Sicinus
whom Oenoe the water nymph bore to her consort Thoas).
For all the women the care of cattle and donning of bronze
as armor and cleaving of wheat-bearing fields were easier
than the tasks of Athena with which they were always busy before.
Often, nevertheless, they peered with grim fear
across the broad sea for the time of the Thracians' coming.
So when they saw Argo rowed near the island, at once,
with all speed, from out the gates of Myrine, clad
in brazen armor, they ran forth to the beach like
flesh-eating Thyiades, for they thought that the Thracians had come.
With them Hypsipyle, the daughter of Thoas, donned
her father's armor, but they in their dismay were afflicted
with speechlessness — such fear hovered about them.

    Meanwhile in turn from the ship the princes had sent forth
Aethalides, the swift herald, to whose care
they entrusted messages and the scepter of Hermes, who was
his sire, and who had granted to him memory
imperishable of everything. Not even now
that he has vanished into the inutterable eddies
of Acheron has oblivion overtaken his soul,
which is forever doomed always to change its abode,
at one time counted among the dwellers beneath the earth,
at another, in the rays of the sun among living men.

But why must I tell at length the tales of Aethalides?
He beguiled Hypsipyle to accept the new arrivals
as day waned into dusk. Nor did they at dawn loose
the cables of the ship at the breath of the northeast wind.

    The Lemnian women went through the city and sat in assembly,
for such were the orders Hypsipyle had given them.
And when they were all gathered together in one throng,
she, straightway, among them spoke and stirred them thus:

    "Oh, my friends, let us proffer these men suitable gifts
of a sort fitting for them to take aboard ship,
provisions and sweet wine, that they securely remain
outside our bastion and not, visiting us for the sake
of need, know us intimately and evil report
go widely about, for we have wrought a monstrous deed,
nor will it be pleasing at all to them should they learn of it.
So stands our counsel now. If any other one
of you can contrive a better scheme, then let her speak,
for it was on account of this that I summoned you here."

    So then she spoke and sat upon her father's seat
of stone, but then her dear nurse Polyxo rose,
limping for age upon her shriveled feet and propped
upon her staff, and she was very eager to speak.
Near her there sat four virgin women, unwed, and crowned
with snow white hair. She took her stand in mid-assembly
and lifting a little her neck from her bent back, she said,

    "Gifts, as it pleases Hypsipyle herself to give,
let us send to the strangers since it is better to do so.
What scheme have you to reap the fruits of livelihood
if a Thracian or some other enemy foe assail
us with violence as frequently happens among men,
as even now this band arrives unforeseen?
If one of the Blessed turns this aside, afterward
myriad other woes worse than battle strife
remain, when the old women die off and you, the younger,
come, childless, to dismal old age. How then will you live,
luckless ones? Do you suppose that your oxen will yoke

themselves for the deep fields and draw the earth-cleaving plow
through the fallow and forthwith, as the year comes round, reap
the sheaves? Indeed, even though till now the Fates
have shuddered at me, I think that in the coming year
I shall put on the dress of earth when I have got
my share of burial gifts, exactly as is right,
before evil's approach. I bid the younger of you
to consider this well, for there is even now escape
already achieved if you will entrust your homes and all
your stock and your shining city as well to the strangers' care."

    She spoke, and the gathering filled with clamor, for her words
were pleasing to them. But after her Hypsipyle
straightway rose up again and spoke this word in reply:
    "If this eager desire is pleasing to all of you,
I shall even now speed to the ship a messenger."
    So she spoke and addressed her serving maid close by,
"Please Iphinoe, rise and go to ask this man,
whoever he is who leads this band, to come to us
that I may speak to him a word that pleases my people,
and bid the men themselves, if they wish, with confidence,
to enter our city and land but only with kindly intent."
    She spoke, dismissed the assembly, and rose to go back home.
And so Iphinoe came to the Minyae, and they asked
with what purpose or need she had come among them. Quickly
she replied with all speed in these words to their questions:
    "The young daughter of Thoas, Hypsipyle, sent me
to come here to summon your ship's captain, whoever
he is, to speak to him a word that pleases her people
and bid the men themselves, if they wish, with confidence,
to enter our city and land but only with kindly intent."
    So she spoke and her fateful speech was pleasing to all.
They understood that Thoas was dead and Hypsipyle,
his darling daughter, was queen and quickly they sent Jason
ahead, and they themselves prepared to go on their way.
    Now Jason around his shoulders had buckled a crimson cloak

of double fold, the Itonian goddess's work, which
Pallas had given him when first she had laid the props
for the ship Argo's keel and taught him how to measure
thwarts with the rule. More easily could you cast eyes
upon the rising sun than behold that blushing red.
For in the center it was fashioned ruby red,
but the borders were all of deeper crimson and at each edge
many intricate schemes had been skillfully woven in.

    In it were the Cyclopes seated at
their imperishable task, forging a thunderbolt
for lord Zeus. It was nearly wrought in its blazing and lacked
only a single ray which they were beating out
with iron hammers as it spat breath of ravening flame.
    In it were the twin sons of Antiope,
Asopus's daughter, Amphion and Zethus, and Thebe,
still unwalled, close by. They were just, in fervent haste,
laying its foundations. Zethus on his back
was hoisting a steep mountain peak, like a laborer.
Amphion went behind, playing piercingly
upon his golden lyre, and a rock twice the size
of Zethus' peak followed along in the prints of his feet.
    Next had been fashioned Cytherea of long locks,
gripping fast the swift shield of Ares. From her shoulder
to her left arm her tunic's fastening was loosed
aslant beneath her breast. Opposite, in her shield
of bronze her image appeared exactly as she stood.
    In it there was a rough pasture of oxen. Around
the oxen, Teleboae raged and Electryon's sons;
the one warding off; the other, Taphian robbers,
hoping to raid them. With their blood the dewy meadow was soaked,
and the many herdsmen were overcoming by force the few.
    And in it had been wrought two chariots, contesting.
The one in front Pelops steered, shaking the reins,
and with him was Hippodameia, mounted at his side,
and in pursuit of him Myrtilus drove his steeds.

With him, Oenomaus grasped his couched spear in his hand,
but then the axle swerved and broke in the nave and he fell,
straining as he was to pierce the back of Pelops.

And in it had been fashioned Phoebus Apollo, shooting,
a big boy, not fully grown, at mighty Tityos,
boldly hauling his mother along by her veil. Elare
bore him, but Earth nursed and gave him birth again.

And in it was Phrixus the Minyan, truly just like one
listening to the ram, which resembled one speaking out.
Looking at them, you would fall silent and cheat your soul,
expecting to hear some shrewd speech from them,
and for a long time would you gaze with that expectation.

Such then were the gifts of Itonian goddess Athena. Jason
took in his right hand a far-shooting spear, which
Atalanta had given him once as a gift on Maenalus
when she met him gladly, for she was mad to follow upon
that expedition, but he, of his own will, forbade
the girl, for he feared grievous strife because of her love.

He went on his way to the city just like a shining star
which young girls kept shut in new-built chambers see
as it rises above their homes and through the blue-black sky
charms their eyes with its lovely red-gold gleam, and the girl
rejoices in her desire for the youth who is kept among
foreign men, for whom her parents keep her as his bride.
Like that star the hero went by the path to the city.
When they had entered the gates and the town, the common women
crowded behind them, taking delight in the stranger, but he
fixed his eyes on the ground and went unheedingly on until
he came to Hypsipyle's gleaming halls. At his appearance
the servants opened the folding doors that were fitted with
panels beautifully fashioned. Here Iphinoe
led him eagerly through a lovely colonnade
and seated him on a burnished bench opposite
her mistress. The young woman cast her glance aslant
and a blush covered her cheeks. Despite her modesty,
she addressed the man with beguiling words and said to him,

"Stranger, why did you sit so long, remaining outside *I. 793*
–830
out walls? For men do not inhabit our town, but they
as sojourners plow the wheat-bearing fields of mainland Thrace.
But I shall tell you all our trouble honestly
that you even yourselves may understand it well.
When my father Thoas was king over the townsfolk,
then the people, setting out from Lemnos, would plunder
from ships the Thracian steadings opposite and bring
boundless booty here, including young girls.
But the deadly wrath of the goddess Cypris prepared to cast
upon them infatuation destructive of souls, for they
conceived a loathing for their lawfully wedded wives
and yielding to folly drove the women from their homes
and slept beside the captives of their spears, cruel
that they were. We endured it long in the hope that in time, though late,
they would change their intent. But always the wickedness and woe
increased twofold. The lawful progeny lost honor
in their halls and bastard offspring blossomed. Unmarried girls
therefore and widowed mothers too wandered neglected
throughout the town. A father would care not even a little
to see before his eyes his daughter slain at the hands
of an arrogant stepmother. Nor did sons as before defend
their mothers from unseemly insult, nor did brothers care
at heart for sisters. Only the young captive girls concerned
them at all in their homes, at dances, the marketplace, and banquets
until some god put overpowering courage in us
to welcome no longer within our walls the men coming back
from Thrace that they might either heed what was right or
set sail with their captive women and go some other place,
and so they begged from us all the male children
left in the city and returned to where even now
they dwell in the snowy plowlands of Thrace. Do you therefore
settle as inhabitants here, and if you should wish
and it be pleasing to you to dwell in this place, then
indeed you shall have my father Thoas' prerogative,
nor do I think that you will scorn this land, for it

is more deep in soil than all the other isles that lie
in the Aegean. But go now to your ship, and tell
your companions my words. Do not stay outside our town."

She spoke, glossing over the slaughter that had been wrought
upon the men, and Jason spoke in reply to her:

"Hypsipyle, it is our hearts' desire we meet
in your offer of help to us, who are in need of you,
and I will return to the city again when I have told
in proper order everything. But let the rule
of the island be yours. Not holding it in scorn do I
shrink from it, but grim trials press me on."

He spoke and touched her right hand, and quickly he went
on his way back. Around him, on this side and that,
myriad girls in their delight whirled in the dance
until he passed through the gates. And then they went to the shore
bearing on smooth-running wagons many guest gifts
when he had told from beginning to end all the speech
Hypsipyle had distinctly made when she summoned him.
And the young women readily led the men to their homes
for hospitality. For Cypris aroused in them
sweet desire for the sake of clever Hephaestus that men
again inhabit Lemnos afterward undefiled.

Then Aeson's son rose to go to the queenly home
of Hypsipyle; the others, each as he happened to go,
except for Heracles, for he had been left beside
the ship, of his own will, with a few chosen companions.
Straightway the city took joy in banquets and dance and was filled
with the savor and smoke of sacrifice. Beyond the other
immortals with sacrifice and song they propitiated
the renowned son of Hera and the goddess Cypris herself.

Always from day to day they made delay of sailing,
and they would have lingered long, remaining there, had not
Heracles gathered together apart from the women his comrades,
and said, chiding them with words of reproach like these:

"Are you out of your minds? Does kindred bloodshed debar
us from our fatherland? In want of wives have we sailed

here from there, scorning our countrywomen, or does
it please you to dwell here and cleave the rich soil
of Lemnos? Glory will not be ours tarrying thus
for long with foreign women. Nor will some god
seize and give to us at our prayers a fleece that moves
of its own accord. Let us each then go to his own affairs,
allowing him to lie all day in Hypsipyle's bed
until he populates Lemnos with males to his great renown."

So did he upbraid the band and no one dared
to raise his eyes or speak a single word in reply,
but prepared to go just as they were from assembly in haste,
and the women came running on as soon as they understood.
As when bees buzz around the lovely anemones,
pouring forth from their hive in the rock, and all around
the dewy meadow takes joy, and they harvest the sweet fruit,
flitting from blossom to blossom, so the women then
fervently poured forth, keening, around the men,
and greeted each one with hands and speech, and offered prayers
to the Blessed Ones to grant them a painless voyage home.
Hypsipyle also prayed, taking the hands of Aeson's
son, and her tears flowed for her loss at his departure.

"Go, and may the gods bring you back again
with your comrades unscathed and bearing the golden fleece to the king,
just as you wish and is your heart's desire. This isle
and my father's scepter await you, if afterward
on your voyage home you should ever wish to return again,
and you could easily gather a boundless host of men
from other towns, but you will not have this fervent desire,
nor do I myself foresee that such will be the future.
Remember Hypsipyle when you are far away
and after you return. But leave me command to fulfill,
gladly, should god grant that I bear a child to you."

The son of Aeson in wonder replied to her and said,
"Hypsipyle, so may all be propitious by
the Blessed Ones, but do you keep a nobler desire
for me. It is enough for me by Pelias' will

to dwell in my fatherland. May the gods only free me from
my toils. But if it is not my fate to return again
to the land of Hellas, sailing afar, and you bear
a male child, send him when grown to Pelasgian
Iolcus to cure the distress of my father and mother should he
find them living still, that apart from the king they may
be comforted at their own hearth in their own home."
  He spoke and boarded the ship first of all, and so
the other princes boarded and grasped in their hands the oars,
seated all in a row, and Argus loosed for them
the hawsers from under the sea-washed rock, and then they
struck the water, powerfully with their long oars.
At evening at Orpheus' behest they anchored at Samothrace,
the isle of Electra, Atlas' daughter, so that learning
by gentle initiation unutterable rites,
they might more safely navigate the chilling sea.
Of these I shall speak no more but nevertheless say
goodbye to the island itself and the deities who dwell
and keep those mysteries there which right forbids me to sing.
  From there they rowed through the depths of the black sea, straining,
and keeping on one side the Thracian land; on the other,
Imbros below, and just at sunset they reached the jut
of the Chersonese. From there a swift south wind blew
for them, and setting their sails to the breeze, they embarked upon
the sheer streams of Athamas' daughter. By dawn the main
to the north had been left behind, and through the night they coasted
within the Rhoeteian shore, keeping the land of Ida
at their right. Leaving Dardania, they sailed ahead
to Abydos and after that they passed Percote
and Abarnis' sandy shore and sacred Pityeia.
And in that night as the ship sped on they sailed straight through
the Hellespont that swirled and gleamed purple-black.
  There is a steep island inside Propontis not far
from the Phrygian continent with its many fields of grain,
sloping seaward where an isthmus is washed by waves before
the mainland, so low does it lie on its face. On it the beaches

are double and lie beyond Asopus' waters. The dwellers
round about call the island the Mount of Bears.
Violent and savage men live there, Earth-born,
giants, a mighty marvel for neighbors to see, for each
overweening man has six hands to raise up,
two from stalwart shoulders and four from below, fitted
to his most terrible ribs. Around the isthmus and plain
the Doliones dwell. Over them Cyzicus,
the hero, Aeneus' son, was king, whom Aenete, daughter
of godly Eusorus, bore. The Earth-born giants did not
plunder them, terrified though they were, because
of Poseidon's protection. The Doliones were sprung from him.
From there the Argo struck forth, pressed by the winds of Thrace,
and Fair Harbor received her as she ran, and there
they hauled up their small anchor stone and at
Tiphys's command left it behind beneath the fountain
Artacie. They took another, fitting for them,
a heavy one, but the first by Apollo's oracles
the sons of Neleus, Ionians, afterward set as sacred,
as it was right, in the Temple of Jasonian Athena.

In friendliness the Doliones and Cyzicus
himself came in a crowd to meet them and when they had heard
of their expedition and lineage and who they were,
they received them happily with hospitality
and persuaded them to row on further and fasten the ship's
hawsers in the city's harbor. Here they built an altar
to Apollo of Disembarking, establishing it upon
the shore and then took care to sacrifice. The king
himself gave them sweet wine in their need and sheep
as well, for he had had an oracle that when
a divine band of hero men should come, straightway
to welcome it with kindliness and take no thought
of war. For him too the soft down was just
blossoming on cheek and chin, nor had it yet
been fated him to take delight in children, but still
in his halls his wedded wife was free of childbirth pangs.

She was the daughter of Percosian Merops, Cleite
of the lovely hair, whom he had recently brought from her father
by wondrous wedding gifts from the continent opposite.
But even so he left his chamber and bed of his bride
and among the men prepared a feast, casting fear
from his heart. They questioned one another in turn. The king
would ask the end of their voyage and Pelias' commands, and they,
of the cities of the dwellers around and all the bay
of broad Propontis. More than that he could not tell
to them although they had such eager hope to learn.
At dawn they climbed mighty Dindymum that they
themselves might gaze upon the paths of that sea
and sailed their ship from its former anchorage to the harbor
Chytus and the course they took is called Jason's Road.

But the Earth-born on the other side rushed from the mountain
and blocked with immense rocks the mouth of Chytus below,
as though in ambush of a sea monster within.
But there had been left there along with the younger men
Heracles, who quickly drew his back-stretched bow
and brought the giants to earth, one upon another,
but they hoisted jagged rocks and hurled them. For those
awful monsters, I suppose, the goddess Hera,
the wife of Zeus, had reared to be a contest of strength
for Heracles. Then the other warrior heroes
returned to engage the foe before they ascended the peak
and fell to slaughtering the Earth-born men, whom they met
with arrows and spears until they had cut them all down
as they rushed headlong and hot to engage in the face to face.
As when woodcutters lay in rows at the surf line
long logs that their axes have just hewn so that,
soaked, the wood accepts the powerful bolts, so they
lay sprawled, row upon row, at the mouth of the foaming harbor,
some, close-packed, dipping their heads and chests into
the brine, their limbs stretched out on the land behind.
Others again propped their heads on the sand of the shore
and so had their feet in the depths of the sea. Whichever way
they lay, they were prey both for birds and fishes alike.

The heroes, when they had completed the journey fearlessly,
loosed the ship's cables then to the breath of the wind
and sped ahead through the swell of the sea, and the ship ran
under sail all day long, but with the coming of night
there was no longer a steady sweep of wind, but gusts
opposing snatched and bore them back until they approached
once more the cordial Doliones. They disembarked
that very night (the rock around which they cast the cables
of their ship in haste is called still the Sacred Rock),
nor did anyone perceptively note that it
was the same island. Nor in the night did the Doliones
realize in truth that the heroes were coming back
but thought that Pelasgian soldiery of Macrians
had beached and so donned armor and raised hands against
the men. With shields and ashen spears they attacked one another
like the keen blast of fire that falls on parched brush
and crests, and battle din, frightful and furious,
fell upon the populace of Doliones.
Nor was Cyzicus destined to escape the fate
of battle, returning home to bridal chamber and bed,
but Aeson's son, as the king turned to confront him,
leapt upon him and struck the middle of his chest,
and around the spear the bone shattered. Rolling upon
the sand, he fulfilled his allotted end. That no mortal
may escape, for everywhere a mighty net
is spread, and so although he thought that he had shunned
sudden death at the princes' hands, he was ensnared
that very night as he fought with them. And many other
champions were slain. Heracles slew Telecles
and Megabrontes. Acastus killed Sphodris. Peleus
slew Zelys and Gephyrus, swift as Ares; and Telamon,
who wielded the fine ashen spear, slaughtered Basileus.
Idas killed Promeus, and Clytius Hyacinthus,
and the two sons of Tyndareus Megalossaces
and Phlogius. The son of Oeneus after these slew
brave Itymoneus and also Artaceus,
a chief of men. All these the inhabitants honor

still with rites appropriate to heroes. The rest
gave ground and fled in terror as doves in flocks fly
in terror from swift-winged hawks. Clamoring, they fell
in crowds upon the gates. Straightway the city was filled
with shouts at the turn of the grim battle. At dawn both sides
realized the incurable and fatal mistake.
Terrible sorrow took hold of the Minyan heroes when
they saw Cyzicus, the son of Aeneus, fallen
before them in dust and blood. For three whole days they moaned
and tore their hair, both they themselves and the Doliones.
Circling three times in brazen arms about his tomb,
they paid funeral rites and contested in games, as right
decrees, throughout the Meadow-plain, where even now
his burial mound rises for later-born men to see.
Nor was Cleite his bride left behind after
her husband's death, but she devised another more
horrible ill to add to this, fitting a noose
to her neck. The nymphs of the groves bemoaned her death, and from all
the tears that fell from their eyes to the ground the goddesses
fashioned a fountain and called it Cleite, the distinguished name
of the luckless bride. Most terrible was that day that came
from Zeus upon the Doliones, both women and men,
nor could anyone bear even to taste of food,
nor for a long time because of their grief did they
take thought of the task of the mill but lived through their days, eating
their food just as it was, untouched by flame. Now here
when Ionians of Cyzicus pour yearly libations,
they always grind the meal for their cakes at the public mill.
     After that severe gales arose and blew
for twelve days and nights together, preventing them
from sailing forth again. But on the next night
the other chiefs, earlier bound by sleep, slumbered
the last watch. Acastus amd Mopsus, Ampycus' son,
kept guard over their deep sleep. A halcyon
fluttered above the blond head of Aeson's son
and prophesied with shrill voice surcease to come

of the rushing winds. Mopsus heard and understood
the fatefully propitious cry of that bird of the shore.
A god turned it aside and it darted high and perched
upon the ornamented curve of the ship's stern.
Mopsus shook Jason as he lay in soft fleeces
of sheep, and waking him at once, he spoke thus:

"Son of Aeson, you must climb to the rugged peak
of Dindymum to propitiate the beautifully throned
mother of all the Blessed Ones, and the furious winds
shall cease. Such was the cry of prophecy I heard
just now from the seabird halcyon, which as it flew
above you while you slumbered uttered each thing.
For by her the winds and the sea and all the earth
below and Olympus' snowy seat have been defined.
Also to her when from the mountains she ascends
to mighty heaven, Zeus, the son of Cronus, yields,
and so do all the other immortal Blessed Ones
revere and serve the dread and awesome goddess Rhea."

So he spoke, and the word pleased Jason when he heard,
and he rose from his bed rejoicing and roused all his companions
urgently and told to them when they were awake
the prophecy of Mopsus, Ampycus' son. Straightway
the younger men drove oxen from their stalls and led
them from there to the mountain's sheer peak, and loosing the hawsers
from the Sacred Rock they rowed to the Thracian harbor, and they
themselves climbed up, leaving a few companions behind
in the ship. To them the Macrian heights and all of Thrace
on the opposite coast appeared close at hand to see.
And there appeared the misty mouth of Bosporus
and the Mysian hills; on the other side, the river Aesepus
and the Nepeian plain of the city Adrasteia.
There was a stout stump of vine grown in the wood,
extremely old. They cut this down to make of it
a holy image of the mountain goddess, and Argus
polished it beautifully. They set it up upon
that rugged hill, roofed above by loftiest oaks,

103

which of all the trees that grow have their roots most deep.
They piled an altar of pebbles and put on their brows wreaths
of oak leaves and concerned themselves with sacrifice.
They called upon the mother of Dindymum, much
revered, inhabitant of Phrygia. Titias
and Cyllenus too, who alone of many more are called
distributors of destiny, coadjutors
of the Idaean Mother, Idaean Dactyls of Crete,
whom once the nymph Anchiale bore in the Cretan cave,
gripping with both hands the land of the river Oaxus.
With many a prayer did the son of Aeson beseech the goddess
to turn aside the tempest, pouring libations upon
the blazing sacrifice. At the same time the youths
at Orpheus' command leapt and whirled in an armed dance
and struck their shields with swords that there disperse in air
the ill-omened cry, the moan that the people made yet
in grief for the king. Always since then with rhombus and drum
Phrygian men propitiate the goddess Rhea.
And she, divinity implored by prayers, inclined
her heart to the sacred sacrifices. Favorable signs
appeared. Trees shed fruit in wondrous abundance. Around
their feet from the tender grass the earth put blossoms forth,
and the beasts left their lairs and thickets and came, wagging
their tails. And she produced still another marvel.
No water had flowed before on Dindymum, but then
for them from the thirsty peak it bubbled forth, unceasing.
The men who dwelt about in aftertime called
that water Jason's spring. Then they prepared a feast
in the goddess's honor on the Mount of Bears with song and dance
for Rhea, most revered. But with the coming of dawn
the winds abated, and rowing off they abandoned the island.

Then rivalry aroused each of the chiefs to see
who should be last to cease from his task at oar, for all
around the windless air made smooth the swirling waves
and lulled the main to sleep. Trusting to the calm,
they forced the ship forward, and as she leapt through the sea

not even Poseidon's storm-footed steeds could have caught her up.
Nevertheless, when the swell was stirred by furious winds,
which rose afresh from the rivers at evening's dusky fall,
worn with their toil, they left off their task, but Heracles,
by the strength of his arms pulled the men along as they labored
with all haste and rattled the well-fitted beams of the ship.
But when, longing for the Mysian mainland, they skirted
and saw the outfall of Rhyndacus and the great tomb
of Aegaeon not far from Phrygia, then, heaving up
in furrows the ruffled swell of the sea, Heracles
broke his oar in two. One piece he held himself
in both hands as he fell aslant. The other the sea
bore away in its backward wash. He sat straight up,
silent, glaring; his hands were unused to idleness.

When from the field a gardener goes or some plowman
happily to his hut, craving his evening meal,
and there on the doorstep, squalid with dust, his worn knees
give way, and he looks upon his hands gnarled with work
and calls down many a wicked curse upon his belly,
then the heroes arrived at the haunts of Cianian land
near the Arganthonian mountain and mouths of the river Cius.
The Mysians, inhabitants of that land, received them
hospitably, for they had come in friendship. Supplies
in their need and sheep and bountiful wine they provided them,
and then some brought wood to kindle; others gathered
meadow grass in abundance to spread. Others still
twisted fire sticks, or, mixing wine in bowls,
prepared a feast and sacrificed at dark to Apollo
of Disembarking. But Heracles, the son of Zeus,
bade his comrades dine well and went to the wood to prepare
first an oar to fit his hand. He wandered and found
a pine, not burdened with boughs, nor abundant in foliage,
but like the trunk of a tall poplar. Such was its length
and breadth to see. Lightly he laid on the ground the quiver
that held his arrows, together with his bow, and took off
his lion's skin. With his club tipped with bronze he shook

the pine loose from the ground and with both his hands he grasped
the trunk, trusting in his strength, and propped it against
his broad shoulder, standing with legs stretched wide apart.
He clung to it and, deep rooted though it was,
he wrenched it from the ground along with clods of earth,
and as when without warning upon a ship's mast
at the stormy setting of deadly Orion a sudden squall
of wind strikes down from above and pulls it from its stays,
wedges and all, so Heracles wrenched the pine from the earth.

He took up his bow and arrows, his lion skin, and his club
and set out on his return. Hylas meanwhile with a pitcher
of bronze, apart from the throng, was seeking the sacred flow
of a spring to draw water for the evening meal
and make all in perfect order for Heracles' return.
In such manner had Heracles fostered him since first
he had taken him, an infant still, from the house
of his father, dreadful Theiodamas, whom Heracles slew,
ruthlessly, among the Dryopians when he
opposed him over a plowing ox. Theiodamas
was cleaving with his plow a field of fallow land
when he was struck with this affliction, but Heracles bade
him offer up against his will the plowing ox.
He wanted pretext for war against the Dryopians
to their destruction, since heedless of right they dwelt there.
But these tales would take me far away from my song.

Quickly Hylas came to the spring which those who dwell
round about call Pegae. The nymphs just then were beginning
their dances. For all of them that roamed the lovely headland
took care to sing songs by night to Artemis.
Those that had by lot the mountain peaks and streams,
all these were ranged far off to keep watch in the woods.
But one was just rising from the fair-flowing spring,
a water nymph. She caught sight of Hylas nearby,
blushing with beauty and sweet grace, for the full moon
cast her beams from the sky upon the boy, and Cypris
fluttered the heart of the nymph so that she was almost helpless

to gather her soul together again. As soon as Hylas
dipped in the stream his pitcher, leaning aside, and the water
sounded loud as it poured against the echoing bronze,
she laid her left arm upon his neck, longing
to kiss his tender mouth, and with her right she drew
his elbow down and plunged him into the whirling depth.
 Alone of his companions the son of Eilatus,
Polyphemus, heard his cry as he went along the path,
for he expected huge Heracles' return. Straightway
he drew his great sword and rushed forth in pursuit,
afraid that Hylas was the spoil of wild beasts
or that men lying in ambush had taken him, alone,
and were leading him away, an easy and ready prey.
He rushed toward Pegae like some wild beast that has heard
the bleating of sheep from afar and, famished, follows after
but does not find the flocks, for the shepherds before have penned
them in the folds. But he growls and roars unceasingly
until he wearies. So then did Eilatides loudly groan
and track back and forth, calling about the spot,
and his shouts were pitiable to hear. Then on the trail
as he brandished his bare sword he met Heracles
himself. He knew him well as he hastened to the ship through the dark.
At once he told the calamity, panting for breath.
 "My poor man, I shall be the first to bring
you bitter pain. Hylas has gone to the spring and not
come safely back again. Either robbers have attacked
and carry him off, or wild beasts maul him. I heard
his cry." So he spoke. When Heracles heard, sweat
poured down his temples, and the blood boiled black beneath
his heart. Enraged, he hurled the pine to the ground and rushed
along the path where his feet themselves bore him headlong.
 As when a bull stung by a gadfly tears along,
leaving the meadows behind and the marshes and pays no heed
to shepherds or flock but rushes headlong on his path, now
without pause, now standing still, and lifting up
his broad neck, bellows, stricken by the wicked fly,

so Heracles, raging, would run with all the strength of his knees,
then rest from his toil and call far off with a piercing cry.
    Just then the morning star rose above the highest
peaks, and the breezes blew down. Tiphys straightway
bade them go on board to profit by the wind.
They embarked at once, eagerly, and drew high
the ship's anchors and hauled the ropes astern. The wind
bellied the sails, and far from the coast they sailed in joy
past the Posideian headland. But when from heaven
the bright-eyed dawn shines, rising up from the East,
and the paths glisten and the plains sparkle with dew at her gleam,
then they realized that they in their heedlessness
had abandoned those men. A mighty quarrel broke out
and unspeakable wrangling because they had gone on board and abandoned
the best of their companions. But Aeson's son, distressed
by their helpless plight, spoke no word of any kind
but sat eating out his heart, weighted with grief.
Anger took Telamon and so he spoke, "Sit there
like that, satisfied, since it suited you to leave
Heracles behind. It was your thought that his glory
not eclipse yours throughout the land of Hellas,
should the gods grant us voyage home again. But what
is the use of words? I shall go alone without those comrades
of yours, who along with you contrived this treachery."
    He spoke, and rushed Tiphys, Hagnias' son, and his eyes
looked like the licks of ravening flame. And now quickly
back to the Mysian land would they have gone, forcing
their way through the gulf and implacable blast of the wind, had not
the two sons of Thracian Boreas restrained
the son of Aeacus with hard words, the villains —
a loathsome vengeance came upon them afterward
at Heracles' hands because they checked the search for him,
for as they came back from the games for Pelias' death,
Heracles slew them in Tenos where the sea flows around
and piled earth upon them and fashioned two slabs
above. One, an immense marvel for men to see,

moves at the blast of roaring Boreas. These things
were all to come then to fulfillment in aftertime.

But now there appeared to them from the salt depths Glaucus,
the subtle interpreter of Nereus, god of the sea.
Lifting his shaggy head and chest from his flanks below,
with sturdy hand he reached for the ship's keel and cried
to the men as they sped eagerly on their way, "Why
despite the will of mighty Zeus do you intend
to take to Aeetes' city the bold Heracles?
At Argos it is his fate to toil for arrogant
Eurystheus, fulfilling for him all twelve of his labors, and dwell
with the gods, sharing their hearth, if only he accomplish
a few more. And so let there be no longing for him.
Just so, it is the fate of Polyphemus to found
at the outfall of Cius among the Mysians a glorious city
and to meet his fate in the boundless land of the Chalybes.
On account of him those two wandered off and were left behind."

He spoke, and then he cloaked himself in the ceaseless wave
and dipped down to the depths. Around him the purple waters
foamed, swirling in eddies, and the leap of the salt sea
washed over the hollow ship, and all the heroes rejoiced,
but Telamon, the son of Aeacus, rushed to Jason.
Grasping his hand in his own, he embraced him and said this:

"Son of Aeson, do not be angry with me if I
in my infatuation did harm, for sorrow took me
to utter a word overweening and not to be borne, but let
us give my sin to the winds and be kindly disposed as before."

The son of Aeson answered him with circumspection:
"O kind friend, certainly with evil words
you did revile me, saying to all these that I
did wrong to a gentle man, but not for long will I
foster bitter wrath, though before I was very vexed,
for not for flocks of sheep nor even for possessions
did you rage in anger but for a man, your own companion,
and I should hope that you would thus do battle for me
against another man should such ever happen to me."

He spoke and they sat down, united as before.
But of those two, by the plans of Zeus, one was to found
and build among the Mysians a town, named for the river,
Polyphemus, son of Eilatus; Heracles,
to return to toil at Eurystheus' tasks. He threatened to ravage
the Mysian land at once should they not discover for him
the fate of Hylas, whether he lived or if he was dead.
They offered pledges to him, choosing the noblest sons
of the people and took oaths that they would never abandon
their labor of search. And so even now the Cians
inquire for Hylas, Theiodamas' son, and are concerned
for well-built Trachis. For there Heracles settled the sons
whom they had sent out from there to be led from Cius as pledges.

Now all that day and all night too a boisterous wind
bore the ship on, but it blew not even a little bit
when dawn came up. Nevertheless, they noticed a beach jutting out
from a curve in the coast, and it was, they saw, very broad to behold,
and so with oars they put to shore as the sun rose.

Book II

Here were the steadings and ox stalls of Amycus,
the headstrong king of Bebrycian men, whom once a nymph,
Bithynian Melie, who lay with Poseidon Begetter,
bore, and he was the most overweening of all men.
Even for strangers he laid down unseemly decree
that none should depart before he had made trial of him
in a boxing match, and he had slain many dwellers about.
Now too he went to the ship and scorned in his arrogance
to ask what the purpose was of their voyaging and who
they were but spoke straightway among them all this word:

"Hear, O sea-roving men, what it behooves you to know.
No stranger who comes near the Bebrycians can by decree
sail off again until he raises his fists with me.
Choose therefore from your host your noblest man to stand
right here alone contending with me in a boxing match.

But if you ignore and trample upon my ordinance,
to your sorrow strong compulsion will come upon you."
    So he spoke, haughtily, and savage wrath
took hold of those who heard, but the challenge struck Polydeuces
especially, and straightway he stood forth
as his companions' champion and cried aloud,
    "Hold now, and show us not, whoever you are,
your brutality. We will yield to your decrees,
as you demand, and I myself of my own accord
will undertake right now to engage you in a match."
    So he spoke, recklessly, but Amycus glared
and rolled his eyes like a lion struck by a javelin
and surrounded by men on the mountains. He, though hemmed in
by the throng, no longer pays it heed but all alone
eyes the man who smote him first and failed to kill.
Thereupon the son of Tyndareus set aside
the closely woven delicate cloak which a Lemnian woman
had given to him as a guest gift, and the king cast down
his dark robe of double fold, buckles and all,
and the rough staff he carried of mountain olive wood.
Spying straightway a pleasing spot nearby, they sat
their companions upon the sands in two separate rows,
nor were they similar to see in stature and size.
The one seemed to be a monster child of either
deadly Typhoeus or like one that Earth herself
brought forth before, enraged with Zeus. But the son of Tyndareus
was like a heavenly star whose sparkle is loveliest
as it shines through the evening sky. Such was the son of Zeus,
the velvety down just blooming and brightness still in his eyes,
but his strength and fury waxed like those of a wild beast.
He poised his hands to try if they were pliant as
before and not completely numb from the work of oars.
But Amycus made no test in turn. He stood apart
in silence and fixed his eyes upon his foe and his fury
crested in him, mad to spatter the blood from his chest.
Between them the squire of Amycus, Lycoreus, placed

III

before their feet on either side two pairs of thongs,
fashioned of rawhide that was dried and exceedingly tough.
The king addressed Polydeuces with overweening words:
"Whichever of these you wish without the casting of lots
I grant to you of my own free will that you not claim
to be defrauded afterward. Bind them about
your hands that you may learn and tell another how I
excel in cutting the parched hides of oxen and how
superior I am at soaking the cheeks of men with blood."
So he spoke, and the other gave no wrangling reply
but smiling slightly took up without hesitation the thongs
that lay before his feet. Castor came opposite
and mighty Talaus, Bias' son, and quickly they bound
the thongs around and often encouraged him to strength.
To Amycus came Aretus and Ornytus. Poor fools,
little did they know that they bound those thongs on the king
for the very last time and to his evil destiny.
Now when they stood apart, prepared in their boxing thongs,
straightway, raising before their bodies their heavy hands,
they encountered one another in a contest of strength. And so
the Bebrycian king, as a rough wave of the sea crests
over the ship and she by the skill of a cunning pilot
just escapes being swamped by the billow that rushes to break
over the bulwark, so Amycus beset Polydeuces,
trying to terrify him, and allowed him no pause.
But he, forever unwounded, would with skill avoid
his rush and quickly studied the rough fisticuffs
to find where their strength was inviolable or inferior
and stood, insatiate, exchanging blow for blow.
As when carpenters with hammers smite and drive
a ship's timbers hard against the sharp nails,
and there is the thud of one pounding after another,
so cheeks and jaws shattered on both sides and there
arose an unspeakable rattling of teeth, nor did they cease
from their alternate thrusts until a dangerous gasping for breath
defeated them both. Standing slightly apart, they wiped

the sweat from their brows in plenty and panted in their exhaustion.
Back again they rushed to confront one another
like bulls that fight in fury for a grazing heifer.
And then Amycus, rising tiptoe, like one who smites
an ox, stretched to full height, swung like an ax
his heavy hand upon him. The hero stepped aside
from his rush, averting his head, and took the king's arm
with his shoulder. Crowding, he slid his knee past Amycus' knee
and struck with a charge above his ear and smashed the bones
inside. In agony Amycus sank to his knees. The heroes
of Minyas gave a shout as his life came gushing forth.
    Nor were the Bebrycian men careless of their king,
but taking up seasoned clubs and spears, all together
they rushed Polydeuces, but his comrades took their stand
before him, drawing their keenly pointed swords from their sheaths.
First Castor struck a man on the head as he charged him,
and it was split in two and fell over either shoulder.
Polydeuces himself slew monstrous Itymoneus and Mimas.
The one he struck beneath the breast, throwing him
with swift foot and cast him in the dust. The other
as he came near he slashed with his right hand over
the left brow and slit the eyelid and left
the eyeball bare. Oreides, the overweening squire
of Amycus, wounded Talaus, Bias' son, in the flank
but did not kill him because the bronze just pierced the skin
beneath his belt and failed to reach his bowels. Just so
Aretus smote with parched club the staunch son
of Eurytus, not yet fated for an evil death.
He himself was destined soon to die by the sword
of Clytius. Ancaeus then, the bold son
of Lycurgus, quickly seized his mighty ax and leapt,
holding a bear's black hide in his left hand and raging,
into the Bebrycians' midst. Together with him
there rushed the sons of Aeacus, and with them
warlike Jason. As when among the sheepfolds
gray wolves on a winter's day terrorize

countless sheep, escaping in their onset the note
of keen-scented hounds and shepherds too and seek for what
they can first leap upon and carry off, often
glancing about from their pack, but the sheep just clump together
and stumble, one upon another, so the heroes
sorely terrorized the arrogant Bebrycians.
And just as when shepherds or beekeepers smoke out
a great swarm of bees from a rock and they meanwhile,
crowded within their hive, hum in great confusion,
until, crazed by the murky smoke, they suddenly stream
far from the rock, so they no longer stayed steadfast
but scattered within Bebrycia, announcing Amycus' death.
Poor fools, they did not realize that another woe,
unforeseen, pressed upon them, for just then
their vineyards and villages were being sacked by
Lycus' hostile spear and the Mariandyni,
since their king was dead, for they were forever wrangling over
the iron-bearing land. They were savaging their stables
and farms, and heroes from all around were slaughtering
countless sheep, and one among them spoke this word:
"Think what they would have done in their cowardice had a god
somehow brought Heracles here. Indeed I expect that had
that man been here, there would have been no boxing match,
but when he approached to announce his rules, the club would have caused
the king to forget his courage, decrees and all. Yes,
we abandoned him to neglect on land and sailed the sea,
and each of us himself will know how destructive was
our folly, now that Heracles is far away."
So he spoke, but all had been wrought by the plans of Zeus.
Then they remained there through the dark and tended the wounds
of the hurt men, and making sacrifice to the gods,
they prepared a mighty meal and sleep took no one
beside the mixing bowl and blazing offerings.
Wreathing their blond brows with leaves of a laurel that grew
near the shore, to which their stern cables were fastened tight,
they sang a hymn in harmony with Orpheus' lyre,

melodiously, and enchanted the windless strand with their song,
celebrating the son of Zeus, Therapnaean Polydeuces.

But when the sun had lit the dewy hills, rising
from far-off lands, and waked the shepherds, then they loosed
from the laurel's stem the cables and put on board the booty,
all that they needed to bring, and with the wind they steered
straight through the swirling Bosporus. Here a wave rose up
like a mountain, sheer before and rushing upon them,
cresting ever above the sails. Nor would you say
that they could escape evil doom since it hangs, voracious,
mid-ship, like a cloud. Nevertheless, it sinks
and is smoothed to calm should it encounter a skilled pilot,
so they by the cunning craft of Tiphys sailed through
unscathed but extremely frightened, and on the next day
they fastened their cables to the coast opposite Thynia.

There Phineus, son of Agenor, had his seacoast home.
He beyond all men endured destructive pain
because of the mantic art that Leto's son had bestowed
on him in times before. Not Zeus himself did he
revere but fearlessly interpreted to men
the god's sacred intent. And so Zeus sent to him
an endless old age and took from his eyes the sweet light
and refused him delight in the countless dainties that dwellers about
brought to his house when they came to find out the oracles.
But through the clouds, suddenly close by, the Harpies
swooped and with their beaks constantly snatched the food
from his mouth and hands — sometimes no food at all was left,
sometimes a little bit that he might live and suffer —
and they poured over all the stench of mold. No one dared
carry food to his mouth or even to stand at a distance,
such was the reek of the banquet leavings. As soon as he heard
the voice and the thudding tramp of the throng he understood
that these were the men passing by at whose coming Zeus
had prophesied that he should enjoy his food. He rose
from his bed, like a lifeless dream. Bent over his staff, he crept
on wrinkled feet to the door, touching the walls, and his limbs

as he went trembled with weakness and age. His parched skin
was squalid with dirt and only his hide held together his bones.
He came from the hall and sat with heavy knees upon
the outer threshold. A dark torpor covered him,
and he thought that the earth reeled beneath, and he lay, speechless,
in a strengthless stupor. And they, when they saw him, gathered around
and were amazed. But he, drawing difficult breath
from the depths of his chest, spoke to them in prophetic words:
  "Hear me, noblest of all the Hellenes, if in truth
you are they whom by a king's chill command
Jason in the ship Argo takes in search of the fleece—
surely you are they, my mind knows everything still
by its prophetic skill—I offer thanks to you,
Apollo, even in my terrible affliction.
By Zeus, god of suppliants, coldest to sinning men,
and for Phoebus' sake and that of Hera herself, by whose
grace beyond that of all the gods you have come here,
I beseech you, succour me, protect an ill-starred man
from misery. Do not set sail, abandoning me
to such neglect. Not only has the Fury ground
her heel in my eyes and I drag to the end tedious age,
but another most bitter evil hangs over me besides.
The Harpies snatch the food from my mouth, swooping down
from some indiscernible aerie or other—sheer destruction!—
and I have no cunning to ward them off. More easily
could I escape my own thought, intent upon
a meal, than those, with such speed do they fly through the air.
If ever they leave to me some little bit of food,
it reeks of mold, and the stench is unendurable.
No mortal man for even a minute could bear to come near,
no, not though his heart were fashioned of adamant.
Insatiate want compels me to endure and put
inside my belly, while I endure, this bitter feast.
These women, the oracle decrees, the sons of Boreas
will restrain. Nor will they be strangers who ward them off,
if I am Phineus, formerly famed among men

116

for my prosperity and gift of prophecy.
Agenor begat me. Their sister, when I was king among
the Thracians, Cleopatra, I brought with my wedding gifts as a bride
to my house." So spoke the son of Agenor. Keen sorrow seized
each of the heroes, especially the two sons
of Boreas. Wiping away a tear, they came near
and Zetes said, taking the hand of the grieved old man,
    "Poor wretch, no man, I say, is more miserable
than you. Why have so many woes been inflicted on you?
Have you sinned against the gods with fatal thoughtlessness
in your art of prophecy? Is it for this that they
are furious with you? We are distressed, for though
we long to help, the reproofs of gods to men on earth
are clear to see. We will not ward the Harpies off,
although we long to, until you swear an oath
that not for this shall we lose favor with the gods."
So he spoke, and toward him the old man opened
his empty eyes and rolled them up and thus replied:
    "Silence. Do not harbor thoughts like these, my child.
Let the son of Leto know, who kindly taught
me prophecy, and the cursed doom that has taken me
and this blind cloud upon my eyes, and the gods below—
may they not be generous to me if I die thus—
that no wrath will come from heaven for your help to me."
    Heeding the oath, the two longed to ward them off.
Quickly the younger men prepared for the old man
a feast, last prey for the Harpies. The sons of Boreas stood
nearby to smite with their swords the Harpies as they streaked down.
As soon as the old man touched his food, suddenly they,
like bitter blasts of wind or lightning flashes that leap
unexpectedly from the clouds, swooped down with a shriek,
raging for food. The heroes saw them and cried aloud,
but they at their shout ate everything up, and over the sea
they sped, far off, and left an unendurable stench.
Behind them ran in equal pursuit the two sons
of Boreas, brandishing swords, for Zeus had inspired in them

unwearying strength. They could not have followed apart from Zeus,
for they in their dashing flight surpassed the very blasts
of the west wind when they came to Phineus or when they left.
Just as when on the slopes of a mountain hounds skilled
in the hunt, tracking horned goats or the roe deer,
run and, though they strain, lag a little behind
and gnash their teeth against their jaws — it does no good —
so Zetes and Calais, though dashing very near, just grazed
the Harpies with their fingertips — fruitlessly.
And now despite the gods they would have torn them to shreds,
overtaking them at the Floating Islands very far off,
had swift Iris not seen them and swept down from the sky,
from heaven above, and held them off with words like these:

    "It is not permitted, O sons of Boreas, to strike with swords
the Harpies, hounds of mighty Zeus, but I myself
will swear that they shall not again approach this man."

    So she spoke and swore by the waters of river Styx,
which is to all divinities most dreaded and dire,
that these creatures should not again approach the home
of Phineus, the son of Agenor, for so it was also fated.
The heroes yielded to her oath and turned again
to the ship for safety. Because of this men call the islands
Turning, which in former times they called Floating.
The Harpies and Iris parted ways. They went down
into their hiding place on Minoan Crete, but she
rose up to Olympus, soaring aloft on her swift wings.
Meanwhile the princes thoroughly washed the old man's
filthy skin and made sacrifice of sheep which they chose
from those they had brought back from plundering Amycus.
But when they had set an enormous feast in the hall, they sat
down to dine, and with them dined Phineus, ravenously,
warming his soul as though he were a man in a dream.
There, when they had had their fill of food and drink,
all night long they stayed awake and waited for
the sons of Boreas. In their midst the old man

himself sat beside the hearth and described to them

the end of their voyage and accomplishment of their journey home.

"Listen now. It is not permitted you to know
all things accurately, but as much as pleases the gods
I shall not hide. I was infatuate before,
thoughtlessly interpreting the will of Zeus
in order and to the end, for he himself intends
to impart to men mysterious words of prophecy
that they may crave something still of the mind of god.

"First of all, setting sail from here, you will see
the two Cyanean rocks in the place where the seas meet.
No one, I say, has escaped between them, for they are not
rooted deep and firm beneath, but frequently float
into one reef, and a great spray of saltwater crests,
heaving high, and the rough beach thunders around.
Obey, therefore, my instructions now, if in truth
with circumspection and reverence for the Blessed Ones
you cleave the waves. Do not press senselessly
to die a self-sought death, obeying the dictates of youth.
First, I command, try with a dove which you have sent
forth from the ship. If she flies safely through the rocks
toward Pontus, no longer yourselves hold back from your path,
but gripping your oars hard in your hands, cleave your course
through the narrow of the salt sea. For the light will come
not so much from prayers as strength of hands, and so
let all else go and labor with profit and courage. Implore
the gods before; I do not prevent you. But if
she flies straight on and perishes midway, turn back
again, since it is better by far to yield to the gods,
for you could not escape an evil fate from the rocks,
not even if the ship Argo were made of iron.

"O wretches, do not dare transgress my divine decrees,
not even if you think me thrice as hated by heaven
as I am, and detested even more. And do not dare
to sail in your ship beyond the omen of the bird.

As these things may be, so shall they be. But if II. 345
–378
you escape the clash of the rocks and come unscathed inside
Pontus, straightway, keeping on your right the land
of Bithynia, sail and beware of the breaking surf until
you round the swift-flowing Rhebas River and Black Beach
and reach the anchorage of the island of Thynias.
There sailing back not very far through the sea, beach
your ship on the opposite land of the Mariandyni.
There is there a downward path to the house of Hades,
and the jutting headland of Acherusia stretches high
and swirling Acheron, cutting through at base the headland
itself and spouting forth streams from a deep ravine.
Close to it, you will sail past the many hills
of the Paphlagonians, over whom at first Pelops
the Eneteian was king. They boast that they are of his blood.

"There is a headland opposite Helice the Bear,
steep on every side. They call the point Carambis.
Around its peak the blasts of Boreas are split,
so very high does it strike the air, turned toward the sea.
When you have rounded it, Great Aegialus lies
before you. At the ends of Great Aegialus
at a jutting point the streams of the river Halys belch
frightfully. Flowing near and next to it
Iris, a smaller stream, rolls with white swirls
into the sea. Forward from there a prominent cape
extends from land, and then the mouth of Thermodon
flows into a fair-weather bay at the promontory
of Themiscyreia, after meandering all through
a broad continent. And there is the plain of Doeas
and close by the three cities of Amazons
and then the Chalybes, the most wretched of men,
possess a stubborn, unyielding soil; laborers,
they busy themselves about the mining and forging of iron.
Near them live the Tibareni, rich in sheep,
beyond the Genetaean promontory of Zeus
of Hospitality. Bordering on them

and next in order, the Mossynoeci inhabit the valleys
and plains of the wooded mainland. They build inside bastions
of wood their huts and well-made walls, which they call
mossynes, and they themselves are named from them.
Passing by them, beach upon a smooth island,
after banishing in every manner of means or way
the shameless birds which in countless numbers haunt
that lonely island. There the Amazonian queens
Otrere and Antiope built a temple of stone
to Ares when they set out upon campaign of war.
Here unspeakable help will come to you from out
of the bitter sea, and so with kindly thought I bid
you to hold back—but what need for me to sin
again, telling every single thing straight through
to the end of my art of prophecy? Beyond the island
and mainland opposite, the Philyres sustain
themselves. Above the Philyres the Macrones live
and after them in turn the endless tribes of Becheiri.
Next in order to them the Sapeires dwell and then
with lands adjoining theirs the Byzeres. Above them
now the warlike Colchians themselves exist.
But sail on until you reach the innermost sea.
Here from Cytaean mainland and Amarantine mountains
far away and from the Circaean plain, Phasis
eddies and spews his broad stream into the sea.
Steer your ship to that river's outfall and you will see
the turreted walls of Cytaean Aeetes and shadowed grove
of Ares. There a serpent, a monster terrible
to see, peers about, protecting the fleece spread
upon the top of an oak tree. But neither day
nor dark does sweet sleep subdue his shameless eyes."

So he spoke. At once fear seized hold of them
as they heard, and long were they stricken with speechlessness. At last
the hero, son of Aeson, spoke, appalled at their plight:

"Old man, now you have come to the ends of our adventures
of voyaging and the sign by which, if we trust in it,

we shall sail through the loathsome rocks. But if in turn,
escaping these, we shall voyage home to Hellas again,
this too I would happily learn from you. What am I
to do, how take again such a long course of the sea,
unskilled myself, my companions unskilled? Colchian Aea
lies at the furthest reaches of Pontus and of the world."

So he spoke, and the old man said in reply to him,
"O child, when once you have fled through the deadly rocks, take heart,
for a deity will lead you by another course
from Aea. To Aea there will be escorts enough.
But heed, my friends, the clever help of the Cyprian goddess,
for in her lie the glorious ends of your adventures.
And do not ask me to tell the future further than this."

So then spoke Agenor's son, and close by
the two sons of Thracian Boreas came, sweeping
down the sky and set their swift feet upon
the threshold. The heroes rose up from their seats when they saw them
          there.
Zetes, still panting hard from his toil, told the men,
who were eager to hear, how far they had driven the Harpies and how
Iris had checked their slaying them and how graciously
the goddess had given oaths and how the Harpies had plunged
in exceeding fear into a cave of the Cretan scar.
And then in the halls all the companions rejoiced and Phineus
himself as well at the news, and quickly the son of Aeson
with the very kindliest of thoughts addressed him thus:

"Surely, Phineus, there was some god who had concern
for your bitter affliction and brought us here from far away
that the sons of Boreas defend you, and if
he should offer light to your eyes as well, truly I
would rejoice as much as if I had voyaged home again."

So he spoke, but Phineus replied dejectedly,
"Son of Aeson, this affliction is past recall,
nor is there after remedy. My empty eyes
are smoldering. May god instead offer death
at once to me. Dead, I shall share in every joy."

So the two of them spoke in reply to one another.
Not long afterward early-born dawn appeared.
Around Phineus gathered the men who dwelt about
and who in earlier times used to come every day
and bring always with them a portion of their own food.
To all of them, however humble the man who came,
he prophesied carefully and freed many
from pain by his mantic art, and so they would come and care
for him. With them came Paraebius, who was
most dear to him, and gladly he marked these men in the house
for once before the seer himself had told of a band
of chiefs to come from Hellas to Aeetes' city
and fasten their stern cables to the Thynian land,
who would restrain for him the Harpies by will of Zeus.
The others the old man pleased with shrewd words and sent
away but bade Paraebius alone remain
with the princes there. Straightway he sent him with orders to bring
to him whichever should be the most choice of his sheep.
And when Paraebius had gone from his halls he spoke
softly to all the oarsmen assembled there:
    "Oh, my friends, not all men are arrogant
or forgetful of benefits. Just so this man came here
as one of those to learn his destiny. For when
he toiled and labored most, then the needs of life
ever more pressing would wear him down, and day would dawn
upon day, each more wretched than the one before,
nor was there any respite for the suffering man,
but he paid the evil penalty for his father's sin.
For once when he was felling trees on the mountains alone,
he scorned the entreaties of a hamadryad nymph
who wept and beseeched him with vehement words not to cut
the stump of an oak of her own age in which she had tarried
for many a season. But he in manly pride of youth
thoughtlessly chopped it down. To him afterward
the nymph made her death a profitless doom, to him and to
his offspring. And I, when he came, knew his sin

123

and bade him build an altar to the Thynian nymph
and make sacrifice of expiation and pray
for escape from his father's fate, and here since he fled from
that god-driven doom he has not once forgotten me
nor treated me with scorn. I send him reluctant from
my doors and yearning to be at my side in my affliction."

So spoke Agenor's son. The man straightway came near,
bringing two sheep from the flock. Jason stood up
and Boreas' sons at instruction from the old man.
Quickly they called upon Mantic Apollo and made
sacrifice upon the hearth, for the day was waning.
The younger companions prepared a feast to please their hearts,
and when they had banqueted well, they slept, some beside
the ships' hawsers, others in throngs throughout the halls.

At dawn the Etesian winds assaulted them. They blow
on every land alike with like abetting of Zeus.
Cyrene, so they say, along the marsh of Peneus
once tended sheep among the men of former times,
for virginity and maiden bed were dear to her,
but Apollo snatched her up as she tended her flocks beside
the river, and far from Haemonia set her down among
the Libyan nymphs who live beside the Myrtosian peak.
And there to Phoebus she bore Aristaeus. The Haemonians,
rich in fields of wheat, call him Hunter and Shepherd.
Because of his love the god made her a nymph there,
of long life and a huntress, and brought his son, an infant
still, to be tended and reared in the cave of the centaur Cheiron.
The goddess Muses betrothed to him when he was grown
a bride and taught him the arts of healing and prophecy.
They made him a keeper of their sheep, all those that grazed
the Athamantian plain of Phthia and around Othrys,
impregnably steep, and Apidanus River's sacred stream.
But when from heaven Sirius scorched the Minoan isles
and there was for a long time no cure for the dwellers there,
then at Far-Archer's suggestion they summoned him
to ward off the plague. At his father's command he left Phthia

and settled in Ceos and gathered together Parrhasian people,
who are of Lycaon's stock, and made a great altar
to Zeus Icmaeus and on the mountains sacrificed
to that star, Sirius himself, and to Zeus,
the son of Cronus. Because of this Etesian winds
from Zeus cool the land for forty days. In Ceos
even now the priests sacrifice before
the rising of the Dog Star. So it is told.

But the princes stayed there, constrained, and the Thynians sent
innumerable guest gifts in gracious favor to Phineus.

Next they built an altar to the Twelve Blessed
beyond the surf line of the beach and laid victims
upon it and went on board their swift ship to row.
Nor did they forget a timorous dove, but Euphemus seized
and bore in his hand the bird, all quivering with fear,
and the heroes loosed from the land the double stern cables.
Nor did they escape Athena's notice as they set forth.
But hurriedly she stepped upon a light cloud
which bore her straight on, sturdy though she was,
and she rushed to Pontus with kindly thought for the oarsmen.
As when one wanders far from his fatherland—as often
we roving mortals do courageously and, troubled,
strain keenly—now here, now there, and no land
seems far away but every city beneath his eyes,
and he imagines his own home, and all at once
the course by land and sea is clear to his eyes, so
quickly then did the daughter of Zeus dart down and set
her foot upon the unwelcoming shore of Thynia.

When they reached the narrow of the crooked passage,
confined on both sides by rough crags where from
below a swirling current washed the ship as she passed,
they sailed forward, much afraid. And now the thud
of the rocks as they clashed constantly struck upon their ears,
and the sea-drenched beach boomed around. Euphemus then
grasped the dove in his hand and rose to mount the prow.
They at command of Tiphys, Hagnias' son, rowed

willingly to steer between the rocks, trusting to
their strength. At once, as they rounded a bend, they saw the rocks
opening up for the last time of all and their hearts
were confounded. Euphemus sent the dove to dart ahead
and they all lifted their heads to look. She flew between
the rocks which then came floating face to face and crashed,
and a great spray of brine boiled up like a cloud, and the sea
thundered terribly, and all around the vault
of heaven rumbled. The hollow caverns roared beneath
the rugged cliffs as the sea surged in, and high above
the bank the froth of the splashing wave spat white. And then
the current spun the ship around, and the rocks sheared
the tips of the dove's tail feathers, but she soared away
unscathed, and the oarsmen shouted aloud. Tiphys himself
roared to them to row powerfully, for the rocks
were opening up again. But they trembled so as they rowed
that the tide, flooding back, bore them within the rocks.
Then a most terrible fear took hold of all of them
for resistless destruction threatened, towering overhead.
And now on this side and that the broad Pontus appeared
and unexpectedly a huge wave rose up
before them, arched, like a sheer cliff. Seeing it,
they bent and bowed their heads, for they thought it would crash down,
engulfing the whole ship, but Tiphys eased her first
as she labored hard with the oars, and the massive wave rolled
away beneath the keel and from the stern raised
the ship far from the rocks and carried it high on air.
Euphemus went up and down the rows of all his companions,
shouting to them to bend to their oars with all their strength,
and they with a cry chopped the water. As far as the ship
gave to the rowers, twice as far did she leap back,
and the blades were bent like curved bows at the heroes' force.
Just then a cresting wave swept upon them,
and the ship exactly like a cylinder ran upon
the voracious billow and plunged ahead through the hollow sea.
The swirling current caught them between the Clashing Rocks,

which on either side thundered and shook, and the ship's timbers
were shackled fast. And then Athena with sturdy left hand
pulled back a rock and with her right thrust the ship
through. She like a feathered arrow swept through the air.
Nevertheless, the rocks, constantly clashing, sheared
the very tip of the stern decoration. But Athena rose
up to Olympus when they had escaped unscathed. The rocks
were suddenly rooted together forever in one spot,
as had been fated by the Blessed Ones should ever
a mortal man pass through them still alive in his ship.

The Argonauts breathed again after their chilling fear
and gazed at the air and at the same time the main
of the sea, spread everywhere, for they thought that they had been spared
from Hades, and Tiphys first of all began to speak:
    "I hope that we have escaped together with our ship,
nor is there other cause for this than Athena, who breathed
divine strength in her when Argus fitted her
together with bolts, nor is it permitted her to be caught.
Son of Aeson, no longer fear so much the command
of your king, since a god has granted us escape through the rocks,
for Phineus said that our after toils would be easily done."
    He spoke, and past the Bithynian land he sped the ship
ahead and through the midst of the main. But Jason spoke
with gentle words. Addressing him in reply he said,
    "Tiphys, why do you comfort me like this in my grief?
I have erred and committed wicked and irreversible folly.
I should when Pelias gave his command have rejected straight out
this expedition, even if I were destined to die,
pitilessly ripped and scattered limb from limb,
but now I am beset by exceeding fear and cares
unendurable, dreading to sail the chilling paths of the sea
in my ship and dreading too to step upon the mainland,
for everywhere are hostile men, and every day
I keep the night moaning to myself since first
you congregated for my sake, and I worry about
every single thing. But you speak easily,

concerned for your own life alone. But I for mine
am distraught not a bit but fear for this man and that and you
and other companions should I not bring you safe to Hellas."

So he spoke, testing the chiefs, but they shouted
encouraging words, and his heart melted within when he heard
their cry, and again he spoke explicitly to them:

"O friends, your valor gives me heart, and therefore now,
not even should I voyage through the underground rivers
of Hades, shall fear fasten upon me, since you stand firm
among such awful terrors. But now that we have sailed
from out between the Clashing Rocks, I think that never
again will we encounter another such frightening thing,
if truly we go on our way following Phineus' advice."

So he spoke, and straightway they left off such talk
and to their rowing gave toil unabating. Quickly
they passed the swift-flowing Rhebas and Colone's peak
and not long after Black Beach and then the outfall
of Phyllis, where Dipsacus once received Athamas' son
when he fled with his ram from Orchomenus. A meadow nymph
gave him birth, nor did violence suit him. Contented he lived
with his mother beside his father's waters and pastured his sheep
along their banks. Straightway they spied and passed his tomb
and the river's broad shores and plain and deeply flowing
Calpe, and by day and windless night alike
they put their strength to their unwearying oars, and just
as laboring oxen toil, splitting the damp soil,
and incredible sweat trickles from flanks and neck, and their eyes
roll askance beneath the yoke, and their scorching breath
roars incessantly from their mouths, and all day long
they toil, imprinting the earth with their hooves — it was like this
that the heroes kept pulling their oars under and out of the sea.

When the ambrosial light has not yet come and yet
it is no longer exceedingly dark but a delicate glimmer
has spread over the night and men wake and call
it the pre-dawn, at that hour they steered into
the harbor of the lonely isle of Thynias and stepped

128

ashore, worn by their many toils. To them appeared
Leto's son, going from Lycia far away
to the countless Hyperborean men. His golden locks
clustered like grapes on either side of his cheeks and flowed
as he walked. In his left hand he wielded a silver bow,
and a quiver hung from his shoulders and back. Beneath his feet
all the island shook and waves washed high on land.
The men were helplessly amazed to see him,
and no one dared to gaze, face to face, into
the lovely eyes of the god, but bowed low to the earth.
But Apollo, far away, swept through the air to the sea.
At last Orpheus spoke to the princes and addressed them like this:
    "Come now and let us call this isle the holy isle
of Dawn's Apollo since he has appeared to all, passing
at dawn. And we shall make what sacrifice we can,
building an altar upon the beach. If afterward
he grant us voyage home unscathed to Haemonian land,
then we shall place on that altar thighs of horned goats.
Now with savor of sacrifice and with libations
I bid you make propitiation to him. Be gracious,
O lord, be gracious in your epiphany to us."
    So he spoke, and straightway they built an altar of stones
and roamed about the island to see if they could spy
a fawn or wild goat that often feeds deep
in the wood, and to them the son of Leto provided prey,
and they burned with pious rites the doubled thigh bones
upon their altar and celebrated Apollo of Dawn.
Around the blazing sacrifice they set up
a wide chorus and danced and sang, "Lovely healer,
hail, healer Apollo, hail," and together with them
the noble son of Oeagrus began a shrill song
upon his Bistonian lyre: how once Apollo slew
beneath Parnassus' stony shelf the monstrous Delphyne—
still a beardless youth, still rejoicing in
his locks. May you be gracious, lord, and may your locks
be ever unshorn, ever unharmed, for so it is right.

Only Leto herself, born of Coeus, strokes
your locks with her own dear hands. Often Corycian nymphs,
daughters of Pleistus, added heart to the song and cried,
"Hië, "Hië." Hence to Phoebus this lovely refrain.
Now when they had with song and dance celebrated him,
with holy libations they swore forever with concord of mind
to aid one another and touched with their oath the sacrifice,
and even now there stands a shrine to kindly Concord
which then the Argonauts built to honor that glorious goddess.
    When the third dawn came, then with a fresh wind they left
the lofty island. Next they spied and skirted the mouth
of the river Sangarius opposite and the flourishing land
of the Mariandyni, and the streams of the river Lycus
and the Anthemoeisian lake. Beneath the breeze the ropes
and all the ship's tackle shook as they sped ahead.
At dawn, since the wind had died during the dark, they reached
gladly the anchorage of the Acherusian cape.
It rises high with precipitous crags, looking toward
the Bithynian sea. Beneath are rooted slippery rocks
washed by the sea and around them thunder the rolling waves,
but above at the very peak spreading plane trees grow.
Away from it and toward the land a hollow vale
slopes away and there there is a cave of Hades,
arched over with wood and rock. From here an icy blast
breathing from the chill recess constantly feeds
a glittering rime, nor does it melt at midday sun.
Nor does silence ever shroud that grim cape,
but it moans with the echoing sea and whispers with the leaves
that quiver from the winds of the cave. And the outfall is here
of the river Acheron, which belches up through
the headland and hurls itself into the eastern sea,
and a hollow ravine brings it down from high above.
Among the later-born the Nisaean Megarians
named it Savior of Sailors when they intended to
inhabit the land of the Mariandyni, for the river
had saved them, ships and all, caught by a wicked storm.

By this and through the Acherusian cape, once
the wind had died, they berthed their ship in sight of it.
Not for long did their mooring escape Lycus, the chief
of that land, nor the Mariandynian men, who had heard of them
before as murderers of Amycus. Therefore
they even made a pact with them, and Polydeuces
himself they welcomed as a god, flocking together
from every side, for they for a long time had warred
with the overweening Bebrycians, and so with all speed,
proceeding to the city, within the halls of Lycus
that day they banqueted in friendship and delighted
their souls in conversation. The son of Aeson told
the name and lineage of each of his companions,
and Peleus' commands, and of the hospitality
of the Lemnian women, and all that they had accomplished at
Dolonian Cyzicus, and how they next had reached
Mysia and Cius, where with unwilling heart they had
abandoned the hero Heracles, and Glaucus' report.
And he told how they had slain the Bebrycians and Amycus,
and Phineus' prophecies and his affliction, and how
they had escaped the Cyanean rocks, and how they had met
Leto's son at the island. And as he told his story,
Lycus' soul was charmed at the hearing, but grief took him
for Heracles left behind, and he spoke like this to them all:
    "Oh friends, from help of what a man have you wandered away,
making a voyage so long to Aeetes, for well I know
that I saw him here in the halls of my father, Dascylus,
when he came on foot through the Asian continent and brought
the warrior belt of battle-loving Hippolyte here,
and he found me with the soft down just fresh on my cheeks.
Here, when Priolas, my brother, had died at the hands
of Mysian men — the people mourn for him still
with piteous elegies — then Heracles engaged
in a boxing match and slew Titias, who surpassed
all youths in beauty and strength, and knocked his teeth to the ground.
Together with the Mysians beneath my father's command

he subdued the Mygdoni, who dwell in fields neighboring ours,
and acquired the Bithynian tribes and their land as far as the mouth
of the Rhebas River and the peak of Colone. Furthermore,
the Paphlagonians of Pelops surrendered all those
that the black water of the river Billaeus breaks around,
just as they were. But the Bebrycians and arrogance
of Amycus have robbed me of these since Heracles
lives far away, cutting off huge chunks of my land
for a long time until they have set their boundaries
at the meadows of the deeply flowing Hypius. Nevertheless,
at your hands they have paid the penalty. I say
that not despite the gods did he, Tyndareus' son,
that day bring war upon the Bebrycians, slaying that man.
And now for this, whatever recompense I can,
I will pay, for that is right for weaker men to do
when others who are stronger begin to help them.
With all of you and in your company I urge
to follow Dascylus, my son, and if he goes,
you will encounter friendly men all along,
as far as the mouth of the Thermodon itself. Besides,
I will set up a steep shrine which all sailors
shall see and reverence from afar upon the main.
And after, for them, before the town, just as for gods,
I shall mark off fertile fields of the well-plowed plain."
     So then they amused themselves all day long at the feast.
At dawn they hurried down to the ship and Lycus himself
accompanied them, when he had given myriad gifts
to carry away with them, and he sent his son from home.
     Here his destined fate struck Idmon, son of Abas,
excellent in prophecy, but not at all
did prophecy save him, since necessity led him on
to destruction, for there lay in the reed-filled river,
gleaming of tooth, a deadly monster, who terrified
even the nymphs of the marsh themselves, and no man
knew it, but all alone it fed in the wide fen.
But the son of Abas was going along the rising banks

of the muddy plain when the boar from some invisible lair

leapt out of the reeds and rushed at him, gashing his thigh,
and severed the sinews, together with the bone, in two.
With a sharp cry Idmon fell to the ground. And as
he bellowed, his comrades crowded about and yelled too.
Quickly Peleus aimed his spear at the deadly boar
as it rushed back to the fen. Again it turned and charged,
but Idmon wounded it, and with a roar it fell
upon the sharp spear. The boar they left on the ground
where it had fallen, but Idmon, gasping for his last breath,
his grieved companions bore back to the ship, where he died in their arms.

   Here they refrained from concern for their voyaging and stayed,
grieved, for the funeral rites for the corpse. For three whole days
they mourned. On the next they buried it, magnificently,
and the people together with King Lycus himself shared
in the funeral rites. They slit the throats of countless sheep
beside the tomb, as the custom is, for the dead and gone.
And so for this man in that land they heaped
a barrow, and there stands upon it for later-born men to see
a sign, the trunk of that ship's timber, the wild olive,
and it flourishes with its silvery leaves a little beneath
the Acherusian height. And if at the Muses' command
I must tell this story bluntly, Phoebus explicitly bade
the Nisaeans and Boeotians to propitiate him
as savior of their city and to lay their city
around the trunk of the ancient wild olive tree,
but they instead of to god-fearing Aeolid Idmon
even until this day pay honor to Agamestor.

   Who was the other who died? For still again the heroes
heaped a cairn for a comrade dead, and two are the tokens
still to be seen of those men. The story is
that Tiphys, Hagnias' son, died. Nor was it his fate
to voyage further, but a brief illness lulled him to rest
right there, far from his fatherland, after the band
had paid funeral rites to the corpse of Abas' son.
They suffered unendurable grief at the cruel blow.

For a long time, when they with honor had buried him,
close by Idmon, falling distraught before the sea
and wrapped closely about in their mantles, they took no thought
of food or drink, and their spirits languished in grief, for they had
no hope of making the voyage home. And now in their mourning
they would have held from further journeying had not
Hera inspired exceeding courage in Ancaeus,
whom beside Imbrasus' waters Astypalaea
bore to Poseidon, for he was especially skilled in steering,
and he addressed Peleus with eager words like these:
    "Son of Aeacus, how is it well to neglect our toils
and linger long in a foreign land? Not so much
for my skill in war did Jason bring me in search of the fleece,
far from Parthenia, as for my knowledge of ships.
And so let there be little fear for the ship, for there are
other clever men here and none we mount
at the helm will harm our voyaging. But quickly, tell
this to all and boldly rouse the men to remember their task."
    So he spoke, and Peleus' soul swelled with delight,
and immediately, with no delay, he spoke in their midst:
    "What is the matter with us? Why do we cling like this
to profitless grief? These two men have perished by
their allotted fate, but we have many pilots yet
in our company. Let us therefore not delay attempt
but stir yourselves to the task and cast your sorrows away."
    Despairing, the son of Aeson in turn replied to him,
"Son of Aeacus, where, may I ask, are these pilots of yours?
For those whom once we vaunted as skilled are more downcast
and grieve even more than I, and so I prophesy
an evil doom together with the dead for us,
if it shall be our luck neither to reach the city
of dangerous Aeetes nor the land of Hellas
again, escaping the rocks, but a wicked fate will enshroud
us here, without renown, and we grow old in vain."
    So he spoke, but Ancaeus eagerly undertook
to steer the swift ship, for the goddess impelled him.

134

After him, Erginus, Nauplius, and Euphemus
rose up, keen to steer, but the men restrained them,
and the many of their companions approved Ancaeus' command.
 And then on the twelfth day they embarked at dawn, for then
a strong west wind began to blow, and swiftly they rowed
out through Acheron and, trusting to the breeze,
let out their linen sails and with their canvases spread,
quickly they passed beside the mouth of the Callichorus,
where they say the Nyseian son of Zeus, when he
had left the Indian tribes and come to live at Thebes,
held orgies, arranging choruses of dancers before
the cave where he spent unsmiling sacred nights. Since then
the dwellers about call the river Callichorus or
"Lovely Chorus" and the cave "Chamber" or Aulion.
 From there they saw the tomb of Sthenelus, the son
of Actor, who, coming back from the bold war against
the Amazons (for he had accompanied Heracles),
shot by an arrow there, died upon the strand.
They sailed no further then, for Persephone herself
sent the ghost of Actor's son, weeping profusely,
begging to behold for a little men like himself.
Stepping upon the tomb's edge, he peered at the ship,
just as he was when he went to war: around his head
there gleamed a lovely four-plumed helmet with crimson crest.
Then he sank again into the black gloom,
and they were amazed at what they had seen, and Mopsus, son
of Ampycus, urged them with mantic word to propitiate
his spirit with libations. Quickly they furled their sail
and cast their cables upon the beach and attended the tomb
of Sthenelus and poured libations and slaughtered sheep
as holy offerings. Apart from that they built
an altar to Apollo Savior of Ships and burned
thigh bones there, and Orpheus dedicated his lyre,
and that is why the place is called Lyra by name.
 Immediately they went on board, since the wind was fresh.
They unfurled the sail and stretched it taut to both sheets,

and the Argo flew flat out toward the main like a hawk that soars
high through the air, giving the wind the flat of its wing,
and is swiftly borne, nor does it swerve in flight but floats
in the clear sky on silent pinions. They passed the streams
of Parthenius that empties into the sea, of rivers
the most gentle. There the daughter of Leto, when
she rises to heaven after the hunt, cools her flesh
in its lovely waters. Then they ran unabating by night
and passed the city Sesamus and steep Erythini,
Crobialus, Cromna, and wooded Cytorus, and then at sunrise
they rounded Carambis and rowed past long Aegialus
all that day and after the day all through the night.

    Soon they stepped upon Assyrian soil, where
Zeus himself established Sinope, Asopus' daughter
and granted her virginity, tricked by his oath,
for he longed for her love and agreed to grant whatever might
accord with her desire. She cunningly asked of him
virginity. So too she beguiled Apollo, who longed
to seduce her, and the river Halys as well. No man
in desirous embrace subdued her. And there the sons
of Tricca's noble Deimachus lived, Deileon,
Autolycus, and Phlogius, ever since they had wandered
away from Heracles. And they then, when they saw
the band of princes, met and told them who they were.
Nor did they wish to linger longer there but went
on board ship, once the northwest wind blew up.

    Together with them, swept along by the swift breeze,
they left behind the Halys and Iris flowing nearby
and the delta land of Assyria. On that very day
they rounded the faraway Amazonian peak that guards
their harbor, where once the hero Heracles caught out
Melanippe, Ares' daughter, in ambush as she went
forth. Hippolyte gave him as ransom for her sister
her glittering belt, and he sent the girl away unharmed.
In this bay at Thermodon's outfall they moored their ship,
for the sea was rough for sailing. There is no river like this,

nor one that casts such enormous streams over the land
from itself. One would lack from a hundred but four should he count
each stream, but the true source is only one, and this
flows down to the plain from lofty mountains which men call
the Amazonians. From there it spreads straight on
into steeper country, and so its streams wind,
forever this way and that, and roll wherever they
can find flatter ground, this one far off,
and this one near at hand. Many streams are nameless,
drained off into the sand, but mingled with a few,
the main stream belches openly beneath
its arching crest of spray into Unwelcoming Pontus.
And now they would have lingered there and engaged in combat
the Amazons and contested not without bloodshed,
for the Amazons were not affable folk and not
honoring custom did they frequent the Doeantian plain,
but violence and Ares' work were their concern,
for they were by birth the daughters of Ares and of the nymph
Harmonia, who bore battle-loving girls
to Ares, when she had lain with him in the wooded glen
of the Acmonian grove, had the northwest wind not blown
again from Zeus, and they with the wind left behind
the curved beach where the Amazons of Themiscyra
were putting on their armor, for not gathered together
in one city did they live but throughout the land,
divided into three tribes: the Themiscyreians,
whom then Hippolyte ruled, the Lycastians, and then
the Chadesians, casters of javelins. On the next day,
when evening came, they reached the land of the Chalybes.
These people have no concern for oxen or plow,
nor do they plant honey-sweet fruit or shepherd flocks
in dewy pastures but cleave the stubborn iron-bearing
soil, exchanging wages for livelihood, and never
does dawn arise for them without labor, but they
in smoke and murky flame suffer heavy toil.

    And then, after the Chalybes, they rounded the cape

of Genetaean Zeus and safely passed the land
of the Tibareni. Here when women bear children
to men, the men collapse in their beds and moan, their heads
closely wrapped, and the women attend the men with food,
and wives prepare for husbands the baths of childbirth.

Next they came to the holy mountain and land where
the Mossynoeci live throughout the hills. Their customs
and laws are peculiar to them. What is customary
to do among the people or in the marketplace,
all this they do at home. What we do at home
they do out of doors, in the streets, without blame.
Respect for the marriage bed is not native to them,
but like grubbing swine, not in the least abashed,
in public they lie in love with women on the ground.
Their king sits in the highest hut, and to his people
in their multitude, he gives judgments that are straight,
poor man, for if he errs at all in his decrees,
his people shut him up and starve him all that day.

Passing them by, they rowed over against the isle
of Ares all day long, for at dark the balmy breeze
abandoned them. And now they saw, swooping through
the air above, one of Ares' birds that haunt
that isle. Shaking its wings over the speeding ship,
it sent against her a sharp feather, which fell upon
the left shoulder of lordly Oileus. He dropped the oar
from his hand at the blow, and the men marveled at the feathered bolt.
Eribotes, who sat beside him, drew it out and bound
the wound, when he had loosed the strap that hung down
from his own sheath. And then another, after the first,
came streaking down, but the hero Clytius, son of Eurytus,
(for he stretched his curved bow and shot a swift bolt
at the bird) struck it first and it spun and fell close
to the swift ship. Amphidamas, Aleus' son, spoke:

"The isle of Ares is near; you know, for you yourselves
have seen the birds. I do not suppose that arrows will aid
our landing. But let us contrive some other device to help,

if you intend to beach your ship, remembering

Phineus' commands. Not even Heracles, when he came
to Arcadia, could with his bow drive off the birds that swam
the Stymphalian lake. (I saw it myself.) But he shook in his hand
a rattle of bronze on a high rock and with such a clatter
that the birds flew far off and shrieked with bewilderment
and fear. And so let us contrive like device,
and I myself, having pondered before, shall give advice.
Place on your heads your high-crested helmets, and half of you
row in turns, and half flank the ship about
with polished spears and shields. Then altogether shout
exceedingly loud so that the unfamiliar howl
and nodding crests and spears held high terrify
the birds. And if we reach the island itself, then make
an enormous din by the clashing together of brazen shields."
  So he spoke, and the saving device pleased them all.
On their heads they set their helmets of bronze that flashed
terribly, and the crimson crests upon them shook,
and some rowed in turn; others wrapped the ship
with spears and shields. As when a man roofs over his house
with tiles to bring brightness to his home and be
a shelter from the rain, and one tile fits tightly
to another, each upon each, so they roofed
the ship with their shields, locking them securely together.
Like the clamor that comes from a hostile throng of men marching
when their phalanxes meet, such was the shout that rose from the ship
high in the air, nor did they yet see a single bird,
but when they reached the island and clashed their shields, then
in their thousands the birds rose and fled, this way and that.
As when the son of Cronus sends from the clouds a storm
of dense hail upon houses and towns and the dwellers beneath
hear the rattling upon the roof but sit at ease,
since the season of storm has taken them not unawares, but first
they had fortified their house, so the birds sent
upon them a dense shower of feathers as they soared
over the sea and toward the hills of the opposite land.

What was in Phineus' mind to bid the godlike band
of heroes beach there? And then, what kind of help
was likely to meet the heroes' hopeful expectations?
The sons of Phrixus were coming to Orchomenus
from Aea and from Cytaean Aeetes, having boarded
a Colchian ship that they might win the miraculous wealth
of their father, for he, as he lay dying, had laid their journey
upon them, and on that day they were very close to the island,
but Zeus roused the might of the north wind to blow,
marking with rain Arcturus' watery path. All day
he shook just a little the leaves upon the mountains, breathing
lightly upon the topmost branches. At night he came,
monstrously, upon the sea, and heaved high
the billows with shrieking blasts. A black mist embraced
the heaven, nor did gleaming stars anywhere
appear between the clouds, but murky gloom pressed
about, and so the sons of Phrixus, dripping wet,
trembled at thought of a horrible death and drifted along,
despairingly, upon the waves. The force of the wind
had snatched their sails away and broken in two the ship
itself, buffeted as it was by the roaring breakers.
There at the gods' command the four of them grasped
an enormous beam of the many that lay scattered about,
fitted with sharp bolts, from the breaking up of the ship.
The billows and blasts of wind bore the men toward
the island, much distressed, within a little of death.
Suddenly unspeakable rain broke forth and fell
upon the sea, the island, and all the opposite land,
where the overweening Mossynoeci have their homes.
The wash of the wave cast the sons of Phrixus together
with their strong timber upon the island's beach beneath
the gloom of the night sky, but the downpour of rain from Zeus
left off at sunrise, and soon the two bands of men
met with one another, and Argus was first to speak:
"We beseech you, by Zeus Beholder, whoever of men you are,
be gracious and help us in our need. For harsh blasts

falling upon the sea have scattered all the beams
of the sorry ship in which we were cutting the swell, embarked
on our task. And so we entreat you now, if you will hear,
to give us clothing to cover our limbs and to take pity
upon men of your own age in such distress.
Respect strangers and suppliants. To Zeus belong
strangers and suppliants, and he beholds even us."

In return the son of Aeson questioned him shrewdly,
for he thought that Phineus' prophecies were being fulfilled.

"All this with good will we shall offer you straightway,
but tell me truly the land where you live and what need
compels you to sail upon the sea and tell me as well
your own names of renown and also your lineage."

Argus, helpless in his distress, addressed him:
"I think that you yourselves have certainly already heard
that a certain Aeolid, Phrixus, came to Aea from Hellas,
Phrixus who came mounted upon a ram that Hermes
had made gold to Aeetes' city. The fleece you may see
even now spread upon the shaggy branches
of an oak. He then sacrificed at its own behest
the ram to Zeus, the son of Cronus, beyond all
the god of fugitives. Aeetes welcomed him
in his hall and with joy of heart bestowed upon him
as his bride his own daughter Chalciope without
asking from him the usual wooing gifts. From them
are we born, but Phrixus died at last, an old man,
in Aeetes' house, but we, heeding our father's commands,
are traveling to Orchomenus to take possession
of Athamas' treasure. And if you want to learn our names,
this one is called Cytissorus; this one, Phrontis;
this, Melas; and me you may call Argus by name."

So he spoke, and the princes rejoiced at their meeting
and attended to them, marveling much, but Jason in turn
replied to him, as was proper and right, with these words:

"Indeed, as kinsmen to us on my father's side, you beseech
that we with good will give help to you in your

adversity, for Cretheus and Athamas were brothers,
and I, the grandson of Cretheus, with these companions go
from Hellas to that same city of Aeetes,
but we shall speak of these things at a later time,
but now, first, put clothing on. By command, I think,
of immortal gods, have you come in your craving need to my hands."
    He spoke, and from the ship he gave to them clothes
to put on. Together then they went to the temple
of Ares to sacrifice sheep. In haste they took their stand
around the altar, which was outside the roofless shrine,
built of pebbles. Inside was set a black stone,
sacred, to which once all the Amazons prayed.
Nor was it permitted them when they came from the continent
opposite to burn on this altar offerings
of oxen or sheep but they slaughtered horses, for them they kept
in abundant number. When they had sacrificed and eaten
the feast prepared, then Jason spoke with these words:
    "Truly Zeus beholds every single thing,
nor do we men, neither the god-fearing nor
the unjust, ever escape his notice, for so he saved
your father from murder at a stepmother's hands and gave him besides
boundless wealth, and so he saved you as well
from the dangerous storm, and you may sail upon this ship
where you will, to this place or that, to Aea
or to the opulent city of divine Orchomenus.
For Athena constructed our ship. With brazen ax she felled
its timbers beside the peak of Pelion, and Argus
helped build. But yours the evil billow shattered before
it reached the rocks that all day long clash together
in the narrows of Pontus. But come, help us, eager to bring
the golden fleece to Hellas; lead our voyage, since I
go to atone for the sacrifice of Phrixus, which was
the cause of Zeus' wrath against the Aeolids."
    He spoke, soothingly. But hearing, they abhorred,
for they did not think that they would find Aeetes kindly,
should they be eager to carry off the ram's fleece,
and Argus spoke, dismayed at involvement in such a quest:

"O friends, our strength, such as it is, shall never fail
in our aid to you, not even a little, should need arise,
but Aeetes is terribly dangerous, ruthless and rough,
and so exceedingly I fear to make this voyage.
He claims to be the son of Helios, and around
dwell countless tribes of Colchians, and he might be
a match for Ares in awful war cry and mighty strength.
To take the fleece despite Aeetes will not be easy.
Such a snake keeps watch around and about it,
deathless and sleepless. Earth herself gave it birth,
on the shoulders of Caucasus near Typhaon's rock, where
Typhaon, they say, struck by the thunderbolt of Zeus,
son of Cronus, when he stretched his sturdy hands
against him, dripped hot blood from his head. And thus he came
to the hills and plain of Nysa, where even now he lies
submerged beneath the waters of the Serbonian lake."
    So then he spoke, and many cheeks turned pale straightway
when they heard of such a task, but Peleus immediately
replied with heartening words and spoke to Argus thus:
    "Do not, good sir, fear too much the tale you hear,
for we are not so lacking in strength or inferior
to Aeetes as not to be able to test him in arms, but I
believe that we too are skilled in war and go
there, born almost of the blood of the blessed gods.
And so, if for friendship's sake, he will not give
the golden fleece to us, then I do not think
that all the Colchian tribes will avail Aeetes much."
    So they spoke to one another in turn until
again they had taken their fill of the feast and fallen asleep.
At dawn, when the men woke, a gentle breeze was blowing,
and they raised the sails which stretched taut at the puff of the wind
and, swift and light, they left behind the island of Ares.
    When night came on, they reached Philyra's island. There
Cronus, son of Uranus, when on Olympus he ruled
the Titans and Zeus was still being nursed in the Cretan cave
by Idaean Curetes, lay beside Philyra,
deceiving Rhea, but she discovered them in their love,

and he in haste leapt up from his bed, in form like a horse
with flowing mane. In shame Philyra, Ocean's daughter,
left the land and those haunts for the long hills
of Pelasgian men, where from her dalliance with the god
transfigured she bore enormous Cheiron, half horse, half man.

From there they sailed past the Macrones and boundless land
of Becheiri and arrogant Sapeires and after them
the Byzeres. Forever forward they quickly cut their way
borne on by the balmy breeze. And now as they sailed on
there opened to their view a deep bay of Pontus,
and Caucasian mountains' lofty crags, where with his limbs
bound around to the stubborn rocks by galling bonds
of bronze, Prometheus with his liver fed an eagle,
forever swooping back to its feast. As evening fell
they spied it high above the ship, soaring near
the clouds with a shrill whistling of flight, but still
it shook all the sails with its fanning of wings, for it had
not the form of a bird of air but poised its pinions
like well-polished oars, and not long after this they heard
Prometheus' tortured cry as his liver was torn away.
The air rang out with his screams until they all marked
the carnivorous eagle sweeping back from the mountain along
the same track. At night by Argus' expertise
they reached the wide-flowing Phasis and Pontus' furthest reach.

Straightway they let down the sails and yardarm
and fitted them within the hollow mast crutch,
and at once they loosed the mast itself until it lay
aslant, and quickly they rowed into the mighty stream
of the river, which splashed their prow as it gave way before.
On their left they had the lofty Caucasus and Aea,
the Cytaean city, opposite the plain of Ares
and that god's holy grove where the serpent guarded
the fleece. The son of Aeson himself from a golden cup
poured into the river libations of unmixed wine
and drops of honey to Earth, the native gods, and the souls
of dead heroes and begged them to be of kindly aid

and graciously to receive as auspicious their ship's cables.
Immediately Ancaeus spoke with these words:

"We have reached the Colchian land and the streams of the river Phasis.
It is time for us to consider whether we shall test
Aeetes with gentleness or whether some other attack
be fitting." So he spoke, and Jason at Argus' advice
ordered them to steer inside a shadowed marsh
and allow the Argo to ride at anchor offshore.
This was nearby. And there they spent the dark hours.
And not long after, dawn appeared to the waiting men.

Book III

Come now, Erato, stand at my side and tell to me
how Jason brought back from there to Iolcus the fleece
with the help of Medea's love, for you share the lot of Cypris,
and with your tender concern you charm unmarried girls.
And so your name too includes the word of love.

Now in the thick of the reeds the heroes, unseen, were waiting
in ambush, but Athena and Hera noticed them there, and apart
from Zeus himself and the other immortal gods they went
into a chamber and plotted together. Hera first
tested Athena. "Now you first, daughter of Zeus,
suggest a plan. What must we do? Can you contrive
some trick by which they can seize the golden fleece of Aeetes
and take it to Hellas, or could they deceive or persuade him
with smooth words? For in truth he is terribly arrogant. Still,
no one ought, I think, to turn away from trying."
So she spoke, and Athena addressed her immediately,
    "I myself was pondering such things in my mind,
Hera, when you asked me bluntly. But not yet do I think
that I have contrived a trick that will help the heart
of the heroes, but I have had my doubts over many plans."
    She spoke, and they fixed their eyes on the ground before their feet
and brooded, each one by herself. Suddenly Hera
spoke forth first and told the plan that she had devised.

"Come, let us go to Cypris and approach her
to beseech the boy, if he will obey, to charm by his arrows
the enchantress Medea with love for Jason. I think that he
by her devices will bring the fleece back to Hellas."

So she spoke. Her shrewd counsel pleased Athena,
and she then answered her in turn with soothing words,
"Hera, my father begat me never to feel the arrows
of passion, nor do I know a charm to work desire,
but if this plan is pleasing to you, certainly I
shall follow along, but you must address her when we meet."

She spoke, and they leapt up and went to the great house
of Cypris, which her lame husband had made for her
when first he had brought her from Zeus to be his bride. They entered
the court and stood beneath the gallery of the room
in which the goddess prepared her husband Hephaestus' bed,
but he had gone at first dawn to his forge and his anvils,
to a broad cave on the island that floats and where with the blast
of his flame he forged all manner of intricate work. She,
alone, sat on a turned chair before the doors.
She had let down her hair on either side of her white back
and was parting it with a golden comb and was about
to braid her long locks. When she saw the goddesses
before her, she stopped and called them in and rose from her chair
and seated them on couches. Then she herself sat down
and with her hands gathered up her uncombed hair.
Smiling, she addressed them with wily words like these:

"Dear ladies, what intent or need brings you here
after so long a time? Why have you come? Your visits
were not too frequent before, distinguished that you are."

Hera answered her and spoke words like these:
"You mock, but disaster disturbs our hearts, for at this moment
at the river Phasis the son of Aeson moors his ship
and all the others that go in pursuit of the golden fleece.
For all of them indeed—for the trial is imminent—
we fear terribly, but most of all for Jason.
Him I shall save even though he sails to Hades

to loose Ixion's brazen bonds down there below,
so long as there is strength in my limbs that Pelias not laugh
at having evaded an evil fate, Pelias who
in his arrogance failed to honor me with sacrifice.
For other reasons too Jason was very dear
to me even before when at the mouth of Anaurus
in full flood he met me making trial of men's
goodwill as he returned from the hunt. All the mountains
were sprinkled with snow and their highest peaks and down them
the winter torrents rushed with a terrible rolling roar.
He pitied me, disguised as an old crone, and lifted
and carried me on his shoulders through the swirling flood.
Therefore I honor him forever, nor will Pelias
pay the penalty for insult unless you grant
Jason his voyage home." So she spoke, and Cypris
stood dumb, bereft of words. She gazed in awe
at Hera, who entreated her, and then replied
in soft words, "Revered goddess, may there be
nothing more evil than Cypris if I make light of you
in either word or deed, whatever my feeble hands
can work. And let there be no favor in exchange."
So she spoke, and Hera again addressed her with cunning:
    "In need of neither force nor strength have we come here.
Just quietly bid your boy to charm Aeetes' daughter
Medea with passionate longing for Jason, the son of Aeson,
for if she will conspire with him, beneficently, I think
that he will easily take the golden fleece and make
the voyage to Iolcus, since she is very clever."
    So she spoke, and then Cypris replied to them both,
"Athena and Hera, he would obey you rather
than me, for shameless though he is, he will have some
little shame in your eyes, but he has no
respect for me but always provokes and ignores me.
Exasperated by his mischief, I long to break
his shrill arrows together with his bow before
his very eyes. In his anger he has made me threats like this:

if I do not keep off my hands until he checks
his rage, I may in time have cause to blame myself."

So she spoke, and the goddesses smiled and gave a glance,
one to the other, but Cypris was vexed again and said,

"To others my troubles are cause for laughter, nor ought I tell
them to everyone. It is enough that I know them myself.
But now since this is dear to the hearts of you both, I shall try
and I shall succeed in coaxing him, and he will obey."

So she spoke, and Hera took hold of her delicate hand
and smiling tenderly, she addressed her in reply,

"Now, Cytherea, accomplish this task, just as you speak,
immediately. Do not be harsh or in your anger
quarrel with your child; he will change his ways."

She spoke and left her seat, and Athena followed her,
and the two of them went hurrying out. Cypris herself
left to go down the folds of Olympus to find her boy,
and she found him apart in the blooming orchard of Zeus, not
alone, but with Ganymede, whom Zeus once established in heaven
among the immortal gods, enamored of his beauty.
They were playing with golden dice, as boy companions do.
Now greedy Eros held the palm of his left hand
quite full of them beneath his breast and stood up straight,
and a sweet blush began to bloom upon his cheeks.
Ganymede crouched nearby, morose. He had two left,
which he threw, one upon the other, again in vain,
and he was angered when Eros laughed out loud.
He lost those dice too, at once, along with the rest,
and went off with empty hands, chagrined, nor did he notice
when Cypris came. She stood before her child and then
she put her hand upon his cheek and said to him,

"Why do you smile, unspeakable rogue? Did you cheat
and dishonestly defeat the innocent boy? But come,
willingly do for me the task that I set for you
and I will give to you Zeus' most beautiful toy.
His dear nurse Adrasteia made it for him when he
was still a little child in the Idaean cave—

148

a well-rounded ball. No better toy than this will you
acquire even from Hephaestus' hands. Its zones
are fashioned of gold and around each one run double seams,
and the stitches are hidden, and a spiral of midnight blue overlays
them all. But if you cast it up with your little hands,
like a star, it sends a blazing trail through the sky. This
I will give you if you with your arrows will smite and charm Medea
with love for Jason. My thanks will be less if you delay."
      So she spoke, and her word pleased the child as he heard.
He threw down all his toys and with both hands caught
at her dress, on this side and that, and excitedly clung to the goddess.
He begged her to put the ball into his hands straightway,
but she with tender words drew him to her and kissed
his cheeks and as she held him close she said with a smile,
      "Let your dear heart and mine now witness this: truly
this gift I will make you nor will I deceive you, if only you
with your arrow will smite Medea, the daughter of Aeetes."
      She spoke. He gathered up his dice and counted them well
and cast them all into his mother's radiant lap.
At once with a golden strap he girded on his quiver,
which lay against a tree trunk, and took up his curved bow.
He left the lushly fruited orchard of mighty Zeus,
and then he went out through the great gates of Olympus
high in the air. From there there is a downward path
from heaven. The two poles of earth thrust up the peaks
of steep mountains, crests of the planet where the risen
sun takes on a rosy blush with its first rays.
Beneath him now appeared the fertile earth and the towns
of men and the sacred river streams, and now again
the hills, and the sea around, as he went through the vast air.
The heroes sat apart in ambush upon the benches
of their ship in a marshy backwater and took counsel.
The son of Aeson himself spoke among them, and they
listened quietly, sitting where they were, in rows.
      "O friends, in truth I shall tell you what pleases me,
and it shall be fitting for you to bring it to fulfillment.

Common is our need, and common too our words
to all alike. Let him know who silently withholds
his thought and counsel that he alone deprives this band
of voyage home. Stay on board, the rest of you,
quietly, with all your gear. I shall go to the house
of Aeetes with the sons of Phrixus and two other
companions, and when I meet him, I shall try first with words
to see if for friendship's sake he will give the golden fleece
or not, but trusting in strength make light of our request.
So, learning first from him of his wickedness,
let us think if we shall join battle with him
or if some other plan will profit us more, should we
hold back from the war cry. Not thus with strength before
making test of words let us deprive him of his possession.
It is better first to please him with words when we meet.
Often speech has easily wrought at need what courage
could scarcely accomplish, smoothing the way, as it is fit.
Aeetes once received blameless Phrixus escaping
his stepmother's guile and his father's sacrifice, for all,
even the most shameless of men, everywhere revere
the law of Zeus, god of strangers, and respect it."

So he spoke, and the youths approved the word of Jason
at once, nor was there one who gave another command.

Then he urged the sons of Phrixus and Telamon
to follow him and Augeias and he himself took up
the wand of Hermes. They went straightway out of the ship
over the reeds and water to dry land to the thrust
of the plain that is called Circe's, where many willows grow,
all in a row, and osiers. From their topmost branches
corpses hang, fastened with cords, for still it is
a sin among the Colchians to burn with fire
the male dead. Nor is it permitted them to put
them in the earth and heap a mound above, but they wrap
them in untanned ox hides and fasten them to trees
outside the town. Earth and air have equal share,
for they bury women in the ground. This is their way.

For their sake as they went Hera with kindly thought
spread a mist throughout the city that they might escape
the myriad host of Colchians as they came to Aeetes.
When quickly they came from the plain to the city and the palace
of Aeetes, then in turn Hera dispersed the cloud.
They stood at the threshold marveling at the courts of the king
and the wide gates and the columns that rose around the walls,
all in order, and high on the palace a coping of stone
was fitted upon triglyphs of bronze. Quietly then
they crossed the threshold. Nearby cultivated vines,
garlanded in green leaves, grew high and blossomed
abundantly. Beneath these were four springs,
forever flowing, which Hephaestus had dug out.
One bubbled up with milk, another with wine,
and a third flowed with fragrant oil. The fourth spouted
water that warmed at the setting of the Pleiades
and again at their rising gushed from the hollow rock like crystal.
Such were the marvels that skillful Hephaestus had contrived
in the palace of Cytaean Aeetes. And he had made
for him bulls with feet of bronze and brazen mouths,
and they would snort forth a horrible flash of fire,
and he forged too of stout adamant a plow,
all of one piece, a payment of thanks to Helios, who
with his horses had rescued him, faint from the fight at Phlegra.
Here had been made an inner court with many doors,
sturdily built, and there were chambers here and there,
and all along, on either side, ran a gallery,
intricately carved. Taller buildings stood
obliquely on both sides. In one of these, the taller,
dwelt brave Aeetes with his wife. In the other Apsyrtus
lived, the son of Aeetes, whom the Caucasian nymph,
Asterodeia, bore before he took Eidyia
as his wedded wife. She was the very youngest born
of Oceanus and Tethys. The sons of the Colchians called him by name
Phaethon, properly, since he outshone all youths.
The other buildings handmaidens had and the two daughters

of Aeetes, Chalciope and Medea. Medea they found
going from room to room in search of her sister. Hera
had kept her inside the house. She did not frequent the palace
before, but all day long attended Hecate's shrine,
since she was herself the priestess of that goddess.
When she saw the heroes quite near, she cried aloud,
and Chalciope was quick to hear, and the serving maids cast
before their feet their yarn and threads and all in a throng
ran out. She, when she saw among them her sons, raised up
her hands in joy. And so did they themselves welcome
their mother when they saw her and embraced her warmly
in their great delight. Weeping, she addressed them with words like these:
    "You did not intend then heedlessly to leave me
and wander far, but destiny has turned you back.
Poor me! What a longing for Hellas from pitiful folly
overtook you at your father Phrixus' commands. He,
when he died, ordained desperate grief for my heart. Why
should you go to the city Orchomenus, whoever this
Orchomenus is, for the sake of Athamas' treasure and leave
your mother to suffer?" So she spoke. Aeetes
came out, last of all, and Eidyia herself came,
Aeetes' wife, when she heard Chalciope's cry. At once
a noisy crowd filled all the court. Certain slaves
were busied about a huge bull, others were chopping
kindling wood with a bronze ax, and others still
were boiling with fire water for baths. Nor was there one
who slacked at all in his toil, doing service for the king.
    Eros, meanwhile, went unseen through the gray mist,
distracting as the gadfly that attacks the heifers
and that the cowherds call the breese. Quickly beneath
the lintel in the entrance he strung his bow and took
from his quiver an arrow, not shot before, to bring much pain.
With quick feet he slipped unseen across the threshold
and glanced sharply around. He crept, crouched down,
past Aeson's son, and fitted his notched arrow end
to the middle of the string, stretched it with both hands,

and shot Medea. She was struck utterly speechless.
But he himself darted away from the high-roofed hall
and laughed aloud, but the shaft burned in the girl's heart,
deep down, like a flame, and she kept glancing at Jason
with sparkling eyes, and her breath came in panting gasps
in her distress. She forgot everything else, and her soul
melted in sweet anguish. As when a toiling woman
piles dry sticks around a piece of burning wood
that she may make a fire beneath her roof by night
if she has waked very early, the flame from the small brand
grows miraculously and consumes all the kindling —
so coiled beneath Medea's heart there burned in secret
destructive love. The color of her tender cheeks
turned now to pale, now to red, she was so distraught.

Now when the servants had laid a ready feast for them
and they had cleansed themselves in warm baths, gladly
did they delight their souls with supper and drink, and then
Aeetes questioned the sons of his daughter Chalciope,
and addressing them with these words, he spoke and said,

"Sons of my child and Phrixus, whom beyond all strangers
I honored in my halls, how have you come to Aea?
Have you returned or did some calamity cut you off
from escape? You did not believe when I put forth for you
the boundless length of your course, for I learned it once, whirled
in my father Helios' chariot, when he brought my sister
Circe to the western land and we reached the shore
of the Tyrrhenian continent where even now
she lives very far away from the Colchian land.
But what delight is there in words? What has happened
to you, tell me openly, and who these are
who follow and where you stepped forth from your hollow ship."

Such things he asked, and Argus before his brothers, because
he feared for the quest of Aeson's son, replied gently,
since he was the eldest born of them all, and said to him,

"Aeetes, that ship furious blasts broke apart
all at once, and a wave washed us, clutching a beam,

to the dry shore of the island of Enyalius
in the murky night, and some god preserved us,
for not even the birds of Ares that haunted that lonely isle
in former times, not even them did we discover,
but these men had driven them off, for they had stepped
from their ship the day before. In pity for us the mind
of Zeus or some fate detained them there, for they
straightway gave to us sufficient clothing and food
when they heard the renowned name of Phrixus and your own,
for they are traveling to your city. And if you wish
to learn their mission, I will not conceal it from you.
A certain king, desperately eager to drive this man
from his wealth and fatherland because he surpassed in strength
all the sons of Aeolus, sends him sailing here,
fruitlessly, and avows that Aeolid stock shall not
escape the soul-racking wrath and rage of implacable Zeus
nor the unendurable sin and punishment of Phrixus
until the fleece returns to Hellas. Pallas Athena
built their ship, not like ships that Colchians have,
of which we chanced upon the sorriest, for the wind
and ravishing wave broke her utterly apart.
But theirs holds with her bolts even when blasts of storm
are buffeting her, and she runs as fast before the wind
as when the men apply themselves tirelessly
to the well-fitted oars, and he has gathered together in her
the noblest of all Achaea's heroes and come to your city
after wandering through many towns and upon the main
of the grim sea to find if you will grant the fleece.
As it pleases you, so shall it be. For he
has come not to wrest it with force but eager to pay
for the gift worthy recompense. Hearing from me
of the hostile Sauromatae, he will subdue them
to your scepter's sway, and if you wish to know the names
and lineage and who these men are, I
will tell you every single thing. This man here,
for whose sake the others gathered from Hellas they call

Jason, son of Aeson, Cretheus' son, and if
he is truly of the stock of Cretheus himself, he would
be thus kinsman to us on our father's side, for both
Cretheus and Athamas were sons of Aeolus,
and Phrixus was son of Athamas, son of Aeolus.
And here, if you have heard of any offspring
of Helios at all, you see Augeias. And this
is Telamon, the son of illustrious Aeacus,
and Zeus himself begat Aeacus. And all
the other companions, as many as follow upon him,
are the sons or grandsons of the immortal gods."

Such was the tale that Argus told. But the king was enraged
when he heard his words, and his heart leapt up high in his wrath.
He spoke, full of rage (he was especially angered
at Chalciope's sons, for he suspected that because
of them the Argonauts had come), and his eyes flashed
from beneath his brows and in his fury he spoke to them:

"Robbers, will you not remove yourselves straightway
from the sight of my eyes, get out of my land, you and your tricks,
before someone sees to his sorrow the fleece and a Phrixus?
You come here in comradeship from Hellas, not
for the fleece but for my scepter and royal prerogative.
Had you not first feasted at my table,
I would have cut out your tongues and sawn off
both your hands and sent you off with only your feet
that you be kept safe from making a fresh start,
such awful lies have you told against the blessed gods."

He spoke then in his rage. The heart of Aeacus' son
swelled enormously from its very depth, and he longed
to speak some lethal word to defy him, but Jason
restrained him, and he himself replied with gentle words,

"Aeetes, bear with me. We have come in this company
to your city and home not as you suspect nor
with such desire, for who would willingly endure
to cross such a swell of sea to acquire a stranger's possession?
But destiny and the chill command of an arrogant king

drove me. Grant favor to them who beseech you
and I to all Hellas will bear wondrous report
of you. Indeed we are eager to pay swift recompense
in war to you whether it be the Sauromatae
or some other people you long to subdue to your scepter's sway."
    He spoke, beguiling him with soft words, but the soul
of the king brooded within his breast a double desire,
whether to rush and slay them upon the spot or try
their force. The latter seemed the better course to him
as he thought, and so he addressed Jason with hidden intent:
    "Stranger, why should you tell every single thing
straight through? If truly you are of divine stock, or if
otherwise you have come not inferior
to me for a stranger's possession, I will give to you
the golden fleece to carry away if you wish but only
after making trial of you. I bear no grudge
against brave men like the one you yourselves
say holds sway in Hellas. The test of your courage and strength
shall be a contest which I myself can accomplish with
my hands, dangerous though it is. I have two bulls
with feet of bronze that feed upon the plain of Ares,
and they blow flame from their mouths. Them I yoke and drive
straight down Ares' stubborn fallow, four fields
in length, and quickly cleaving it to the boundary
with my plow, I cast into the furrows for grain not
Demeter's seed but the teeth of a dreadful dragon that grow
in form like those of armed men. I slaughter them
on the spot, cutting them down with my spear as they spring up
all around. I yoke the oxen at dawn and cease
at the evening hour from my harvesting. If you accomplish
the same, that very day you shall bear away the fleece
to the king's palace. Before that I will not give—
do not expect—it, for it would be unseemly
for a noble man to give way to one more base."
    So he spoke, but Jason, fixing his eyes before
his feet, sat exactly as he was, speechless, dismayed

at his wicked plight. For a long time he pondered over
a plan, but in no way could he undertake the work
courageously, for the task seemed very great. At last
he replied to the king, addressing him with cunning words,
    "With that justice of yours, Aeetes, you constrain me too much.
And so I shall endure that contest, outrageous though
it is, even if it be my destiny
to die, for nothing yet more chill is allotted men
than evil necessity, for this is what it was
that fated me to sail here at a king's command."
    So he spoke, stricken with helplessness, but the king
addressed Jason in his distress with grim words:
"Go now to the gathering, since you are keen on the task,
but if you fear to yoke the oxen or shrink from
the fatal harvesting, then I shall see to this
that another may shudder to come to a man better than he."
Aeetes spoke very bluntly. But Jason rose from his chair,
and Augeias and Telamon too, at once, and Argus followed,
alone, since he had nodded to his brothers to stay
yet in that place meanwhile. But they went from the hall,
and marvelously distinguished among them all was the son
of Aeson for his beauty and grace. The young girl looked aslant
at him, holding aside her shining veil, and her heart
smoldered with pain. Her mind crept like a dream and fluttered
in the tracks of the man as he walked. They went then from the palace,
distressed. Chalciope, guarding against Aeetes' wrath,
quickly had gone with her sons to her own chamber. Just so
did Medea follow in turn. She pondered in her soul
all the many concerns that the loves arouse in one.
Before her eyes everything was vivid still—
how he looked, what clothes he wore, how he spoke,
how he sat on his chair, and how he moved to the door.
In her excitement she thought that there could be no other
such man. In her ears there rang continuously his voice
and the honey-sweet words that he spoke. She feared for him lest the bulls
or even Aeetes himself destroy him. She grieved for him

as though he were already dead, and a delicate tear
trickled down her cheek in her very terrible pity and grief.
Weeping softly, she lifted her voice and cried aloud,
"Why does this agony take me, unhappy that I am?
Whether he perish, the best of all heroes or worst,
let him go. I hope that he will escape unharmed—yes,
may this happen, revered goddess, daughter of Perses,
may he make the voyage home, escaping doom, but if
it be his fate to be worsted by oxen, may he know
this first, that I do not rejoice in his disaster."

So then the girl's mind was racked by anxiety,
but when the men had gone out from the people and town
on the road by which they had earlier come from the plain, then
Argus addressed Jason and spoke with these words:

"Son of Aeson, you will scorn the advice I give,
but it is not fit to forgo the attempt in adversity.
You have heard before from me of a girl who deals in drugs
with instruction from Hecate, the daughter of Perses. If we
could persuade her to help, there would be no fear, I think,
of your defeat in the test. But terribly I dread
lest my mother not somehow undertake this task for me.
Nevertheless I shall go back once more to beseech
her help, for a common destruction hangs over us all."

He spoke with kindly intent, and Jason answered him:

"Oh, dear friend, if this is pleasing to you, I grudge
it not. Go, entreat your mother with shrewd words.
Pathetic indeed is our hope to entrust our return to women."

So he spoke, and quickly they returned to the marsh.
Their companions rejoiced and questioned them when they saw
    them arrive.
The son of Aeson, sorrowing, spoke this word:

"O friends, the heart of ruthless Aeetes is utterly filled
with rage against us, for there is no way that I
or you who question me can obtain the goal. He said
that two bulls with feet of bronze feed in the plain
of Ares and blow flame from their mouths. He ordered me

with these to plow a fallow four fields in length,
and he would give me seed from a serpent's jaw which would
shove up Earth-born men with arms of bronze, and I
that very day must slay them. This toil I undertook
outright—there was no better plan at hand."

So he spoke. The task seemed impossible
to all. Speechless and silent, they looked at one another,
dejected by disaster and despair. At last
Peleus spoke to all the princes courageously:

"The hour has come to contrive what we shall do, though I
do not suppose that help lies so much in plans
as in the might of hands. If you now intend
to yoke the oxen of Aeetes, hero son
of Aeson, and are so keen on the toil, surely then
you will fulfill your promise and gird yourself for the task.
But if in fact your heart does not entirely trust
its bravery, then neither rouse yourself, nor peer
about for another one of these men, for I
shall not hold back, since the boldest pain will be but death."

So spoke the son of Aeacus. Telamon's soul was stirred,
and hastily he rose, and Idas stood third,
very proud, and the two sons of Tyndareus. With them
Oeneus' son, numbered among vigorous men,
though the soft down had not so much as bloomed on his cheeks,
with such strength was his soul inspired. The others yielded
to these and guarded their silence. Straightway Argus spoke
this word to those who hoped to take on the task:

"O friends, this is a last resort, but I think some help
will come opportunely from my mother, and so hold back
a little while and stay in your ship as you were before
since it is better to refrain than recklessly
to die by an evil doom. There is a young girl,
reared in Aeetes' halls, whom the goddess Hecate
taught before all others the skill of mixing drugs,
all those the continent and flowing waters bear.
With them she quenches the blast of unwearying flame

and stays at once the roaring rivers rushing on
and binds fast the stars and sacred paths of the moon.
We thought of her as we came here on the track from the palace,
and if perhaps my mother, her sister, could persuade
the girl to help us in the contest, and if this pleases
you as well, I shall go this very day again
to Aeetes' house to make the trial. Perhaps too
I shall make the attempt with the aid of some divinity."

So he spoke, and the gods graciously gave them a sign.
A timorous dove in flight from the mighty force of a hawk,
terrified, fell from above into Jason's lap,
and the hawk was impaled upon the ornamented stern.
Quickly Mopsus prophesied among them all:

"For you, my friends, this sign was wrought with the gods' will,
nor is there any way to interpret it better than
to approach and attend the girl with cunning of every kind.
I do not think that she will scorn us if with truth
Phineus foretold that our voyage home should be within
the Cyprian goddess's power. Hers was the gentle bird
that escaped its fate, and as my heart prophesies
according to this bird of omen, so may it be.
But, my friends, summon Cytherea to help,
and heed now at once the persuasive counsels of Argus."

He spoke, and the young men approved, remembering
Phineus' commands. Aphareian Idas alone leapt up,
filled with rage, and roared horribly, and said,

"For shame! Have we come here in company with women
that we call upon Cypris to be of help to us
and not the mighty strength of Enyalius?
And do you look to hawks and doves to save yourselves
from tests? Off with you! May your concern be not
for war but for cajoling strengthless girls with prayers."

He spoke, passionately. Many of his companions
murmured, very softly, but no one contradicted.
Then, angered, he sat down. But Jason stirred the men
straightway; speaking to them his own mind, he said,

"Let Argus set out from the ship since this is pleasing to all,
but we ourselves from the river upon the shore will fasten
our hawsers openly, for it is no longer fitting
that we hide here and cower in fear of the battle cry."
  So he spoke and sent Argus to go swiftly
back to the city, and they hauled the anchors on board
at command of Aeson's son and rowed to beach the ship
upon the shore a little way from the meadow marsh.
  Straightway Aeetes called an assembly of Colchians
apart from his house, exactly where in former times
they sat contriving insufferable tricks and trouble for
the Minyae. He threatened when first the oxen had torn
apart the man who had taken on the heavy toil,
he would rip out the coppice of oak that grew above
the wooded hill and burn the ship's timbers and crew
that they might boil away their bitter violence,
devising lawlessness. For never would he have received
in his halls the Aeolid Phrixus, though sore his need, Phrixus
who surpassed in gentleness and fear of god all
foreigners, had not Zeus himself sent
from heaven Hermes, his messenger, that Phrixus meet
an affectionate host. Nor would pirates coming to
his land go long unscathed—whose care it was to stretch
their hands for a stranger's possession, devising deceits of stealth,
and to batter the steadings of herdsmen in bellowing raids—and that
apart from that the sons of Phrixus should pay to him
fit and pleasing recompense for having returned
in company with men who wrought evil that they
might heedlessly drive him from scepter and throne, for once
he had heard from Helios a dismal prophecy
that he must avoid the clever trickery and schemes
of his own seed and their cunning deceit. And so he was
sending them, as was their wish, to the land of Achaea
at their father's command, a long journey, nor had he
the slightest fear lest his daughters devise some loathsome plan
or Apsyrtus, his son, but Chalciope's sons were working this bane.

Angered, he promised outrageous deeds against the people
and threatened loudly to guard the ship together with
its crew that no man escape calamity.
Argus, meanwhile, went to Aeetes' house to beguile
his mother with every argument to beseech Medea
to help them. Chalciope herself had already planned
the same, but fear held back her heart lest somehow
fate intervene and she entreat in vain a Medea
in fear of her father's fatal wrath, or, if she agreed
to her beseechings, the deeds be discovered and revealed.
A deep sleep relieved the girl of her agony
as she lay on her bed. But deceptive dreams, such as come
to one who suffers, destructively provoked her.
She thought that the stranger had undertaken the contest not
because he was so eager to fetch the fleece of the ram
and that not for this had he come to the city of Aeetes
but to carry her to his own home as his wedded wife.
She thought that she herself contended with the oxen
and did the labor easily and that her parents
made light of their promise, for it was not the girl they had ordered
to yoke the oxen but the stranger himself. Because of that
a quarrel broke out between her father and the strangers.
Both turned to her to settle the matter as she thought best.
She suddenly chose the stranger, in disregard of her parents.
They were seized with terrible pain and called out
in their anger. At that cry sleep released her. She rose,
quaking with fear, and gazed about the walls of her chamber.
With difficulty did she gather her soul in her breast
as it had been before. Then she raised her voice and said,

  "Miserable that I am, how these depressing dreams
have frightened me. I fear that this journey of the heroes
will bring great evil. My heart quivers in fear for the stranger.
Let him court an Achaean girl far away among
his people. Let me take care for my virginity
and my parents' home. Nevertheless, no longer aloof,
with shameless heart, I shall make trial of my sister
to see if she will entreat me to help in the contest

because she sorrows for her own sons. This
would quench the gloom and pain in my heart." So she spoke.
    She rose and opened the doors of the house, barefoot,
in a single robe, and she longed to go to her sister and crossed
the threshold of the court. For a long time she stood
at the entrance of the chamber, restrained by shame, and then
she turned and went back again. Again she came forth from within
and then shrank inside. Her feet took her vainly
this way and then that. When she set straight out, shame
would hinder her. Checked by shame, bold desire
would urge her on. Three times she tried, three times held back.
The fourth, she fell prone upon her bed, writhing.
As when a bride in her chamber mourns for her young husband
to whom her brothers and parents have given her, but some doom
has destroyed him before they have enjoyed one another's
charms—her heart burns within and she weeps in silence
as she looks on her widowed bed, nor does she mingle at all
with her attendants because of her shame and her thought for him,
but sits in a corner and grieves, fearing that the women
will scoff at her—like that bride did Medea grieve.
Suddenly one of the serving maids passing by,
a young girl who was her attendant, noticed her
in the midst of her weeping and told Chalciope straightway.
She was sitting among her sons devising ways
to win her sister. She did not disbelieve when she heard
from the serving maid the unexpected tale but rushed,
astonished, from her own room straight to that in which
the young girl lay, anguished, with both her cheeks torn.
When Chalciope saw her eyes drenched with tears she said,
    "Goodness me, Medea, why do you shed these tears?
What has happened? What dreadful sorrow afflicts your heart?
Has some disease, destined by god, encompassed your limbs,
or have you learned of some deadly threat from our father
against my sons and me? I wish that I had never
seen the home of my parents nor their city but dwelt
at the ends of the earth where "Colchians" is never heard."
    So she spoke. Medea's cheeks flushed red, and long

did a young girl's modesty restrain her, though she yearned
to reply. Now the word would rise to the tip of her tongue,
now would flutter down to the depths of her chest. Often
it rushed for utterance up to her lovely lips, but her voice
would proceed no further. At last she spoke words like these,
cunningly, for the bold loves were urging her on:
"Chalciope, for your sons my soul shakes lest my father
destroy them straightway with the strangers, such lurid dreams did I have
as I slumbered just now in my short-lived sleep. May some god
prevent their fulfillment and you have no painful concern for your sons."
　　She spoke, trying her sister to see if she would beseech
her first to help her sons. Unendurable grief engulfed
Chalciope's soul, utterly, with fear for the nature
of what she had heard and she replied in these words:
"I myself have come pondering all these things,
whether you would contrive and arrange with me some aid.
But swear by heaven and earth to keep what I tell to you
in your heart and promise to work with me. I beg you
by the blessed gods, by yourself, and our parents not to see
them destroyed, pitiably by an evil doom, or else
may I, dying with my sons, come afterward,
a ghastly Erinys from out of Hades, to haunt you."
　　She spoke, and straightway many a tear welled forth.
With both hands she embraced her sister's knees below,
and both allowed their heads to sink to their breasts, and made
piteous lament for one another and there arose
through the house the delicate cry of women grieving in anguish.
Medea first addressed her sister in her distress,
"Are you possessed? What cure can I work for you for the things
that you describe, curses and loathsome avenging Furies?
Would that I had the power secure to save your sons!
Let the overpowering oath of the Colchians know,
by which you urge me to swear, let mighty Heaven know
and Earth beneath, mother of gods, so long as strength
is mine, you shall never be in want for your prayers' fulfillment."
　　She spoke, and Chalciope replied in these words:

"Would you not dare to contrive for the stranger who craves it himself III. 719 –762
some trick or plan for success in the contest for the sake
of my sons? From him Argus has come beseeching me
to make trial of your help. I left him in the palace
while I came here." So she spoke. Medea's heart
fluttered for joy within, and at the same time
her lovely complexion flushed and a mist descended upon
her eyes. She came close to fainting but spoke words like these:
     "Chalciope, as is pleasing and dear to you and your sons,
so will I do. May the dawn not shine in my eyes nor may
you see me longer alive if I should prefer
anything at all to your life or the life of your sons,
who are brothers to me, kinsmen as well as friends and companions
of my own age. And I say that I myself am your sister
and your daughter too, since along with them you lifted me
to your breast as a little child. So I always heard
from my mother in time gone by. But come, conceal my favor
in silence that I may fulfill my promise unknown to my parents.
At dawn I shall come to Hecate's temple and bring to the stranger,
for whom this quarrel arose, drugs to charm the bulls."
     Chalciope went back from the chamber and shared with her sons
the report of her sister's help. But again shame overtook
Medea when she was alone and loathsome fear that she
should devise such schemes for a man in secret from her father.
Then night drew darkness over the earth, and on the sea
sailors looked from their ships to Helice and the stars
of Orion, and now the traveler and the gatekeeper
longed for sleep, and a deep slumber enwrapped the mother
whose children are dead, nor was there a barking of dogs throughout
the town, nor the murmuring sound of a crowd of men, but silence
pervaded the blackening night. But sweet sleep did not
capture Medea. In longing for Jason, her many cares
kept her awake. She feared the mighty strength of the bulls
by which he was destined to die by an unfitting doom in the field
of Ares. For pity a tear flowed from her eye. Always
within her agony bored, smoldering through the flesh

and her delicate nerves and deep beneath the nape of her neck
where pain enters most piercingly when the unwearied
loves plant in the heart their shafts of suffering.
And quickly did her heart leap within her breast
as when in a house a sunbeam quivers when it darts
from water just poured in a cauldron or pail perhaps; now here,
now there, on the quick eddy it flickers and bounces along.
So did the young girl's heart quiver within her breast.
At one time she said that she would give him the drugs
to charm the bulls, at another not, that she herself
would die. Then again that she would not herself die,
nor give the drugs, but quietly endure her fate,
just as she was. Then she sat, thinking, and said,

    "Am I, poor thing, to choose between this evil and that?
My heart is utterly helpless, nor is there any aid
for my pain, but it burns just as it did before.
Would that I had been subdued by the swift shafts
of Artemis before I saw him and before
the ship brought Chalciope's sons to Achaea. God
or some Fury brought them here from that land to be
a cause of many tears and suffering to us.
Let him perish in the contest, if it is his fate
to die in the field. For how could I escape my parents
contriving charms? What story could I tell? What trick,
what cunning plan could I devise to bring him help?
Shall I go to greet him alone apart from his companions?
Ill-fated, I do not hope, even though he dies,
to find relief from my pain: for even deprived of life,
that man will be a bane to me. Let modesty go,
let glory go. Let him, saved by my desire,
unscathed, go wherever it pleases his soul to go.
May I, on the very day that he completes the task,
die, either fastening my neck to the roof beams
or tasting drugs to destroy my life. Even so
they will mock me afterward when I am dead, and every
far-off city will shout my doom. Colchian women

will blame my impropriety, gossiping,
'Who cared so much for a foreign man that she died? Who
disgraced her parents and house giving way to a raging passion?'
What shame will not be mine? How infatuated I was!
Far better this very night to abandon life in my chamber,
escaping by an unexplained fate all wicked reproach
before I bring to utter fulfillment such nameless disgrace."
    She spoke and brought a chest in which lay many drugs,
healing and also fatal. Placing it on her knees,
she wept. Her dress she drenched with tears that fell in torrents
as she mourned her own doom. She yearned to choose and taste
a fatal drug and was already making loose
the bonds of the chest, eager to take one out, poor girl.
But suddenly a deadly fear of grim Hades
gripped her heart. For a long time she hesitated,
speechless. All the pleasant cares of life thronged
around her. She thought of all the joys the living have,
and remembered her happy age-mates, as a young girl does.
The sun was sweeter for her to see than ever before,
since truly she yearned in her heart for every single thing.
She put the chest aside from her knees again, prompted
by Hera to change her mind. No longer of two minds,
she longed for the first rays of dawn to appear that she
might give to him the enchanting drugs as she had promised
and meet him face to face. Often she would loose
the bolts of the door, looking for the first gleam.
Welcome to her was the light cast by the early dawn
when all the people began to move throughout the town.
    Argus ordered his brother to stay there still to learn
the mind and plans of the young girl. He himself
first turned about and then went back again to the ship.
    Then when first the young girl saw the shining dawn,
she fastened up with both her hands her tawny hair,
which, let down, drifted now in disarray.
She soothed her tear-worn cheeks and anointed her skin with oil
that smelled sweet as nectar, put on a lovely robe,

fitted with well-bent pins, and upon her ambrosial hair
she cast a silvery veil. So attired, she wandered
back and forth throughout the palace and trod the floor,
forgetful of her woes, those, god-sent, that were
at hand, and those that were to grow in after time.
She called her serving maids, who, twelve altogether,
lay all night in the forecourt of the fragrant chamber,
of her own age, not sharing yet their beds with men,
quickly to yoke to the four-wheeled wagon the mules that would take
her to the exceedingly beautiful shrine of Hecate.
There then the serving maids were fitting out the wagon.
Medea, meanwhile, chose from out of the hollow chest
a drug which they say is called Prometheus' drug.
If with this he should anoint his body, after
making nocturnal sacrifice to please Daira,
the only-born, he could not be broken by strokes of bronze
nor would he yield to blazing fire, but for that day
would prove the better man in strength and force alike.
It shot up, first begotten, when the eagle that feeds
on raw flesh let drop upon the ground along
the rugged crags of Caucasus the bloody ichor
of suffering Prometheus. Its blossom as much as a cubit
high appeared in color much like the Corycian crocus
and rose on double stalks. But in the earth the root
resembled newly cut flesh. Its dark juice, like that
of a mountain oak, she had gathered up in a Caspian shell
to concoct the drug, after bathing in seven running streams
and calling seven times upon Brimo, nurse
of youths, who wanders by night, chthonic queen of the dead,
in the murky night, dressed herself in dusky robes.
The black earth bellowed and shook beneath when the Titan's root
was cut, and Iapetus' son himself moaned, distraught
in his soul with pain. This drug she chose and put it in
the fragrant band that was bound about her ambrosial breasts.
Then going out the door, she mounted the swift wagon.
With her went two serving maids on either side.

She herself took the reins and the well-made whip in her hand
and drove through the city. The other serving maids touched
the wagon behind and ran along the wide track
and tucked their delicate dresses up to their snow-white knees.
Just as in the warm waters of Parthenius
or when she has bathed in the river Amnisus, Leto's daughter
stands on her golden car and drives over the hills
with her swift deer to greet a savory hecatomb
from afar—her nymphs follow in attendance; some
gather at the spring of Amnisus; others abandon
the groves and peaks with their many springs, and all around
the wild beasts whine and fawn, trembling at her approach—
so they sped through the city, and all around the people
made way, averting their eyes from those of the young princess.
But when she had left behind the well-paved streets of the city
and arrived at the temple, driving there from out of the plains,
then she stepped down from out of the well-running wagon,
hurriedly, and to her serving maids she said,

 "Dear friends, truly I have committed a great sin.
I paid no heed to avoiding foreign men, who roam
over our land. The whole city has been struck
with helplessness, and so no one of the women has come
of those who used to gather here every day before.
But since we have come and no other now is present here,
come, let us satisfy our souls, unsparingly,
with sweet song, and when we have plucked the lovely blooms
from the tender grass, at that very hour, we shall return.
And with many gifts you will arrive at home this day,
if you will please me in this eager desire of mine.
For Argus persuades me with words as does Chalciope.
But keep silent in your heart what you hear from me,
that the story not reach the ears of my father. They order me
to accept gifts from the stranger who has taken on
the challenge of the oxen and then to rescue him
from the dangerous contest. I approved this speech and have
  summoned him

to come alone apart from his companions to meet me
face to face that we may divide among ourselves
the gifts he may bring, and to him in turn I may offer
another, more evil charm. But stand apart when he comes."
      So she spoke, and the cunning plan pleased them all.
      At once Argus drew the son of Aeson away
from his companions, alone, as soon as he heard from his brothers
that she had gone at dawn to Hecate's sacred shrine,
and he led him through the plain, and Mopsus followed them,
the son of Ampycus, skilled to interpret prophetic birds
and skilled to counsel well those who were journeying.
Never was there such a man of those who lived before,
neither of those born to the race of Zeus nor of all
the heroes who sprang from the blood of other immortal gods,
as the wife of Zeus that day made Jason to see and address.
His companions marveled as they gazed at him, shining
with grace, and the son of Ampycus rejoiced in their journey,
already presaging somehow all the events to come.
      There is beside the path that borders the plain and near
the temple a poplar wearing a crown of countless leaves,
and there cawing crows come frequently to roost.
One of them while flapping her wings up and down
high in the branches gave reproof with the counsel of Hera:
      "A pathetic seer is this who knows in his mind not even
what children know, that a young girl will say to a youth
not a single sweet or loving word so long as strangers
accompany them. Go away, you pitiful prophet, witless.
Neither Cypris nor the tender loves inspire you."
      She spoke, chastising, and Mopsus smiled when he heard the voice,
divine and sent by god, of the bird and he spoke these words:
      "Son of Aeson, go to the goddess's temple, where you
will find the girl and she will greet you very kindly
at command of Cypris, who will be your fellow combatant
in the contest, even as Phineus, Agenor's son, foretold.
We, Argus and I, will stand apart, expecting
your return, in this very spot. You yourself,
all alone, beseech and beguile her with clever words."

He spoke shrewdly, and they both at once approved his plan.
Nor did Medea's heart turn to other thoughts,
though she sang and danced. But no song that she sang, no game that she
  played,
pleased her for very long, but she would stop, distraught,
nor did she keep her eyes steadily upon
the throng of her serving maids, but she would peer at the paths
far-off, turning her face aside. Often her heart
broke within her breast when she thought that she heard the fall
of a footstep or the sound of the wind passing by. But soon,
even as she yearned for him, he appeared to her
striding high into view, like Sirius from Ocean,
which rises lovely and conspicuous to see
but brings unspeakable disaster to flocks. So Jason
came to her, beautiful to see, but he,
when he appeared, provoked lovesick suffering.
Her heart fell from her breast, her eyes were misted over,
and a hot blush covered her cheeks. She had the strength
to lift her knees neither forward nor back, but her feet beneath
were fixed fast. All her serving maids meanwhile
had drawn aside from them. So they two stood
opposite one another, speechless and silent, like
oaks or tall pines which, rooted side by side,
are silent for the want of wind, but then again
stirred by the breath of a breeze murmur ceaselessly—
so they were about to speak, stirred by the breath of Eros.
The son of Aeson recognized that she had fallen
into disaster, destined by god, and beguilingly said,
  "Why, my girl, are you in such awe of me, since I
am alone? For I am not boastful as other men are,
nor was I even before, when I dwelt in my own land.
Do not therefore be too bashful before me, my girl,
either to ask or to take whatever is pleasing to you.
But since we have come with good will toward one another,
in this very sacred place, where it is not right to sin,
speak openly and ask; do not with pleasant words
deceive me, since from the first you promised your sister to give

the drug that I desire. By Hecate I beg
and by your parents and Zeus who holds his hand above
suppliant strangers; as suppliant and stranger both
I come, bending my knee in need, for apart from you
and Chalciope I shall not prevail in the strenuous contest.
I shall pay my thanks to you for your help in aftertime,
as it is right and proper for men who live abroad,
making beautiful your name and your fame. Just so, the other
heroes will spread your glory when they return to Hellas,
and the wives and mothers of heroes, who even now perhaps
sit upon the shore and mourn for us. You could
dissipate this bitter affliction. Once Ariadne,
the maiden daughter of Minos, whom Pasiphaë, daughter
of Helios, bore, rescued Theseus from evil toils.
She, when Minos had lulled his wrath to sleep, boarded
his ship with him and left her fatherland behind.
The immortal gods themselves loved her, and as a sign
a crown of stars, which men call Ariadne's, wheels
all night long among the heavenly constellations.
So will thanks from the gods come to you, if you
will save so great a band of heroes. For from your beauty
you are likely to excel in kindly courtesy."
    He spoke, flattering her. She cast her eyes askance
and smiled as sweetly as nectar. Her soul melted within.
Elated by his praise, she gazed up at him,
face to face, and did not know what word to say
first, she was so eager to tell him everything
at once. Ungrudgingly she took from her fragrant sash
the drug, and he at once accepted it with joy.
And now she would have drawn all the soul from her breast
and put it into his hands, delighting in his desire,
so did love flash forth from Jason's blond hair,
a sweet flame, and he captured the sparkle of her eyes.
Her heart warmed within and melted away, as the dew
melts around the roses, warmed by the rays of dawn.
And now both would fix their eyes upon the ground,

bashfully, and now again would cast glances
at one another, smiling with all the light of desire
beneath their radiant brows. After a long time
the young girl very hesitantly addressed him and said,
        "Now give me heed that I may devise help for you.
When my father gives to you as you come the deadly teeth
from the jaws of the snake to sow, then watch for the hour when the night
is divided in two, bathe in the streams of the restless river,
alone, apart from others, in dark robes, and dig
a rounded pit. Slaughter in it a female sheep
and sacrifice it whole, heaping well the pyre
upon the pit itself. Propitiate Hecate,
the only begotten daughter of Perses, pouring from
a goblet honey from the hives of bees. And there when you
have remembered and appeased the goddess, withdraw from the pyre,
and let neither footfall nor howling of dogs turn you back
again lest you blemish the rites and fail yourself to return
in good order to your companions. At dawn dampen
this drug and, naked, anoint your body, as if with oil.
You will have unlimited strength and tremendous force, nor will
you compare yourself to men but to the immortal gods.
In addition, let your spear, your shield, and your sword be spattered.
Then the spears of the Earth-born men will not cleave you
in two, nor the irresistible flame that flashes from
the fatal bulls. Not for long will you be such,
but for this one day you must not shrink from the contest.
But I shall provide for you still another aid.
As soon as you have yoked the powerful oxen, and have plowed
with your skill and strength all the stubborn fallow field,
and have sown the dragon's teeth upon the dark clod,
and already the giants are shooting up along the furrows,
when you see them rising up in number from the fallow,
secretly cast a massive stone among them, and they
over it, like snarling dogs over their food, will slay
one another. But you yourself press on and rush to the fray,
and as a result you will bear the fleece to Hellas from Aea

far away, at last. But go, where it pleases your heart
or where it is dear to you to return after setting sail."

So she spoke, and silently cast her glance before
her feet and wet her heavenly cheek with warm tears,
weeping because he was destined to wander far from her
over the wide sea. Again she spoke to him
with sorrowing words and took his right hand in hers,
for now all shame had abandoned her eyes, and she said to him,

"Remember, if you should return home, the name of Medea.
So in turn shall I remember yours though you
are far away. But kindly tell me this. Where
is your home? Where now will you go in your ship over the sea?
Will you come perhaps near rich Orchomenus or the isle
of Aea? Tell me of the maiden whom you have named,
the renowned daughter of Pasiphaë, kin to my father."

So she spoke. At the tears of the girl destructive love
stole over him too, and in return he said,

"Neither by night nor day do I think that I shall forget you
should I escape death—if in fact I shall escape
unscathed to Achaea and Aeetes not set some other task
more difficult than this. If it pleases you to know
my fatherland, I will tell it to you. For my heart itself
compels me. There is a land surrounded by steep mountains,
very rich in sheep and pasture, where Prometheus,
the son of Iapetus, begat noble Deucalion,
the first to found cities, the first to build temples,
and first to be king over men. This land the dwellers about
call Haemonia. In it is Iolcus itself, my city,
and in it too are many others, where those who live
have never heard the name of the island of Aea. Minyas,
setting out from there, Minyas, the son of Aeolus,
the story goes, once built the city Orchomenus,
bordering on the Cadmeians. But why do I tell you all
these trifling things about my home and the daughter of Minos,
far-famed Ariadne, by which glorious name they called
that lovely maiden of whom you ask? I hope that just

as Minos was then well pleased with Theseus because of her,
so your father will be united in friendship with us."

So he spoke, soothing her with soft words,
but agony, most acute, provoked her heart, and she,
suffering, spoke to him with impassioned words and said,

"In Hellas, no doubt, it is noble to care for covenants,
but Aeetes is not such among men as you say Minos,
the husband of Pasiphaë, was, nor am I at all
Ariadne. Do not therefore speak of the love of guests,
but only do you, when you reach Iolcus, remember me,
and I shall remember you, despite the will of my parents.
And may there come to me from afar some rumor or some
messenger bird if you forget me. Or may swift blasts
of wind snatch me up and bear me over the sea
myself from here to Iolcus that I may cast rebuke
into your eyes, reminding you that you made your escape
at my will. Unexpectedly then may I be a guest in your halls."

So she spoke, and piteous tears poured down her cheeks,
and Jason himself then spoke to her in reply and said,

"Dear girl, allow the empty blasts of wind to wander
and also the messenger bird, for what you say is foolish.
If you should come to those haunts and to the land
of Hellas, you would have honor and respect among
men and women, who would defer to you as a goddess,
because their sons came home again by your counsel,
and their brothers and kinsmen and youthful husbands were saved from
     doom.
In our bridal chamber you shall prepare our marriage bed,
and nothing else shall divide us from our love for one
another before the death that is destined enshrouds us both."

So he spoke, and her soul melted within when she heard.
Nevertheless, she shuddered to see the deeds that were clear
to come, poor girl. Not for long was she to refuse
to dwell in Hellas. For this was Hera's plan, that Aeaean
Medea come to sacred Iolcus to be a bane
to Pelias, abandoning forever her native land.

Now her serving maids were gazing anxiously
at them from a distance and were silently distressed.
It was the hour of the day for the young girl to return
home to her mother. But not yet did she think of leaving,
for her soul rejoiced in his beauty and beguiling words
alike, but Jason took caution and spoke, though late, and said,
  "It is the hour to go away before the light
of the sun sinks and we not notice, but some stranger
observe everything. We shall come to meet here again."
  So far did the two of them make trial of one another
with tender words, and then they went their separate ways.
Jason returned in haste to his companions and ship,
rejoicing, and she to her serving maids. They all came near
together to meet her, but she took no notice of them
as they crowded about, for her soul had flown up to the clouds.
With feet that moved of themselves she mounted the swift wagon.
In one hand she took the reins, in the other the whip
of intricate workmanship to drive the mules, and they rushed
toward the city and pressed on to the palace. When she arrived,
Chalciope, in distress for her sons, questioned her,
but Medea, confused and distraught, heard not a word that she said,
nor was she eager to reply to her questioning,
but she sat on a low stool at the foot of her bed and leaned,
resting her cheek on her left hand, and her eyes were full
of tears, for she was disturbed at the wicked deed that she planned.
  The son of Aeson, when he mingled again with his companions,
in the place where he had left them behind, hurried to go
with them, telling them every single thing, to the band
of heroes. Together they approached the ship. And they welcomed him
warmly when they saw him, and questioned him, and he
told to all of them the plans of the girl and showed them
the terrible drug. Idas, apart from his companions,
sat alone, biting down his wrath. The others
were glad then when the dark of night gave check to them
and they could take their ease. But at the first dawn
they sent two men to go to Aeetes and ask for the seed.

Telamon himself first, who was dear to Ares
and with him Aethalides, the illustrious son of Hermes.

They went, nor was their journey fruitless, for the lord Aeetes
gave them for the test when they came the jagged teeth
of the Aonian dragon which Cadmus slew in Ogygian Thebes
when he went there in pursuit of Europa. It guarded the spring
of Ares. There he dwelt by escort of the cow
that Apollo offered to him by his prophetic art
to guide him on the road. But the teeth the Tritonian goddess
tore from the jaws and made them a gift to Aeetes and also
to the slayer himself. Cadmus, the son of Agenor,
sowed them in the Aonian fields and founded a people,
Earth-born, and all who were left by the spear of Ares, the reaper.
These teeth Aeetes offered them to take to the ship,
willingly, since he did not suppose that Jason would
complete the contest even if he should yoke the bulls.

The sun far-off was sinking beneath the black earth
above the lowest peaks of western Ethiopia,
and Night was yoking her horses. The heroes were preparing
their beds beside the hawsers. But Jason, as soon as Helice,
the brilliant stars of the Bear, had set, and the air from heaven
was perfectly still, went to a lonely place, like a thief,
with all that he needed. For by day he had thought of everything.
Argus came and brought a ewe and milk from the flock,
which he had taken from the ship. But when Jason saw
a place that was far from the path of men in pure meadows
beneath a fair sky, there first of all he bathed
his delicate body, reverently, in the divine river,
and wrapped himself in a blue-black robe, which Hypsipyle
of Lemnos had given to him before to be a memento
of their passionate lovemaking. Then he dug a pit
of a cubit's depth in the plain and piled up split wood,
and over that he slit the throat of the lamb. The body
he stretched out well above. He kindled the logs, thrusting
fire beneath and poured upon them mixed libations,
summoning Hecate Brimo to be his help in the contest.

When he had called her up again, he stepped back,
and, hearing him, the terrible goddess from the lowest hollows
approached the rites of Aeson's son. Around her were wound
among the young branches of oaks horrible serpents,
and there flashed the light of countless torches. Around the goddess
the hounds of hell were loudly baying. All the meadows
trembled at her step. The marsh and river nymphs,
who dance about the meadow of Amarantian Phasis,
howled. Fear took hold of Jason, but even so
his feet bore him forward, nor did he turn back until
he had met with his companions. But now early-born dawn
arose and cast her light above snowy Caucasus.

Then Aeetes girt about his chest the sturdy corslet
which Ares had given him when he with his own hands
had slain Phlegraean Mimas. Upon his head he put
a golden helmet with four plumes. It shone like the sun's
circled light when first it rises from Ocean. He brandished
his shield of many hides and his dread irresistible spear.
This not one of the heroes could have withstood since they
had abandoned Heracles, who alone could have met its force
in battle. Phaethon nearby held for him
to mount his well-built chariot with its swift-footed steeds,
and he himself mounted and took the reins in his hands.
From the city they drove along the wide wagon trail
that he might stand by at the contest. With him there rushed
numberless people. As Poseidon goes to the Isthmian games
upon his chariot, or to Taenarus or the water
of Lerna or to the grove of Hyantian Onchestus and then
goes often even to Calaureia with his steeds
and to the Haemonian rock or to forested Geraestus,
such then to see was Aeetes, king of the Colchians.

Meanwhile, at Medea's instruction, the son of Aeson,
moistening the drug, sprinkled with it his shield
and his stout spear and his sword all around. His companions about
made trial by force of his arms but could not bend that spear,
not even a little, but in their strong hands it remained

unbroken, and just as sturdy as it had been before.
But in his insatiate rage with them Aphareus' son,
Idas, struck at the butt of the spear with his mighty sword.
The point leapt back, repelled, like the hammer from an anvil,
and the heroes shouted loud with joy in their hope of the contest.
Then he sprinkled himself, and an awful strength entered
his body, ineffable and intrepid, and both his hands
gained power and swelled with might on either side, as when
a war-horse in anticipation of battle neighs
and prances about and smites the ground with his hoof and lifts
his neck high, rejoicing, with ears erect, just so
did the son of Aeson exult in the strength of his limbs. Often
now here, now there, he leapt high in the air and brandished
his brazen shield and Ares' spear in his hands. Then,
not for long after that were his men to hold back from the contest,
but seated on benches in rows they pressed swiftly on
to the plain of Ares. It was as far in front of them
on the opposite side of the city as is the turning post
that a chariot must achieve from the starting line whenever
a king has died and his kinsmen arrange funeral games
for foot soldiers and horsemen. They came upon Aeetes
and the Colchian tribes stationed along the Caucasian crags,
but the king himself upon the bank of the winding river.

The son of Aeson, when his companions had made fast
the stern cables, with spear and shield leapt from the ship
and came to the contest, and he had with him a brazen helmet,
all shining and full of the sharp teeth and a sword about
his shoulders, and he himself was naked, in one way
like Ares, and in another, Apollo of the golden sword.
Gazing over the fallow, he saw the brazen yokes
of the oxen and nearby the plow of one piece,
made of sturdy adamant. He came near and fixed
his stout spear straight up on its butt and took off his helmet
and braced it against the spear. Then he advanced with the shield,
alone, seeking out the countless tracks of the bulls.
They, from some unknown hollow beneath the earth, where

their sturdy ox stall was, wrapped in murky smoke,
came forth, both together, breathing flame of fire.
You would say that from the lowering sky winter lightning
flashed and leaped frequently from the clouds whenever
they bring blackest rain. The heroes were terrified when
they saw the bulls, but Jason, with legs well astride,
withstood their assault, as in the sea a reef of rock
withstands the waves billowed by the constant blasts.
He held his shield before him. Both the bulls bellowed
and struck at him with their mighty horns, but in their assault
they heaved him aside not even a little bit. As when
in the pierced melting pots the leather bellows of smiths
move quickly now to kindle the fatal flame and now
again leave off their blowing, and a terrible roar
comes from them when the fire leaps up from below, so
both the bulls, blowing quick flame from their mouths,
roared. The devouring fire licked about him and hit
like lightning, but the drugs of Medea protected him.
He with his right hand pulled at the tip of the bull's
horn and dragged it, powerfully, with all his strength
toward the brazen yoke and forced the bull to the ground on its knees,
and suddenly with his foot struck the foot of bronze.
So also the other he threw to its knees as it rushed him headlong,
thrusting it down with a single blow. His broad shield
he cast to the ground and stepping, now here, now there, on this side
and that, he held the bulls down where they had fallen
upon their foreknees and passed at once through the flame.
Aeetes marveled at the strength of the man. Meanwhile,
the sons of Tyndareus—for it had been foretold of old
for them—nearby handed the yoke to him from the ground
to put upon themselves. He bound their necks well,
and lifting the brazen plow pole between he fitted it
to the yoke by its sharp tip. The two withdrew from the fire
and went back to the ship. But Jason took up again his shield
and cast it to his back and took the stout helmet
full of the sharp teeth and his irresistible spear

with which like some plowman with Pelasgian goad

he pricked the bulls, piercing them beneath their flanks.
   Very firmly he steered the well-fitted plowhandle
that was made of adamant. The bulls meanwhile kept raging,
blowing furious flame of fire, and their breath rose
like the roar of blustering winds which sailors especially fear
and furl therefore their large sail. Not long after,
urged by the spear, they moved on. The rough fallow
was broken behind, split by the plow and the mighty strength
of the bulls. At the same time along the furrows the clods
screamed terribly as they were rent by the plow,
each one the size that a man could carry. Jason followed,
pressing down the field with stout foot, and far
from himself he cast along the plowed clods the teeth,
turning back for fear that the deadly crop of Earth-born men
spring up first to meet him. The bulls kept laboring on,
plodding with hoofs of bronze. But when the third part
of day, waning from dawn, remains, and the weary plowmen
long for the sweet ox-loosing hour to come to them soon,
then the fallow was plowed by the tireless plowman, though
it was four fields deep, and the oxen were loosed from the plow. Them
he frightened to flee to the plain, but he himself went back
again to the ship while he saw still the furrows empty
of the Earth-born men. His companions around emboldened him
with their shouts. From the river streams with his helmet he drew water
and quenched his thirst. He bent to limber his knees and filled
his mighty heart with strength, raging like a boar
that sharpens its teeth against hunting men, and all
around much foam drips from its furious mouth to the ground.
   But now over the plowed field the Earth-born men
were shooting up. The precinct of Ares, slayer of men,
bristled with stout shields and double-pointed spears
and gleaming helmets. The beams reached Olympus, flashing
from below through the air. Just as when abundant snow
has fallen upon the earth and then blasts of wind
scatter the wintry clouds beneath the gloomy night

and all the constellations appear in throngs, shining
through the dark, so did they shine, springing up
above the earth. But Jason remembered wily Medea's
advice. He grabbed from the ground a huge boulder, round,
an awesome quoit of Ares. Four vigorous men
could not have raised it from the earth even a little.
But Jason lifted it with ease and shot it far
into their midst. He himself crouched in secret,
confident, beneath his shield. The Colchians roared
as the sea roars when it thunders over the sharp reefs.
Aeetes was speechless at the cast of the sturdy quoit,
but the Earth-born men like fleet hounds leapt about
and, howling, slew one another. They fell upon the earth,
their mother, by their own spears like pines or oaks that squalls
of wind shake down. Like a fiery star that leaps from heaven
blazing a furrow of light, a marvel for men who see it
dart and sparkle through the dusky sky, such was the son
of Aeson as he rushed the Earth-born men and drew
from its scabbard his bared sword and smote left and right,
mowing them down, many in the belly and flanks
who were half-risen to the air and others as far
as the knees and others still just standing upright and some
even now running to battle. As when a quarrel arises
between neighbors and the farmer fears that they
will plow his fields first and seizes in his hands
a sickle, newly sharpened and well bent, and hastens
to shear the unripe sheaves and does not wait for them
to be dried in due season by the rays of the sun,
so did Jason cut down the crop of the Earth-born men.
The furrows were filled with blood as watering channels are filled
with streams from springs. They fell, some of them prone, biting
the broken clod with their teeth, some on their backs, and some
on the flat of their hands and sides like sea monsters to see.
Many, struck before lifting their feet above earth, were as bent
to the ground as they had risen in air, and were propped there
with damp brows. So when Zeus sends rain in torrents,

fledgling shoots in the vineyard droop to the earth, cut off *III. 1400*
–1407
at the root—the work of the gardeners—but heartache and dreadful pain
overtake the man who owns the plot and planted them.
So then did heavy anguish enter the heart of the king,
Aeetes, and he returned to the city and the Colchians,
pondering how he might more quickly encounter them.
Daylight waned, and for Jason the contest was completed at last.

Book IV

The suffering and artful plans of the Colchian girl *IV. 1–27*
now tell yourself, goddess Muse, child of Zeus.
For my mind reels within and I am speechless when
I wonder whether to call it lovesick anguish of madness
or disgraceful flight by which she left the Colchian tribes.
Aeetes with the bravest men of his people all night long
within his halls was contriving sheer cunning against
the Argonauts, for his heart was angered insatiately
because of the abominable result of the contest,
nor did he suppose at all that these deeds were accomplished without
the help of his daughter. But into Medea's heart Hera
put most troublesome fear, so that she trembled like
a delicate fawn that the baying of hounds has terrified
in the thickets of a deep wood. At once she knew
infallibly that her aid had not escaped her father
and that soon she would fulfill all her allotment of woe.
She feared her knowing attendants. Her eyes were filled with fire,
and her ears rang terribly. Often she clutched at her throat, and often
pulled out her hair at the roots and moaned in agony.
Now the girl, then and there, would have taken the drugs and perished
before her time and foiled the designs of Hera had not
the goddess forced her to flee distraught with the sons of Phrixus.
Her fluttering heart was warmed within her breast, and then
she poured back again from her dress all the drugs together
into the chest. She kissed her bed and the folding doors
on either side and touched the walls. Tearing off

with her hands a long lock, she left it behind in her room
for her mother, a memento of her maidenhood,
and then, lamenting with passionate voice, she sobbed and said,
    "Leaving this long lock in my place I go, my mother.
Accept this goodbye from me as I set out afar.
Goodbye Chalciope too and all the house. I wish
that the sea had dashed you to pieces, O stranger, before you arrived
at the Colchian land!" So then she spoke and from her eyes
poured floods of tears. As a captive slave slips away
from a rich house, whom fate has recently deprived
of her native land, nor has she yet attempted at all
hard labor, but unaccustomed still to misery
and bewildered by her slavish tasks, she goes about
at the harsh hands of her mistress, so the lovely girl
rushed forth from the palace. For her the bolts of the door gave way
themselves, leaping back at the shrill strains of her magic song.
    With bare feet she rushed along the narrow paths,
with her left hand holding her robe before her brow
to hide her face and her lovely cheeks, and with her right
lifting up high the hem of her dress. Swiftly along
a secret track outside the walls of the spacious town
she went in fear, nor did one of the guards recognize her,
but she escaped them all as she sped by. From there
she intended to go to the temple, for well she knew the way.
Often before had she wandered there in search of corpses
or for noxious roots of the earth, just as a sorceress does.
Her soul trembled with quivering fear. The Titanian goddess
the Moon, just rising now from a distant land, saw
the girl as she ran distraught and exulted savagely
over her and spoke words like these to her own heart:
    "Not I alone then stray to the Latmian cave, nor do I
alone burn for the lovely Endymion. Often have I,
mindful of love, been driven to hide by your guileful spells
that you in the murky night might compound your drugs at ease,
the deeds that are dear to you. Now you yourself it seems
have a share of disaster. A malicious god has given

Jason to be your distressing affliction. But go, learn,
clever though you are, to endure your grievous pain."

So she spoke. Medea's feet bore her hastening on.
Gladly she reached the height of the riverbank and saw
opposite her the light of the fire that the heroes burned
all night long in their joy at the contest. Then through the dark
with voice loud and shrill she called from the opposite shore
to Phrontis, the youngest of Phrixus' sons. He, together
with his brothers and Aeson's son, recognized the voice
of the girl, but his companions were silently amazed
when they realized that it was true. Three times she called
aloud, and three times at urging of the throng
Phrontis shouted back in reply. Meanwhile, the heroes
were rowing with swift oars in search of her. Not yet
were they casting the ship's cables upon the opposite shore
when Jason leapt nimbly upon dry land from the deck above,
and afterward Phrontis and Argus, the sons of Phrixus, jumped
to the ground. She embraced their knees with both hands and said,

"Save me, ill-starred, and yourselves as well, my friends, from Aeetes,
for all has been revealed and no remedy comes, but in
the ship let us take flight before Aeetes mounts
his swift steeds. I will give you the golden fleece, lulling
to sleep the guardian snake. And do you, stranger, among
your companions make the gods witness to promises
you made to me so that as I set out from here
for a distant land you need not make me for want
of kin an object of blame and disgrace." She spoke in anguish,
and greatly did the heart of Aeson's son rejoice.
He lifted her at once, gently, from where she had fallen
upon her knees and embraced and encouraged her with words:

"Dear girl, let Olympian Zeus himself be witness to
my oath and Hera of bridal yoke, consort of Zeus:
I shall make you in my halls my lawfully wedded wife,
when we have made our voyage home to the land of Hellas."

He spoke and straightway took her right hand in his.
She bade them row the swift ship to the sacred grove

185

close by that they might take the fleece while night remained
and carry it off despite the will of Aeetes. From there
word and deed were one and the same to the eager men,
for they took her on board and at once thrust the ship from the shore.
There was a mighty din as the chiefs pressed on with their oars.
She leapt up and stretched her hands toward land, in despair,
but Jason heartened her with words and checked her grief.
    At the hour when men have cast sleep from their eyes—hunters
trusting in their hounds, who never slumber the night
away till day, shunning the light of dawn for fear
that it efface the fresh track and scent of the prey,
striking with its bright rays—then Aeson's son
and the girl stepped from the ship upon a grassy spot
called the Ram's Bed, because there first it had bent
its weary knees, bearing upon its back the son
of Athamas of Minyas. Nearby was the sooty base
of the altar which once Aeolid Phrixus set up to Zeus
of fugitives, sacrificing that marvel of gold
at Hermes' behest when that one kindly encountered him.
There at the counsel of Argus the captains put them ashore.
They came by the path to the sacred grove, searching for
the enormous oak on which the fleece was hung, like a cloud
that blushes red with the blazing beams of the rising sun.
But opposite them the serpent with its keen sleepless eyes
stretched its long neck when it saw them coming and hissed
horribly, and all around the long banks
of the river and grove rang unspeakably. Those heard it
who far from Titanian Aea inhabit the Colchian land
beside the outfall of Lycus, which spreads abroad from the river,
roaring Araxis, and mixes its sacred stream with Phasis,
and they together, made one, flow toward the Caucasian sea.
Mothers, newly delivered, awoke in terror and put
their hands upon their infant sons who slept in their arms
and trembled at that hissing—the women were so distressed.
As when above smoldering wood sooty eddies
of smoke roll endlessly, one ever rising up

186

soon after another, billowing from below in spirals,
so then did that monster unwind his countless coils
covered with horny scales. As he writhed, the girl came
before his eyes, calling with sweet voice upon
her helper Sleep, highest of gods, to charm the monster,
and she called aloud to the queen, wanderer by night
of the world below, to grant her a welcome outcome.
The son of Aeson followed, though he was afraid.
But the snake, already charmed by her song, began to relax
the long spine of his giant coil, lengthening out
his myriad spires, like a black wave that rolls, silent
and dumb, over an indolent sea. But nevertheless
he lifted up his horrible head, raging to
embrace them both in his deadly jaws. But she with a sprig
of juniper, newly cut, dipping from her brew,
sprinkled unmixed drugs with her spell of songs upon
his eyes, and all around the powerful smell of the drug
cast sleep. On that very spot he let his jaw drop down,
and his countless coils were stretched far behind throughout
the forest of many trees. Thereupon Jason took
the golden fleece from the oak at the young girl's command,
but she stood steadfast, smearing the head of the beast with the drug
until Jason himself bade her turn back to the ship,
and they left the shadowy grove of Ares. As a young girl
catches the beam of the full moon as it rises above
her high-roofed chamber upon her delicate robe, and her heart
rejoices to see the lovely gleam, so then did Jason
rejoice as he took the great fleece in his hands, and on
his fair cheeks and brow from the glittering of the wool
there rested a rosy flush like a flame. As large as is
the hide of a yearling ox or a stag that hunters call
a brocket, so large was the fleece, and all golden above
and heavy with its cover of flocks. The earth beneath
his feet reflected the gleam of the fleece as he walked. And now
he would go, cloaked with it from the left shoulder, from
high on the neck down to the feet, and now again

187

he would take it up in his hands, for he feared excessively
that some god or man, encountering him, would take it away.

Dawn was beginning to spread over the earth when they came
to the band of heroes. The young men marveled to see the fleece
gleaming like the lightning of Zeus, and each rose up,
hoping to touch and to take it up in his own hands.
But the son of Aeson prevented them and covered it
with a cloak, newly made. Then he took Medea to
the stern and seated her there and spoke like this to them all:

"No longer, my friends, refrain from return to your fatherland.
Now the need for which we endured this painful voyage,
suffering wretchedly, has handily been fulfilled
by the skills of the girl. I shall take her home, since this is her wish,
to be my lawfully wedded wife. Protect her as
the noble savior of all Achaea and of yourselves
as well, for I think that Aeetes surely will come with his throng
to prevent our passage from river to sea. Throughout the ship,
some, sitting man beside man, row with the oar blades,
and half of you, holding before you your ox-hide shields,
a ready defense against the enemies' bolts, protect
our voyage home. Now in our hands we have our children,
our dear native land, and our aged parents, and Hellas depends
upon our venture, to gain either shame or great renown."

He spoke and put on his armor of war, and they shouted out,
wonderfully eager. Drawing his sword from its sheath, he cut
the stern cables away from the ship. Near the girl,
fully armed, he stepped beside the helmsman Ancaeus.
With their rowing the ship sped forward as they pressed in haste
and desperation to steer at once outside the river.

To overweening Aeetes and all the Colchians
Medea's love and her deeds were now notorious,
and in assembly they gathered together in arms, as many
as the waves of the sea that crest beneath a wintry wind
or as many as the leaves that fall to the ground from a wood
branched all around in the month of shedding leaves—who
could mark them?—so countless did they throng the banks

188

of the river, clamorous in their rage. In his well-built car
Aeetes was conspicuous with the steeds, swift
as the breath of wind, that Helios had given him.
In his left hand he raised his rounded shield. In the other,
a high pine-wood torch. Beside and facing him
was propped his monstrous spear. Apsyrtus held in his hands
the horses' reins. But already the ship was cleaving the sea
before her, pressed on by the powerful oarsmen,
and by the mighty river stream that rushed on down.
But the king in manifold anguish raised his hands and called
on Helios and Zeus to witness their wicked deeds
and straightway he threatened terribly all his people
that, unless they should themselves discover the girl, either
upon the land or finding the ship still upon
the swell of the navigable salt sea, and bring
her back to him that he fulfill his furious soul
with vengeance for all these deeds, with their lives they would learn to
      endure
all his rage and accept total calamity.

    So Aeetes spoke, and on that same day
the Colchians drew down their ships and put their gear
on board and set forth upon the sea. Nor would
you say that such was a fleet of ships but that a flight
of birds in countless flocks clamored over the sea.

    The Argonauts, with a light wind, at the goddess Hera's plan
that Aeaean Medea most quickly reach Pelasgian land
and be a bane to Pelias' house, at the third dawn
bound their ship's hawsers to Paphlagonian shores
before the mouth of the river Halys. For there Medea
bade them disembark to propitiate Hecate
with sacrifice, and what the girl prepared for this
(let no one know nor may my soul bid me to sing)
I am in awe of saying. And still since then the altar
the heroes built the goddess upon the beach remains
until today for later-born men to see from afar.
Straightway Aeson's son recalled, and the other heroes

with him, how Phineus had foretold that their voyage from Aea
would be otherwise, but to all alike his prophecy
was obscure. Then Argus addressed them, and they were eager to hear:
   "We go to Orchomenus to where that infallible seer
whom you met before foretold your sailing, for there exists
another course shown by the priests of immortal gods,
born of Tritonian Thebes. Not yet in heaven did all
the constellations wheel, nor yet could one, should he
inquire, hear anything at all of the sacred race
of the Danai. Apidanean Arcadians
alone existed, who, they say, lived even before
the moon, eating acorns upon the mountain tops; nor then
did Deucalion's glorious sons rule the Pelasgian land
when Egypt, mother of lusty earlier-born, was called
Morning Mist of many fields of corn, and the river
wide-flowing Triton by which all the Morning Mist
is watered, and never does rain from Zeus moisten it,
but from the floods abundant sheaves of wheat spring up.
From there, they say, a certain king journeyed around
through all Europe and Asia, trusting the might, the strength,
the courage of his people. Where he went he founded
myriad towns. Men live in some, in others not,
for much time has passed since then. But Aea abides
secure, even now, and the sons of those men
whom that king Sesostris established to dwell in Aea.
They preserve their fathers' inscribed pillars on which are carved
all the roads and limits of water and land for those
who travel around. There is a river, the highest horn
of Ocean, broad and very deep, that a merchant ship
can cross. They call it Ister and marked it far off.
For a time it cleaves the boundless plowland alone,
in one stream, for springs beyond the northwest wind
among the Rhipaean Mountains faraway roar
as they boil forth. But when it enters the boundaries
of Scythians and Thracians, it splits in two and casts
its water into our sea and back into

a deep gulf projecting from the Trinacrian sea,
which lies along your land, if in truth indeed
it is from your land that the Achelous flows."

So then he spoke, and to them the goddess granted a sign
of auspicious portent, and all when they saw shouted assent
that this was the path to take. For before them formed a furrow
of a heavenly ray of light to show where they might pass.
Rejoicing, they left behind the son of Lycus there,
and spreading their sails, they sped across the salt sea,
fixing their gaze upon the Paphlagonian mountains,
nor did they round Carambis, for gleam of the heavenly flame
and the winds remained until they reached the mighty Ister.

Now some of the Colchians, searching in vain, sailed out from Pontus
between the Cyanean rocks; the others went to the river.
These Apsyrtus led; turning aside, he entered
the Fair Mouth, and so outstripped the Argonauts
by crossing a neck of land into the uttermost gulf
of the Ionian Sea. For there is an island enclosed
by Ister, Peuce by name, three-cornered, its width
stretching along the beach with a sharp angle toward
the river. Around it the outfall splits in two. One
they call Narex' mouth; the one at the lower end,
the Fair. Through this Apsyrtus and the Colchians
swiftly rushed, but the heroes went to the highest part
of the island, far off. In the meadows the rustic shepherds left
their countless flocks in fear of the ships, for they supposed
they were beasts emerging from the monster-teeming sea.
For never yet before had they seen sea-going ships,
neither Scythians mixed with Thracians nor Sigynni
nor Graucenii nor Sindi, who dwell now around
the large deserted plain of Laurium. But when
they had passed Mount Angurum and far from it beside
the cliff of Cauliacus, around which the Ister
splits and casts its stream on this side and that, into
the sea and the plain of Laurium, then indeed
the Colchians put forth for the Cronian Sea and cut off

all the paths to prevent the Argonauts' escape.
But the Argonauts came down the river behind and reached
the twin Brygean islands of Artemis nearby.
On one of them there was a sacred shrine. On the other,
guarding against Apsyrtus' band, they set foot,
for the Colchians had left those of the many islands
just as they were, in awe of the daughter of Zeus. The others,
thronged by Colchians, closed the courses to the sea,
and so on the shores of the other isles close by Apsyrtus
left his band up to Salangon River and Nestian land.

    Then the Minyae would have given way, fewer
to more, in grim strife, but before that they made
a covenant, averting mighty conflict, that they
should keep the golden fleece, secure as justly won,
whether they had taken it by trickery
or even openly in the Colchian king's despite,
since Aeetes himself had promised it them should they fulfill
the terms of the contest, but that they give Medea in trust
to Leto's daughter apart from the band until someone
of the king, upholding right in his decrees, decide
whether she must return again to her father's house
or follow the princes in their return to the land of Hellas.

    Now when the girl had considered each of these things in her mind,
straightway she called Jason forth alone to her side
and led him apart from his companions until they had drawn
faraway, and, moaning, she spoke this word to his face:
    "Son of Aeson, what is this plan that you prepare
concerning me? Or has your glory caused you
utter forgetfulness and you have no regard
for all you said when bound by necessity? Where
are the oaths sworn by Zeus, the god of suppliants?
Where have your honey-sweet promises gone?—for which I,
improperly, with shameless desire deserted my land,
my illustrious home, and my parents themselves, and all these
were most important to me. Alone and far away
I am borne over the sea with lamenting halcyons

for the sake of your toils that I might keep you safe while you
fulfilled the terms of the contest with oxen and Earth-born men.
Finally, you took the fleece, for which you made
the voyage, by my folly, and I shed fatal shame
on womankind, and so I say that as your child,
your sister, your bride, I follow you to the land of Hellas.
Stand ready now at my side. Do not abandon me
alone, apart from you, as you go to visit the kings,
but save me even so. Let justice and right, to which
we both agreed, stand secure, or else then
shear straightway with your sword through this throat of mine
that I may reap acceptable recompense for my lust,
wretch that I am. And if this king to whom you both
commit your sorry covenant decrees that I
belong to my brother, how shall I come to my father's eyes?
With fair name, no doubt. What retribution, what crushing
revenge will I not bear in agony because
of the awful deeds I have done? Now would you choose to have
the voyage home that is your heart's desire? May the wife
of Zeus, queen of all, in whom your glory lies,
not bring this to pass. May you remember me
one day, when wrung with troubles, and may the fleece like a dream
be gone below with the breath of the wind to the nether dark,
and may my Furies drive you from your fatherland
straightway for all that I suffered myself at your hardness of heart.
Right will not permit this curse to fall to the ground
without accomplishment, for you have violated
a mighty oath, ruthlessly. But not for long
will you and your companions sit at your ease and wink
in mockery of me because of your covenants."

So she spoke, seething with ominous wrath. She yearned
to torch the ship, to shatter it utterly and fall
herself into the ravening flame. But Jason, alarmed
for her, spoke with gentle words and said to the girl,

"Dear child, refrain. Neither am I pleased at this,
but we seek some delay of strife, so great a cloud

of hostile men blazes around because of you.
For all that dwell in this land are mad to assist Apsyrtus
that he may lead you home to your father, some prize of war,
and we would all ourselves perish in grim destruction
should we join battle with them. More bitter will be the pain
if we should die and abandon you as booty to them.
This covenant will contrive a trick by which we shall
entice him to ruin. Nor will the dwellers-about object
to please the Colchians on your account, apart
from their prince who is your brother and champion, nor I
withdraw from doing battle with the Colchians,
face to face, if they refuse my sailing forth."
     He spoke, comforting her, but she made a murderous speech:
     "Consider now—one must for unseemly deeds take
counsel like this, since at first, infatuate
with sin, by the gods' design, I fulfilled evil desire.
Do you in the battle moil ward off the Colchian spears
and I will entice Apsyrtus to come to your hands, and do you
welcome him with gleaming gifts, if only I
can persuade the heroes as they go away to bring
him alone to attend to my words. And then if this deed is pleasing
to you, kill Apsyrtus—I do not grudge it you—
and raise with the Colchians the hostile battle strife."
     So concurring, they two devised a great deceit
for Apsyrtus and proffered many gifts of host to guest.
Among them they gave Hypsipyle's sacred crimson robe.
The Graces themselves had woven it for Dionysus
in sea-girt Dia. He gave it afterward to his son
Thoas, who left it to Hypsipyle, and she
gave it to Aeson's son with many marvels to wear,
a beautifully wrought gift of hospitality.
Neither by touching nor gazing upon it could you fulfill
sweet desire. From it ambrosial fragrance breathed,
ever since the Nyseian lord himself lay
wrapped in it, slightly drunk with nectar and wine,
and clasped the lovely breasts of Minos' maiden daughter,

whom Theseus abandoned once on the isle of Dia when she
had followed him from Cnossus. When she had pressed her plan
upon the heralds to cozen him to come, as soon
as she reached the temple of the goddess, according to
the covenant, and murky night surrounded them,
that she devise with him deceit by which she might
take the great golden fleece and go again
back to Aeetes' house, for the sons of Phrixus, she said,
by constraint had given her to the strangers to lead away.
With such beguiling words she scattered to air and wind
the bewitching charms which would have brought from faraway
the wild beast down from the lofty mountaintop.
Savage Love, mighty bane, abomination
to humankind, from you there come like storms at sea
lethal quarrels, groans and sighs and lamentation,
and boundless misery besides. Against the sons
of foes, O demon god, don your helmet and rise
as when you inspired Medea with loathsome insanity.

How did she subdue with evil death when they met
Apsyrtus? For this must be the next event of our song.

Now when they had left Medea on Artemis' isle, in accord
with the covenant, they separately beached their ships.
Jason went to lie in ambush, awaiting Apsyrtus,
and then his companions in turn. But he, deceived by these
most dire of promises, quickly crossed in his ship the swell
of the sea. Beneath the gloom of night he stepped upon
the sacred isle. Meeting her alone, he tested
his sister with words, just as a tender child tests
a stormy torrent not even stalwart men can cross,
to see if she devised deceit for foreign men.
The two of them agreed on every single thing.
Straightway the son of Aeson leapt from his dense ambush,
hefting his bared sword in his hand. Quickly the girl
cast her eyes aside and covered them with her veil
that she not behold her brother's blood when he was struck.
And Jason smote him, like a butcher that smites a mighty

strong-horned bull, sighting him near the temple which
the Brygi who dwell on the opposite coast had once built
to Artemis. In its forecourt he fell to his knees. At last
the hero, breathing his life away, scooped up in his hands
the black blood from the wound and crimsoned the silvery veil
and robe of the girl as she shrank away. With quick glance
aslant the implacable Fury saw the murderous deed
they had done, and the hero, Jason, Aeson's son, cut off
the dead man's extremities and thrice licked up his blood
and thrice spat the defilement from out his teeth just as
a murderer must in right to expiate a slaying
by treachery, and the clammy corpse he hid in the earth,
where even now those bones lie among the Apsyrtians.

 As soon as they saw before them the gleam of the torch the girl
had raised as a signal for them to follow after, the heroes
placed their ship near the Colchian ship and slew the band
of Colchians as hawks slay tribes of doves or as
savage lions, springing upon the folds, drive
in confusion a mighty flock. Nor did anyone
of them escape death, but they rushed the whole host,
like ravaging flame. At last Jason met them, keen
to help, but they needed no aid and were now concerned for him.

 So then they sat, devising a shrewd plan of voyage,
and Medea came upon them as they took their counsel,
but Peleus was first to speak his word and said to them,

 "I urge you now while still it is night to embark and row
the passage opposite that the enemy holds, for when
at dawn they behold all, no word, I believe, that urges
further pursuit of us will be persuasive to them,
but like men bereft of their king they will scatter in grievous dissent.
And easy for us, once the people divide and scatter,
will be the path when we return in aftertime."

 So he spoke, and the youths agreed with Aeacus' son.
Nimbly they boarded the ship and bent unceasingly
to their oars until they reached Electris, a sacred isle,
the highest of all and near the river Eridanus.

But when the Colchians learned of the death of their lord, in fact
they longed to follow Argo and the Minyans through all
the Cronian Sea, but Hera held them in restraint
with terrible lightnings from the sky. Finally,
(for they loathed their haunts in Cytaean land, quaking before
Aeetes' savage wrath), they sailed forth and settled
securely, some here, some there. Some disembarked upon
the very islands the heroes had held and live there still,
bearing Apsyrtus' name. Others built a bastion
upon the Illyrian river of the black depths and where
there is the tomb of Cadmus and Harmonia,
who dwell among the Encheleans, and others live
among the mountains called the Thunderbolts from the time
that the thunders of Zeus, the son of Cronus, prevented them
from sailing across to the island that lay opposite them.

The heroes, when their voyage home seemed safe to them,
sailed forth and bound their hawsers to Hyllean land,
for the islands, scattered thick, made the course hazardous
for sailors. Nor did the Hylleans, as they had before,
devise danger for them, but themselves contrived a course
and took as wage a huge tripod of Apollo.
For Phoebus had given two tripods to Aeson's son
to carry afar as he journeyed, compelled, when he had come
to sacred Pytho to ask about this very voyage.
And it was fated that the land in which they stood
be ever free of ravaging by invading foes.
And so even now this tripod is hidden there
in that land near the city Pleasant Hyllus, far
beneath the earth that it be always invisible
to mortal men. Nor did they find there still alive
the lord Hyllus, whom lovely Melite bore in the land
of Phaeacians to Heracles, for he had come to the house
of Nausithous and Macris, the nurse of Dionysus,
to cleanse himself of his children's bloody murder. There
he loved and ravished the river Aegaeus' virgin daughter
Melite, the water nymph, and she gave birth

to mighty Hyllus. When he grew up, he did not care
to live on that island beneath the beetling brows of the king
Nausithous but went to the Cronian Sea with a host
gathered of native Phaeacians, for King Nausithous,
the hero, prepared a path for him. There he settled.
The Mentores murdered him protecting his rustic oxen.

But goddesses, how outside this sea and near
Ausonian land and Ligystian isles, called Stoechades,
are the measureless traces of Argo ship so truthfully told?
What compulsion and need carried them so far
astray? What breezes blew to waft them on their way?

At Apsyrtus' monstrous thudding fall, wrath took hold
of Zeus himself, king of gods, at what they had done,
and he decreed that by the arts of Aeaean Circe
they wash away the murder blood and suffer before
returning home myriad woes. Not one of the princes
was aware of this. But they ran afar, setting out
from Hyllean land, and left behind all the isles
the Colchians had formerly thronged — the Liburnian isles,
Issa, Dysceladus, and lovely Pityeia,
all in a row, and after these they came to Corcyra,
where Poseidon brought to dwell Asopus' daughter, Corcyra
of the lovely hair, far from the land of Phlius, when he
for love had carried her off. Sailors beholding it
from the sea, darkening everywhere the black woods,
call it Corcyra the Black. They passed by Melite,
rejoicing in balmy breezes, and steep Cerossus, Nymphaea
far beyond, where the queen Calypso, Atlas' daughter,
dwelt. They imagined they saw the misty mountaintops
of the Thunderbolts. Then Hera remembered the mighty wrath
and counsels concerning them of Zeus, and she contrived
an end of their voyage, stirring up squalls against them,
which snatched them up and carried them back to the isle Electris.
Suddenly, straightway, there cried in human voice
in the midst of their course the beam of the hollow ship which Athena
had fitted mid-keel, made of Dodonian oak.

Deadly fear took hold of them as they heard the voice
that told the heavy wrath of Zeus. For it declared
that they would not escape the long paths of the sea
nor terrible tempests until Circe should wash away
the guilt of blood from Apsyrtus' pitiless murder and bade
Polydeuces and Castor to beg the immortal gods to provide
paths through the Ausonian sea where they should find
at home Circe, the daughter of Perse and Helios.
      So the Argo cried through the gloom, and there rose up
Tyndareus' sons, raising their hands to the gods immortal
and praying for everything, but dejection held the other
Minyan heroes. The ship under sail sped far ahead,
and the Argonauts entered the furthest reach of Eridanus' stream,
where once struck to the chest by the blazing thunderbolt,
Phaethon, half-consumed, fell from Helios' car
into the mouth of that lake of many depths,
which even now from the smoldering wound spouts up steam
in clouds and no bird can spread its nimble wing
to cross that water. Midway it flutters and falls into
the flame. All around the daughters of Helios,
enclosed in lofty poplars, grieve and wretchedly keen
and shed from their lids upon the ground gleaming drops
of amber. These are dried by the sun upon the sands,
but when the flood of the black lake washes the shores
before the blast of the howling wind, they roll in a mass
to Eridanus with the billowing tide. But the Celts report
that these are the tears of Leto's son, Apollo, borne
on the swirling tides, which he shed by thousands before when he came
to the Hyperborean tribe and left the glittering sky
at his father's rebuke, angered about the son whom
divine Coronis bore in shining Lacereia
at the mouth of Amyrus. Such is the tale that these men tell.
The Argonauts had no desire for food or drink,
nor did their minds rejoice, but they were tortured all day,
faint and depressed at the loathsome unendurable stench
that Eridanus' streams sent up from the smoking Phaethon.

By night they heard the piercing lament of Helios' daughters,
keening shrilly. And as they wept their tears were borne
like drops of olive oil along the watery tides.
  From there they sailed into Rhodanus' deep flood,
which flows into Eridanus, and where they meet
their waters tumble and roar; but from the furthest reaches
of earth, where there are the gates and precincts of night,
it rises and here erupts upon the shores of Ocean,
while there it pours into the Ionian Sea,
and there through seven mouths it hurls its stream
into the Sardinian sea and its boundless bay.
From Rhodanus they sailed into stormy lakes which spread
ineffably large throughout the Celtic continent,
and there they would have met with unseemly disaster, for a branch
of the Rhodanus bore them toward a gulf of Ocean which
with no knowledge before they were about to enter.
From there they would not have returned alive, but Hera leapt
from heaven and shrieked aloud from atop the Hercynian rock,
and they were all alike shaken with fear at her cry,
for terribly rang the mighty firmament. And back
they turned again because of the goddess and marked the path
by which they would voyage home. After a long time
they reached the beaches of the salt-surging sea
by the counsels of Hera, passing unscathed through countless tribes
of Celts and Ligyans. For the goddess shed about them
an awful mist day by day as they traveled on.
And so steering their ship through the midmost mouth,
they reached the Stoechades, safe because of the sons
of Zeus. Altars and shrines are built steadfast for them,
and not this voyage alone did they attend as saviors,
but Zeus granted them to ships of later-born men.
Abandoning the Stoechades, they sailed to Aethalia,
where with pebbles they wiped away much sweat
after their labors. Like skin in color, the pebbles are strewn
along the beach and their quoits and wonderful clothing too,
and the harbor there is called Argoan after them.

Swiftly from there they went through the swell of the sea of Ausonia
and saw the Tyrrhenian headlands and came to the famous harbor
of Aeaea. From the ship they cast the stern cables
upon the shore close by. There they found Circe
washing her hair in the salt seawater, for so frightened
had she been by her dreams in the night. The rooms and all the walls
of her house appeared to run with blood, and flame was devouring
all the drugs with which she bewitched any strangers that came.
She herself with murderous blood quenched the blaze,
drawing it off with her hands, and was cured of deadly fear.
And so at the coming of dawn she awoke and was washing her hair
and her clothes in the sea. Beasts, not like carnivorous beasts
of the wild nor human in form, but mingled of limb, went
in throngs as sheep from the fold follow the shepherd in crowds.
Such creatures in time before did earth herself engender
from mud, composed of mingled limbs, before she was
compressed by thirsty air. Not yet had she acquired
so much as a drop of rain from the rays of the parching sun.
But time compounded these forms and marshaled them in rows.
So these creatures, formless of nature, followed her.

    Enormous wonder seized the heroes. At once as each
gazed at the form and face of Circe, they easily guessed
that she was Aeetes' sister. When she had banished the fear
from her dreams of the night, straightway she turned and stepped back
and cunningly bade them follow, caressing them with her hand.
The band of heroes at the command of Aeson's son
remained steadfast, but he drew with him the Colchian girl.
Both followed the same road until they came to the hall
of Circe. She bade them sit on gleaming chairs, astonished
at their coming, and both of them, speechless and silent, hastened
to sit at the hearth, the right of mournful suppliants.
Medea put her face in both her hands, but Jason
fixed in the ground the huge hilted sword with which he had killed
Aeetes' son. Nor did they raise their eyes to meet
her glance. Circe knew at once a fugitive's doom
and the sin of murder. Therefore, in reverence of the law

of Zeus, the god of suppliants, who is mighty in wrath
but mighty too in his help to murderers, she began
the rite with which ruthless suppliants are cleansed
when they approach the hearth. First as atonement for
irreparable murder she held above them the young of a sow
whose teats were flowing still from the labor of her womb,
and severing its neck, she wet their hands with the blood.
With other libations she made propitiation, invoking
Zeus who Purifies in response to murderers' prayers.
And all the defilements together her servants bore forth from the house,
the Naiads, river nymphs who prepared each thing for her.
Circe, inside, was burning propitiatory cakes
at the hearth and with offerings and prayers without wine
that she might stay the wrath of the horrible Furies and Zeus
himself might be propitious and kindly disposed to them both,
whether with hands stained by the blood of a stranger or
as kin stained by kindred blood they should supplicate him.

But when she had done all her work, then she raised them up
and sat them upon the polished chairs and she herself
sat down nearby, face to face with them. At once
she asked them precisely about their quest and their voyage and then
from where they had come to her land and palace to sit like this
at her hearth, for the memory of her unseemly dreams entered
her mind as she pondered, and she longed to know the kindred voice
of the girl as soon as she saw her lift her eyes from the ground.
For all the race of Helios was conspicuous
to see, since by the sparkle from afar of their eyes
they cast a beam of gold, as it were, opposite them.
Medea then recounted all that she asked, gently,
in the Colchian tongue, the daughter of melancholy Aeetes:
the heroes' quest, their journey's path, and all that they labored
in the quick contests and how she had sinned in her counsels with
her sorrowing sister and how she had fled with the sons of Phrixus
the frightening force of her father, but she shunned speaking
of the murder of Apsyrtus, but she did not deceive
Circe, who nevertheless pitied the grieving girl

and spoke to her with words like these: "Poor girl,
it is an evil and unseemly voyage home
that you have contrived, for I do not expect that you will escape
the heavy wrath of Aeetes, for soon he will go even
to the haunts of Hellas to avenge his son's murder,
for intolerable are the deeds that you have done. But since
you are a suppliant and kinswoman to me,
no further evil shall I devise for your coming here,
but go from my halls in company with this stranger, whoever
he may be, this unknown man whom you have chosen
without your father's consent. But do not kneel to me
as suppliant at my hearth, for I shall not approve
the counsel that you gave nor your disgraceful flight."

She spoke, and dire anguish overtook the girl.
She cast her robe over her eyes and moaned until
the hero took her by the hand and led her through
the door and out of the halls, quivering with fear,
and they left the palace of Circe. But they did not escape
the spouse of Zeus, son of Cronus, for Iris told
when she saw them go from the hall. For Hera had commanded
that she keep watch for their return to the ship. And so
again, urging her, she said, "Iris dear,
now, if ever you have fulfilled my commands, go
again on swift wings and bid Thetis to come
here to me, rising up out of the salt sea,
for I have need of her. Then go to the beaches where
the bronze anvils of Hephaestus are beaten by
sturdy hammers. Tell him to lull the blasts of flame
until the Argo passes them by. Then go to Aeolus,
the king who rules the winds born of the clear air,
and tell him of my intent that he may make still
all the winds beneath the dawn and that no breeze
ruffle the sea, but let the west wind blow until
the Argonauts reach the Phaeacian isle of Alcinous."

So she spoke, and at once Iris leapt from Olympus
and cleft the air, spreading wide her light wings.

She dived into the Aegean Sea, where the home
of Nereus is, and approached Thetis first and at Hera's
command repeated her words and urged her to come to her.
Next she went to Hephaestus and quickly made him stay
from his iron hammers, and the sooty bellows left off from their blast.
Last she went to Aeolus, the famous son
of Hippotas. When she had reported to him and rested
from her journey her swift knees, then Thetis, abandoning
Nereus and her sisters, went from the salt sea
to Olympus and the goddess Hera, who sat her beside her and said,
    "Listen now, divine Thetis, to what I long
to say. You know how much in my heart I honor the hero,
son of Aeson, and all the others who helped me in the contest,
and how I saved them all when they set their course between
the Wandering Rocks, where roar awful blasts of flame
and waves foam around the rough reefs. Now past
the huge rock of Scylla and Charybdis, belching
horribly, their path awaits them. But truly you
from your infancy I myself have cherished and loved
beyond all others who dwell in the salt sea because
you did not agree to share the bed of Zeus despite
his desire (for such deeds are ever his delight—
to pass the night with women—mortal or divine).
But in respect for me and with fear in your heart, you shunned
his love. He then swore a monstrous oath, that you
should never be called the bride of an immortal god.
Nevertheless, he did not cease to watch you
against your will until ancient Themis told
everything to him, that it was fated for you
to bear a son stronger than his father. And so,
though he longed for you, he let you go for fear
that another be his equal and rule the immortal gods
and so that he might preserve forever his own power.
But I gave you the best of the men of earth to be your husband
that you might make a marriage to please your heart and bear
children. I called to the wedding feast all the gods

together, and I myself raised the bridal torch
with my own hands because you graciously honored me.
But come, and I shall tell you a true story. When
your son comes to the Elysian field, whom now
the river nymphs tend, though he craves your milk, he must be
the husband of the young Medea, Aeetes' daughter.
You as mother-in-law must help your daughter-in-law,
and Peleus himself as well. Why is your wrath so fixed?
He was deluded, and delusion visits even
the gods. Yes, at my command I think that Hephaestus
will cease to blow his force of flame and Aeolus,
Hippotas' son, will stay the swift rush of the winds,
except for the favoring west wind, until they reach
Phaeacian harbors. Do you devise a safe return.
The rocks and overpowering waves are my only fear
and these you and your sisters could turn aside. Do not
allow them to fall helplessly into Charybdis for fear
that she gulp them down, one and all, or to approach
the grim lair of Scylla (Ausonian Scylla, the deadly,
whom Hecate, called Crataeis, who roams by night
bore to Phorcys), lest swooping upon them
with her horrible jaws she destroy the best of the heroes. Steer
the ship where there will be narrow escape from destruction."
   So she spoke, and Thetis replied with words like these:
   "If the wrath of the ravening flame and the furious blasts leave off
in truth, then I can say that I will bravely save
the ship from the encountering wave if the west wind
blows even a little. But the hour has come to make
the journey, immeasurably long, to my sisters who will help,
and to where the ship's hawsers are fastened, so that at dawn
the Argonauts may make their plans to voyage home."
   She spoke and sweeping down from the sky she sank into
the swirling dark blue sea, and she called the Nereids,
her sisters, to help. They heard and met with one another,
and Thetis told them the command of Hera and sent
them all swiftly to the Ausonian sea. And she

herself, more quickly than a glitter or than the rays
of the sun when it rises above a far-off land, sped
lightly through the waves until she reached the beach
of Aeaea on the Tyrrhenian mainland. Beside the ship
she found the heroes taking delight in the quoit and shooting
of arrows. She stood near and touched with her fingertips
Peleus, the son of Aeacus, for he was her husband.
No one else was able to see her clearly, but she
appeared to his eyes alone, and she spoke to him and said,

    "No longer now on Tyrrhenian beaches must you sit
and wait, but at first dawn make loose the stern cables
of your swift ship, obeying Hera, who is your helper.
For at her command with all speed the Nereids meet
to draw your ship through the rocks which are called the Wanderers.
For that is the path that is fated for you. But show my form
to no one when you see me approaching with them, but keep
it secret in your mind lest you anger me even more
than you so recklessly angered me in time before."

    She spoke, and then, invisible, she sank into
the depths of the sea. Peleus was struck with terrible anguish,
for he had never before seen her return since first
she had left his chamber and bed, angered because of her son,
noble Achilles, who was still an infant, for she
always burned around his mortal flesh by night
with blazing fire, and by day in turn she would anoint
with ambrosia his tender flesh that he might be immortal
and she ward off from his body hideous old age.
But he leapt up from his bed when he spied his dear son
gasping through the flame. He uttered a horrible cry,
great fool that he was. She, when she heard, caught up the child
and threw him screaming to the ground, and then like a breath
of wind or a dream went swiftly from the hall and leapt
into the sea, angered. Afterward she did not
return again. And so astonishment bound his soul.
Nevertheless, he told his companions all the command
of Thetis. And they left off in the midst and stopped their games

hurriedly and were busied about their meal and their beds,
and then after their supper they slept all night as before.
    When dawn that brings the light touched the lowest tip
of heaven, then at descent of the swift west wind
they went from the land to their rowing benches, and joyfully
they drew from the deep their anchors and readied all the rigging
properly, and spread the sail above, as they stretched
it taut with the sheets from the yardarm. A gentle breeze
bore the ship on, and soon they saw the lovely island
of Anthemoessa, where the shrill Sirens, daughters
of Achelous, used to enchant with their sweet songs
and then destroy whoever cast his cables there.
Beautiful Terpsichore, one of the Muses, bore them
to Achelous, her consort, and once they waited upon
Demeter's comely daughter, still unwed, and sang
to her, all together. Then they were in part
like birds, in part like young women to see, and always
on the watch from their lookout place of good anchorage,
often had they deprived many of sweet return,
wasting them with consuming desire. To the Argonauts too
they endlessly sent their lily voices, high and sweet,
and the men would have cast from the ship to the shore their hawsers
        had not
Thracian Orpheus, Oeagrus' son, strung in his hands
his Bistonian lyre and made it ring with a hasty refrain
of melodious song that their ears might hum with the sound of his
        strumming,
and the lyre overpowered the women's voices. The west wind
and the roaring wave washing astern sped the ship on,
and the Sirens kept singing their endless song. But even so
the noble son of Teleon, alone of his comrades,
leapt first from the polished rowing bench into the sea,
Butes, his soul melted by the Sirens' shrill voice,
and he swam through the roiling swell to step upon the shore,
poor man. Then and there, would they have deprived him
of voyage home, but the goddess, ruler of Eryx, Cypris,

taking pity, rescued him, still in the eddies,
and so in gracious encounter saved him to dwell upon
the Lilybean point. The heroes, in anguish, abandoned
the Sirens, but worse destruction of ships awaited them
at the meeting place of the seas. For on one side there appeared
Scylla's smooth rock; on the other Charybdis spouted
and roared insatiably. Elsewhere the Wandering Rocks
beneath the enormous waves were thundering where, before
the blazing flame spat forth from the peaks of the crags above
the glowing rock, the air was smoky. Nor could you have seen
the rays of the sun. Again, though Hephaestus had left off his labors,
the sea was still giving off a hot blast. There
the daughters of Nereus, some on this side, others
on that, approached them, and behind the glorious Thetis
put her hand to the oar to steer them through the Wandering Rocks,
and as when dolphins from out of the sea in fine weather
spiral in throngs about the ship as it sails along
and are seen, now in front, now behind, and now
at either side, and bring delight to sailors, so
the Nereids, close thronged, leapt up and played about
the ship Argo, and Thetis directed its course. And when
they were about to reach the Wandering Rocks, at once
they raised the hems of their dresses to their gleaming white knees,
and above, on the rocks themselves and where the wave breaks,
they hurried along, this way and that, separately.
The current struck the ship headlong, and all around
the turbulent wave, towering high, kept crashing down
upon the rocks, which now like beetling crags reached
the sky, and now stood fixed in the uttermost depths of the sea
when the furious surge swept over them in floods.
The Nereids, as young girls near a sandy beach
roll their dresses up to their waists, out of the way,
and play with a rounded ball—and one catches it
from another and sends it back again high in the air,
and it never touches the ground—so they, one from another
in turn, sent the ship through the air above the waves

as it sped always away from the rocks. Around them the water
spouted and seethed. The lord Hephaestus stood upon
the peak of a bare cliff, propping his heavy shoulder
upon his hammer handle, and watched them. Standing above
the gleaming heaven the wife of Zeus threw her arms
about Athena, such fear did she feel as she gazed. As the time
of a day in spring grows long, just so long did they toil,
hoisting the ship between the echoing rocks. The heroes,
enjoying the wind, sped forward. Quickly they passed the meadow
of Thrinacia, pasture for the cattle of Helios.
There the Nereids plunged to the depths like sea gulls
when they had fulfilled the commands of the wife of Zeus. Just then
there came through the mist the bleating of sheep, and near at hand
the lowing of cattle struck their ears. Through the thickets
covered with dew Phaethusa, the youngest of Helios' daughters,
herded the sheep. She held in her hand a silver staff.
Lampetia, tending the kine, brandished a shepherd's crook
of glowing orichalc. These cattle the Argonauts saw
feeding beside the river streams over the plain
and the meadow marsh. Not one of them was dark of hide
but all were white as milk and gloried in golden horns.
These they passed by day. At the coming of night they cut
a great gulf in the sea, joyfully, until
once more early-born dawn cast her light on their course.

   Facing the Ionian strait is an island, rich
and spreading, in the Ceraunian sea. Beneath it, the story
goes, there lies the sickle (be gracious, Muses, for not
willingly do I tell the tale of earlier men)
with which Cronus pitilessly castrated his father,
but some call it the reaping hook of chthonic Demeter,
for Deo once dwelt in that land and taught the Titans to reap
the sheaves of wheat because of her love for Macris. Therefore,
it is called Drepane by name, the Phaeacians' sacred nurse,
and so the Phaeacians themselves are by birth of Uranus' blood.
To them came Argo, distressed by many troubles, borne
by breezes from the Thrinacian sea. Alcinous

and his people with kindly sacrifice received them gladly
and for them all the city laughed aloud. You would say
that they rejoiced for their own sons. The heroes themselves
greeted the throng, as delighted as though they had stepped into
the heart of Haemonia. But they were about to arm
themselves with the battle cry, so near appeared a host
of countless Colchians, who had passed down the mouth
of Pontus and through the Cyanean rocks in pursuit of the princes.
They intended to take Medea, alone, immediately
back to her father's house, or, they threatened, to raise
the awful war cry with harsh intractability,
both then and afterward with the coming of Aeetes.
But Alcinous restrained their eagerness for war,
for he longed to resolve the wanton quarrel for both sides
without the strife of battle. Medea in deadly fear
often appeased the companions of Aeson's son and often
touched with her hands the knees of Arete, Alcinous' bride:

    "I implore you, Queen, be gracious. Do not betray me
to the Colchians to take to my father, if you yourself
are one of the race of mortals whose soul runs swiftly to ruin
from trifling transgressions. My shrewd wits betrayed me.
It was not for the sake of lust. Let the sacred light of Helios,
let the rites of the night-wandering daughter of Perses know:
not willingly did I set sail with alien men,
but a horrid fear persuaded me to think of flight,
because I had sinned. There was no other recourse. But still
my virgin sash remains, as in my father's house,
unsullied and undefiled. But pity me, my lady,
and beseech your husband, and may the immortals grant you joy
and a perfect life and children and glory of a city unsacked."

    So, shedding tears, she implored Arete, and so
also with words like these each of the princes in turn:

    "For your sake, bravest of men, and because of your contests
am I now distraught. By my will you yoked the bulls
and sheared the crop of the Earth-born men. Because of me
you will bear straightway on your voyage home to Haemonia

the golden fleece. Here am I who have lost my country,
my parents, my home, and all the joy of life. But you
because of me will dwell again in your native land
and your homes and see once more your parents, a sight sweet
to your eyes. But from me a stern deity has taken
all happiness and, hated, I wander with alien men.
Fear your covenants and your oaths; fear the Fury
of suppliants and the gods' retribution. If I fall
to Aeetes' hands to be slain with dire outrage, to no
temples, no bastion of protection, no other shelter
do I appeal, but only to you yourself. Cruel
and pitiless that you are, you have in your heart no respect
for me, though you see me helplessly stretching my hands toward the knees
of a foreign queen. Yet, when you were eager to take
the fleece, you would have done battle with all the Colchians
and haughty Aeetes himself. But now you have forgotten
bravery, since they are cut off and all alone."
    She spoke, beseechingly. Whoever she implored
would give her heart, restraining her anguish, and in their hands
they brandished their well-pointed spears and the swords from their
        sheaths and promised
not to withhold their help should she meet with wrongful judgment.
Upon the host there came night that puts to rest
labors for weary men, and she calmed all the earth.
But sleep did not lull the girl at all. In her breast
her heart was twisted in anguish, as when a working woman
twists her spindle all through the night and around her wail
her orphaned children, for she is a widow. The tears course
down her cheeks as she thinks of what a gloomy fate
has taken her. So, Medea's cheeks were wet
and her heart within tormented, pierced with bitter pains.
    Now in the city, within their house, just as before,
the king Alcinous and his honorable wife, Arete,
were making plans on Medea's behalf as they lay in their bed
through the dark night. Her wedded husband the wife embraced
and then addressed with impassioned words like these and said,

"Yes, my dear, come now, save the suffering girl
from the Colchians, for my sake, and show grace
to the Minyans. Argos lies near our island and the men
of Haemonia, but Aeetes lives far away, nor do
we know him at all except for what we hear. This girl
who suffers so terribly has broken my heart completely
by her appeal. Do not, my lord, betray her to
the Colchians to take to her father's house. She was
infatuated when first she gave the drugs to him
to charm the oxen, and then to cure one evil with
another (as often we do in our sinning) she made her escape
from the heavy wrath of her haughty father. But Jason, I hear,
is held by mighty oaths to make her in his halls
his lawfully wedded wife. And so, my dear, do not
yourself make Aeson's son forswear his oath, nor let
the father, with angered heart, if you can prevent it,
do his child insufferable harm. For fathers are
excessively jealous against their own children. What pain
did Nycteus contrive for Antiope of the lovely face,
what did Danae endure on the sea at her father's
reckless rage? Recently, not far away,
cruel Echetus fixed goads of bronze in his daughter's eyes,
and she is withered by a hideous doom, grinding grain
of bronze in a gloomy barn. So she spoke, beseeching,
and his heart melted at his wife's words and he spoke like this:
"Arete, I could with arms drive out the Colchians
and so show the heroes grace for the sake of the girl,
but I fear to dishonor the straight justice of Zeus, nor is
it good, as you advise, to discount Aeetes, for there
is no one more lordly than Aeetes, and if he wishes,
he could bring war, though from afar, upon Hellas.
And so it is fitting for me to utter judgment that will
be best for all men, nor will I conceal it from you.
If she is a virgin, I decree that they take her back
to her father. But if she shares her bed with a man, I shall not
separate her from her husband, nor if she bears a child

in her womb will I give it up to the foe." So he spoke,
and soon sleep lulled him to rest. But she put away
in her heart his shrewd words. At once she rose from her bed
and went through the house, and her serving women hurried together,
bustling about to attend their mistress. Quietly
she summoned her herald and spoke to him. With her own wisdom
she urged that the son of Aeson marry the girl Medea
and not beseech the king Alcinous, for he
himself would decree to the Colchians that if she were
a virgin, he would return her to her father's house,
but if she shared her bed with a man, never would he
separate her from her married love. So then did she speak,
and his footsteps took him straightway from the hall to announce to Jason
Arete's fateful advice and pious Alcinous' counsel.

He found the men on watch beside their ships with their gear
in the harbor of Hyllus near the city, and he told them the whole
of his message. And each of the heroes rejoiced in his heart, for he spoke
a word that was exceedingly pleasant to them. At once
they mixed a krater of water and wine to the Blessed Ones,
as it is right, and piously led sheep to the altar,
and for that very night prepared for the young girl
a marriage bed in the sacred cave where once lived Macris,
the daughter of Aristaeus whose kingdom is honey, for he
found out the labor of bees and the oil of the olive, the fruit
of much toil. She it was who first took
to her heart the Nyseian son of Zeus in Abantian Euboea
and wet with honey his parched lip when Hermes brought him
out of the fire. Hera saw and, angered, drove her
out of all the island. She therefore dwelt
in the Phaeacian sacred cave, far away,
and offered ineffable wealth to the inhabitants.
There then they spread an enormous bed, and over it
they laid the glittering golden fleece that the marriage might be
honored and worthy of song. For them the nymphs gathered
blossoms of every color and carried them to the couch
in their snow-white bosoms. And a gleam, as of flame, played about

them all, such a light glittered from the golden tufts. It kindled
in the eyes of the nymphs a sweet longing, but shame restrained
each one, much as she yearned, from touching it with her hand.
Some were called the daughters of river Aegaeus, and some
dwelt about the peaks of the mountain Meliteius.
Others from the plains were nymphs of the groves. For Hera,
the wife of Zeus, had called them forth to honor Jason.
Even now that sacred cave is called the Cave
of Medea, where they brought them together with one another,
spreading covers, fragrant and finely woven. The heroes,
brandishing in their hands spears for war, so that
a hostile throng not fall upon them, unforeseen,
in battle, their heads garlanded with leafy sprays,
melodiously, while Orpheus played his lyre, sweet
and shrill, were singing at the entrance of the cave,
their marriage chamber, the bridal song. But not in the house
of Alcinous did the hero intend to complete his marriage
but in the halls of his father, sailing back to Iolcus.
Such too was the thought of Medea. But necessity
led them to marry then. For never do we tribes
of suffering men step upon the path of joy
with whole foot, but always some bitter anguish keeps step
with our delight. And so, they too, although they melted
in sweet desire, feared the decree of Alcinous.

Dawn with ambrosial gleam rose up and scattered through
the mist the black night; and the island beaches laughed
and the dew-drenched paths of the plains far off, and a clamor
filled the streets and the inhabitants stirred throughout
the town and the Colchians far away at the boundaries
of the island Macris. Straightway Alcinous in accord
with the covenant met with them to tell his intent about
the girl. In his hands he held a scepter of gold, the staff
of judgment with which he meted to many straight decrees
throughout the city. With him in ordered ranks and dressed
in battle array there marched in throngs the Phaeacian princes.
The women in crowds came out of the bastion to look upon

214

the heroes, and rustic men to meet them when they heard,
for Hera had sent forth unerring report, and one
led the choice ram of his flock, another a heifer
that had not toiled. Others set up nearby jugs
of wine for mixing. The murky flame of sacrifice
fumed far away, and women, as women will, bore
linens, white and finely wrought, and gifts of gold,
and many another adornment as well, befitting brides.
They marveled when they saw the beauty and shapeliness
of the splendid heroes and among them Oeagrus' son, who
to the time of his well-strung lyre and song frequently beat
the ground with his glittering sandaled foot; and all the nymphs
together, when he recalled the wedding, cried aloud
the lovely bridal song. Again, each would sing
alone, as they whirled in the circular dance, Hera, for you,
for you inspired Arete to speak the shrewd word
of Alcinous; and he, as soon as he had uttered
decrees of straight judgment and consummation of
the marriage had been announced, then took care that it
remain forever secure, and neither lethal fear
nor Aeetes' heavy wrath intervened with him, but he
held fast bound to his unbroken oaths. And so
when the Colchians learned that they petitioned in vain, and he
bade them keep their ships far away from his harbors and land,
then fearing rebukes of their own king, they entreated him
to receive them as allies, and there on the island they dwelt long
among Phaeacian men until after a time
the Bacchiadae, a race of Ephyra, settled there,
and the Colchians crossed to an island opposite. From there
they were destined to reach the Ceraunian Mountains of the Abantes,
the Nestaeans and Oricus. But this all came to be
after many an age had passed. And still the altars there
that Medea built in the sacred precinct of Apollo,
lord of shepherds, receive annual sacrifice
to the Fates and Nymphs. Many gifts of host to guest
did Alcinous make to the Minyans when they left, and many

Arete made, and to Medea she gave from the palace
twelve Phaeacian serving maids to attend her as well.

On the seventh day they left Drepane. There came at dawn
a fresh fair-weather breeze and sped by the breath of the wind
they ran forward, but not yet were the heroes fated
to set foot upon Achaea until they had suffered
in even the furthest reaches of Libya. And now
with sails spread they had left behind the gulf named
for Ambracians and now the Curetes' land, the narrow islands,
Echinades and all, quite in a row, and the land
of Pelops barely appeared. And then a fatal blast
of Boreas snatched them up midcourse and bore them
toward the Libyan sea for nine whole nights and just
as many days until they came far within
Syrtis, from where there is no voyage home for ships
once forced inside that bay. Everywhere are shoals,
everywhere clumps of seaweed from the depths,
and over them flows the mute foam of the wash of the sea,
and dunes of sand lie along a misty horizon
where there stirs no creature that creeps or flies. Here the tide
(for often the flood withdraws from the land but erupts again
upon the strand with a ravenous roar) suddenly
thrust them upon the innermost shore. Only a little
of keel was left in the water. They leapt from the ship, but anguish
took hold of them as they gazed out upon the mist
and flats of the vast earth that stretched far beyond
and continuously, as though it were the hazy air.
No watering place, no path, no herdsman's stall did they see
far off but all the land was oppressed by a silent calm.
And so, sorrowing, one man would ask another,

"What land is this? Where has the hurricane thrust us?
Would that we had dared, despite our deadly fear,
to rush through the rocks by that same course. Better it were,
overstepping the destiny of Zeus, to die, striving
for something big. But now what are we to do,
held in check by the winds to linger here if only

a little time? How barren there spreads before us
the desolate edge of this enormous continent."

   So he spoke. Then Ancaeus, the steersman, himself
in distress at their evil plight, addressed the despairing men:
   "We perish by a terrible fate, nor is there escape
from doom, but we must suffer horribly, fallen
upon this desert place, even if breezes should blow
from land, for I see as I gaze far about shoals
on every side and water, lightly rippled, runs
over the hoar sands, and wretchedly would our ship
have shattered utterly long ago and far from land
had the flood tide itself not swept her high from the main of the sea.
But now it rushes back to the deep and only the brine
no ship can sail swirls about, just covering
the soil. And so I say all hope of a voyage home
is cut off. Let someone else show his skill,
sit at the tiller with fervent desire for our return.
Zeus does not will a homecoming day for all our toils."

   So he spoke, in tears, and all who were skilled in ships
agreed with him in his distress. But the hearts of all
were chilled and pallor spread over their cheeks, as when
men like bloodless phantoms wander through a town
awaiting the outcome of war or pestilence or some
incredible storm that washes out the work of oxen,
when wooden images of their own volition run
with sweat and blood, and bellowings are heards in the shrines,
or the sun at high noon draws on from heaven the night,
and stars sparkle through the hazy mist, so then
the princes wandered distraught along the endless beach,
feeling their way. Straightway dusky evening came
upon them. Pitiably they embraced and caressed one another
with tears that each apart might fall upon the sands
and perish. One went here, another there, to find
further off a resting place. Wrapping their heads
in their cloaks, fasting, unfed, they lay all that night
and day, awaiting piteous death. The young women

apart clung together and moaned with Aeetes' daughter,
as when abandoned and fallen from a hollow of rock
unfledged nestlings shrilly chirp, or when by the banks
of the lovely-flowing Pactolus swans raise their songs
and all around resounds the meadow, drenched in dew,
and the rivers lovely streams, so these women lay
their tawny hair upon the dust, and all night long
they keened and wailed aloud their pitiable lament.

And there now all would have slipped away from life, nameless,
obscure to mortal men, bravest of heroes, their mission
unaccomplished. But as they wasted in despair
the tutelary heroines of Libya
pitied them. They once, when she leapt all gleaming from
her father's head, encountered Athena, anointing her
after her bath beside the waters of Triton lake.
It was high noon, and the sun's most piercing rays were parching
Libya. They stood near Aeson's son and gently
took with their hands the cloak from his head, but he cast his eyes
aside, abashed before the goddesses, but they
addressed him, bewildered and all alone, with soft words:

"Ill-starred, why are you struck with such despair? We know
that you went for the golden fleece. We know each of your toils,
all the overwhelming tasks you wrought as you wandered
over the land and sea. We are solitary
goddesses of earth, speaking with human voice,
Libya's daughters and tutelary heroines.
But up, no longer wail nor despair so much but rouse
your comrades. When Amphitrite looses straightway
Poseidon's beautifully running chariot, then pay
to your mother recompense for the suffering that she
endured when she bore you so long in her womb and so may you
yet make your voyage home to the very divine Achaea."

So they spoke and disappeared together with
the voice just where they stood, but Jason sat upon
the ground and gazed about as he spoke aloud like this:

"Be gracious, illustrious goddesses who guard the desert,

concerning our return. I do not understand
completely yet your oracle, but I shall gather
my comrades and speak to them to see if we can find
some token of our escape. The scheme of many is better."

He spoke and, squalid with dust, leapt up and shouted far
to his companions, like a lion that roars through
the forest, pursuing his mate, and at the depth of his voice
the glens rumble throughout the mountains far away,
and oxen that dwell in the fields and their herders shudder with fear,
but the voice of their companion, calling out to them,
his friends, was not horrible at all. Nearby
they gathered together, dejectedly. But Jason sat
them near their anchorage, grieving that they were,
women mixed with men, and told them everything:

"Listen, my friends, As I despaired, three goddesses
girt with goatskins from high on the neck around
the back and waist, like young girls, stood at my head,
close by, and drew aside my cloak with light hand,
uncovering me, and bade me rise and go to rouse
you as well and pay our mother recompense
in plenty for all she suffered bearing me in her womb
so long, whenever Amphitrite looses Poseidon's
beautifully running chariot. But I do not
completely understand about this oracle.
They said that they were tutelary heroines
and daughters of Libya, and all that we endured
on land and sea—they claimed to know everything.
I saw them no more in their place, but a mist or cloud came
between and covered them as they had appeared to me."

So he spoke, and they all marveled when they heard.
Then the greatest of portents occurred for the Minyans.
From sea to continent there leapt a monstrous horse,
enormous, that tossed a golden mane about his neck.
Nimbly he shook from his limbs the briny salt spray
and rushed to speed ahead with feet like the wind. At once
Peleus rejoiced and addressed his companions assembled together:

"I say that Poseidon's chariot has now been loosed
by the hands of his beloved wife. I realize
our mother to be none other than our ship itself,
for she carries us in her womb continuously and groans
in grievous labor. But with unflinching strength and shoulders
unwearying we shall lift her high and carry her
within this land of sands to where that swift steed
sped ahead, for he will not sink beneath
dry land, and his hoofprints, I suppose, will point
us toward some gulf extending down from the sea above."
      So he spoke. The befitting counsel was pleasing to all.
This is the Muses' story, and I sing attentive to
the Pierides, and this the tale I have heard most truly,
that you, O bravest by far of the sons of kings, by your strength,
your valor over the lonely dunes of Libya
lifted aloft on your shoulders the ship and all that you brought
within the ship and bore her twelve whole days and nights
as well. Who could tell the anguish and misery
that they fulfilled in their laboring? Certainly
theirs was immortal blood, such a task, compelled
by necessity, they undertook. How gladly, how far
they bore the ship to the waters of Triton's lake! How
they strode in and set her from their sturdy shoulders!
      Then like ravening hounds they leapt to search for a spring,
for a parching thirst with their suffering and agony
lay upon them, nor did they wander fruitlessly
but reached the sacred plain where Ladon till yesterday
guarded the golden apples in Atlas' garden, and all
around the nymphs, Hesperides, bustled about
and sang their lovely song. But now, at that time,
the guardian snake, mutilated by Heracles, lay
stricken beside the trunk of the apple tree, and only
the tip of his tail was twitching still, and from his head
down his black spine he lay breathless, and where
the arrows had left in his blood the bitter bile of the Hydra
of Lerna, flies shriveled and died in the festering wound.

The Hesperides, nearby, raising their gleaming arms
above their tawny heads, made shrill lament. The men
suddenly approached, but the nymphs, as they hurried near,
turned to dust and earth on the spot. Orpheus marked
the divine portent and thus addressed the nymphs with prayers:
     "O deities, lovely and kind, be gracious, queens,
whether you are counted among the goddesses
of heaven or those beneath the earth or whether you
are called the solitary nymphs, come, O nymphs,
sacred race of Oceanus. Appear before
our hopeful eyes and show some gush of water from rock
or some sacred stream of water bubbling from
the earth, goddesses, with which we may abate
our savage burning thirst, and if we ever again
reach Achaean land in our voyaging, then
we will offer you, first among the goddesses,
graciously, libations, banquets, and myriad gifts."
     So he spoke with fervent voice, and the nymphs nearby
pitied their suffering and first of all they made
grass spring up from earth. Above the grass there sprouted
tall shoots, and then saplings flourished and grew
straight up, much above the earth. Hespere
became a poplar, Erytheis an elm, Aegle
a willow's sacred trunk. Now from those trees, just
as they had been, exactly as such again did they
appear, an exceeding miracle, and Aegle spoke
with gentle words, replying to their craving need:
     "Surely there has come here an altogether
mighty aid to your labors, a most audacious man,
who deprived our guardian snake of life and took away
with him the golden apples of the goddesses
and left behind abominable pain for us.
For yesterday there came a man most destructive
in violence and form. His eyes blazed beneath
his scowling brow, pitilessly, and he wore the hide
of a monstrous lion, raw, untanned. He bore a branch

of olive wood and a bow with which he shot and killed
this enormous snake. He came too, traveling
the earth, parched with thirst, and rushed wildly about
this place, looking for water, which he was not likely
anywhere to see. There was a rock near
the Tritonian lake. This, of his own thought or by prompting
of god, he struck below with his foot, and water gushed
in plenty. He, propping his chest and hands upon
the ground, gulped from the cleft rock until, bent
like a grazing beast, he sated his capacious maw."
   So she spoke, and happily they ran, rejoicing,
to where Aegle had pointed out the spring until
they found it. As when earth-tunneling ants teem
about a narrow cleft, or flies, insatiate,
swarm fervently around a tiny drop
of honey, so then in throngs the Minyae teemed
about the spring from the rock. And, overjoyed, one
spoke to another from moistened lips and said this:
   "Amazing! Heracles, though far away, has saved
his companions, half-dead with thirst. If only we could meet
with him striding through the continent as we go!"
   So they spoke, and of the assembly those who were fit
for the task replied and rushed, one here, one there, to search.
For the night winds had effaced the prints of his feet by shifting
the sands. The two sons of Boreas started up,
trusting their wings, Euphemus with faith in his nimble feet,
Lynceus casting afar his keen eyes, and a fifth
with them, Canthus rushed. The destiny of gods
and his own manliness urged him on that course that he
might learn outright from Heracles where he had left
Polyphemus, son of Eilatus, for he was very anxious
to ask about his comrade every single thing.
But he had founded an illustrious town among
the Mysians, and homesick now, went in pursuit of Argo,
far over the continent, until he came to the land
of the Chalybes who live near the sea, and there his fate

overcame him. Beneath a tall poplar a monument
is built, a little before the sea. But Lynceus then
thought he saw Heracles all alone
and far away on the endless land as when a man
in the new month sees or thinks he sees the moon
dimmed by mist. Returning, he told his companions that no
other seeker would find Heracles striding on,
and they themselves came back and Euphemus, swift of foot,
and the two sons of Thracian Boreas, after they
had labored in vain. But you, Canthus, the Fates of Death
took in Libya. You encountered pasturing flocks,
but there followed a shepherd who on behalf of his sheep, while you
were herding them off to your companions in need, cast
a stone and killed you. For he was scarcely feeble, Caphaurus,
grandson of Lycoreian Phoebus and the modest girl
Acacallis, whom once Minos drove to Libya
when she was pregnant by the god, his own daughter.
She bore to Phoebus a glorious son, Amphithemis
by name or Garamas. Amphithemis married
a Tritonian nymph, who bore to him Nasamon
and mighty Caphaurus, who then slew Canthus, defending his sheep.
But he did not escape the princes' harsh hands
when they learned what he had done, and after they had learned,
the Minyae took up the corpse and buried it
in the earth and mourned. The sheep they took away with them.

 And then, that same day, pitiless destiny
took Mopsus too, the son of Ampycus, nor did
he escape by his prophecies a bitter fate: there is no
averting of death. There lay in the lands, shunning the blaze
of noon, a terrible snake, too torpid himself to strike
at an innocent foe, nor would he lash full face at one
who cowered. But into whom of any living creature
of all those the fostering earth gives nurture and life
he once injects his black venom, his path to Hades
becomes not so much as a cubit long, not even
if Paeëon (if it be permitted me to speak

223

bluntly) should treat him when the teeth have merely grazed
the skin. For when the god-like Perseus Eurymedon
(for by that name his mother called him) flew above
Libya and carried to the king the Gorgon's
newly severed head, all the black drops
of blood that oozed to earth sprouted that brood of snakes.
Now Mopsus trod upon the end of his spine, planting
upon it the flat of his left foot. It writhed around
and with its teeth bit and carded the flesh between
the muscle and shin. Medea and her serving maids
fled in terror. But he touched the bloody wound,
bravely, for no overpowering pain tortured
the poor wretch. Already a paralyzing torpor
was creeping beneath the skin, and a thick mist obscured
his eyes. Straightway his sluggish limbs sank to the ground,
and he grew hopelessly cold. His companions gathered around,
and the hero, Aeson's son, and wondered exceedingly at
the crowding doom. Not even a little while was he
to lie beneath the sun, though dead, for the venom at once
began to rot the flesh within, and the hair decayed
and dropped away from the skin. Quickly they dug out,
and hastily, with mattocks of bronze a deep grave.
They tore out their hair in clumps, the young women and men
together, bewailing the piteous corpse's suffering.
Thrice in armor they circled the grave when he had got
the proper burial rites and heaped a mound of earth.

But when they boarded the ship and the south wind blew over
the deep and they were seeking passages out
of Tritonian lake, for a long time they had no plan
but all day long were borne on aimlessly, and as
a snake goes writhing along his crooked path, scorched
by the fiercest blaze of the sun, and hisses and turns his head,
now this way, now that, and, furious, his eyes glow
like sparks of fire until he slips to his lair through a rift
in the rock, so Argo seeking a navigable mouth
of the lake, drifted about for a long time. Straightway

Orpheus bade them dedicate from the ship's hold
Apollo's mighty tripod to the indigenous gods
as propitiating gifts for their voyage home. And so
they disembarked and dedicated Phoebus' gift.
There encountered them there in disguise as a vigorous youth Triton,
wide in sway of strength. Lifting a clod of earth,
he proffered it as guest gift to the princes and said,
    "Accept this, friends, for I have no guest gift of worth
to give to strangers who entreat me, but if you seek
passage through this sea, as often men need
when traveling through a foreign land, I will tell it to you.
For my father Poseidon made me practiced in this sea,
and I am king of the shore—perhaps though far away
you have heard of Eurypylus, born in beast-rearing Libya."
    So he spoke, and eagerly Euphemus reached
with his hands for the clod and spoke words like this in reply:
    "O hero, if now you know at all of the sea of Minos
of Apis, tell us unerringly who ask it of you.
Not willingly did we come here but by the blasts
of Boreas we touched the borders of your land.
We carried our ship aloft to the waters of this lake
over the mainland, a heavy burden, nor do we know
where a passage leads for us to go to Pelops' land."
    So he spoke, and Triton stretched his hand and showed
the sea, far off, and the deep mouth of the lake and said,
    "That is passage to the sea where the depth lies
especially black and calm. On either side breakers
shudder, translucent and topped with foaming white. The course
between is narrow for sailing out. That main extends
in mist to Pelops' divine land beyond Crete.
On the right hand, when you enter the swell of the sea from the lake,
hug the land as you steer your course as long as it stretches
north, but when the coast curves the other way,
then your course is safe if you sail from the jutting cape.
But go, rejoicing. Let there be no agony for toil,
that, laboring, youthful limbs be weary and worn."

He spoke with kindly intent, and they at once embarked,
eager to go forth from the lake with oars, and forward
they sped with fervent desire. Triton, meanwhile,
taking up the mighty tripod, was seen stepping
into the lake. No one afterward saw how
he disappeared, tripod and all, so near to them.
But their hearts were cheered because one of the blessed gods
had encountered them propitiously, and they bade the son
of Aeson sacrifice to him the choicest of sheep
and sing, when it was slain, a song of praise. At once
he chose in haste and lifting the victim he slaughtered it
above the ship's stern and spoke with these prayers:
     "O god, who appeared upon the shores of this lake, whether
the sea-born daughters call you Triton, wonder of
the brine, or Phorcys, or Nereus, be gracious and grant to us
the end of the voyage home that is our hearts' desire."
     He spoke with prayers and slit the victim's throat into
the water and hurled it from the stern, and there appeared
from the depth the god such as he was truly to see.
As when a man trains a swift horse for the broad
racecourse and runs along beside with a grasp upon
the shaggy mane and the steed follows, obedient,
but lifts its neck, haughtily, and the gleaming bit
rings in reply as he champs it from side to side in his jaws,
so Triton grasped the hollow Argo and guided it toward
the sea. His body, from high on his head around his back
and waist until his belly, was wondrously like that
of the Blessed Ones in form, but below his flanks the tail
of a sea monster forked and trailed on this side and that,
and he would smite the water's rippling surface with spines
that split below to curving fins like the horns of the moon.
He guided the ship until he sent her into the sea,
speeding away, and plunged straightway into the depths.
The heroes shouted when they saw the awesome portent.
     There are Argo's harbor and signs of the ship and altars
of Poseidon and Triton. For that day they held back.

But at dawn, with sails spread, keeping on their right *IV. 1622*
–1659
the desert land, with the west wind, they sped ahead.
By morning they saw the angle and inlet of the sea,
curving inward beyond the jutting cape of land.
Straightway the west wind ceased and there came at the stern a breeze
from the south, and their hearts rejoiced at the sound of the whispering
      wind.
But when the sun set and the shepherd's star returned
which brings pause to worn plowmen, then the wind
abating in the black night, they furled their sails and lowered
the very tall mast and bent to their well-polished oars
all night long and through the day until again
another night came on and rugged Carpathus far
away welcomed them. From there they were to cross
to Crete, which rises above all other isles in the sea.
Talos, the man of bronze, as he broke rocks off
the rough cliffs, prevented them from fastening
their cables to land when they came to Dicte's anchorage.
The son of Cronus offered him, born of root
of bronze from men of ash-tree stock, the last left
among the demigods, to Europa to be a guard
and thrice each day to circle Crete with feet of bronze.
The rest of his body and limbs were made of bronze and were
unbreakable, but beneath the tendon beside the ankle
there was a duct of blood, and this a thin skin
covered with its confines of life and death. The men,
though overcome with woe, quickly backed their ship
from shore with oars in terror. And now in sore distress
would they have sailed far from Crete, suffering thirst
and pain, had Medea not addressed them as they withdrew:

    "Listen to me. I think that I alone will subdue
for you that man, whoever he is, though his body be all
of bronze unless his life is invincible too. But keep
your ship willingly here beyond the throw of his rocks
until, overcome, he yields in humble submission to me."

    So she spoke, and they withdrew their ship from range

of his bolts and rested upon their oars, expectant to see
what she would contrive unexpectedly. And she,
holding a fold of her crimson robe over both her cheeks,
stepped upon the deck. Clasping her hand in his,
the son of Aeson guided her along the thwarts.
There with songs she appeared and charmed the soul-devouring
Spirits of Death, the swift hounds of Hades, who
through all the air whirl down upon living men.
Kneeling, thrice she called upon them with song, thrice
with prayers. Intent on wickedness, with hostile glance
she cast a spell upon the eyes of brazen Talos
and gnashed hateful wrath with her teeth against him
and launched annihilating wraiths in her violent rage.

Father Zeus, great wonder inspires my soul that not
from wounds and disease alone does destruction encounter us
but even from afar it crushes us, so he,
though made of bronze, yielded to the might of Medea
the sorceress and was subdued. As he was heaving up
the heavy rocks to keep them from reaching the anchorage,
he grazed his ankle upon a pointed crag; the ichor
poured forth like molten lead, and not for long did he stand
planted upon the jutting scar. But just as high
in the mountains some giant pine woodsmen left behind,
hewn half through by sharp axes, when they returned
from the wood, at first is shaken at night by blasts of wind,
and then at last breaks at the stump and comes
crashing down, so Talos stood for a while and swayed
back and forth upon unwearied feet, but at last,
enfeebled, he came crashing down with a mighty thud.

In Crete then the heroes spent the dark of night,
but at the first glow of dawn they built a shrine
to Minoan Athena and drew water and went on board
to row first of all beyond Salmone's point.
Straightway as they ran over the great Cretan gulf
there frightened them the night they called the Deadly Shroud.
No stars pierced it nor gleam of moon, but a black void

228

extended from heaven, or some other dark arose
from deepest gulfs below. The men knew not at all
whether they drifted in Hades or on the waters above
but entrusted to the sea their voyage home, helpless
in their direction. But Jason lifted his hands and cried
to Phoebus with mighty voice and called to him for rescue,
and tears ran down his cheeks in his distress. Often
he promised to bring boundless gifts to Pytho, often
to Amyclae; to Ortygia he promised often again.
Son of Leto, quick to hear, nimbly you came
down from heaven to the Melantian rocks which lie
in the sea. Leaping up upon one of the two,
you held on high in your right hand a golden bow,
and the bow flashed a dazzling beam all around,
and there appeared to them to see a little island
of the Sporades, near the small isle Hippuris, and there
they cast their anchors and lay by. Straightway the dawn
came up and shone and they made Apollo a glorious precinct
in a shady grove and a shadowed altar and called on Phoebus
the Gleamer because of the beam that shone afar, and that
bare island they called Anaphe, the Revealer, because
Phoebus revealed it to them in their bewilderment.
They sacrificed whatever men could provide for that
upon a barren beach. Medea's serving maids,
therefore, who came from Phaeacia, had no longer the strength
to contain the laughter within their breasts when they saw them pour
libations of water upon the blazing brands, so frequent
the slaughters of oxen that they had seen in Alcinous' halls.
The men rejoiced in the jest and kept scoffing at them
with indecent words, and kindled among them were scurrilous taunts
and merry mockery, and from that sport of the heroes
such taunts do women toss at men on that island
when with sacrifice they propitiate Apollo,
called the Gleaming One and guardian of Anaphe.
     But when from there and under fair skies they loosed
the cables, Euphemus remembered a dream of the night, in awe

of Maia's illustrious son. The divine clod, it seemed
to him, held in the palm of his hand beneath his breast,
was suckled by streams of gleaming white milk and that
from the clod, little though it was, a woman grew,
and she was like a virgin to see. He lay with her
in love, helplessly enamored. In his embrace
he pitied her as though she were a young girl
whom he was cherishing and nursed with his own milk,
but she kept comforting him and spoke with gentle words:
    "Triton's daughter am I, dear friend, and nurse of your sons,
no virgin girl. My parents are Triton and Libya.
Put me down beside the maiden daughters of Nereus
to dwell in the sea beside Anaphe. In aftertime
I shall come to the rays of the sun, to your children a ready aid."
    He held the memory of this in his heart and mentioned it
to Aeson's son, who pondered the prophecies in his soul
of the Far-Archer and raised his voice and said aloud:
    "My dear friend, great and glorious honor has been
allotted you. This clod the gods will make an island
when you cast it into the sea, and there your children's children
shall live, since Triton put this in your hands as a guest gift
from the Libyan continent. No other immortal than he
offered you this clod upon encountering you."
    So he spoke, nor did Euphemus make void
Aeson's son's reply, but cheered by the prophecy,
he cast the clod beneath the sea. There rose from it
the isle Calliste, holy nurse of Euphemus' sons,
who dwelt once in times before in Sintian Lemnos.
Driven from Lemnos by Tyrrhenian men, they arrived
at Sparta as suppliants. When they abandoned Sparta,
Theras, Autesion's son, led them to the isle
Calliste and named it from himself Thera. But this
happened after Euphemus' time. In steady course
from there, cleaving the measureless swell, they put in
at Aegina's beach. At once they wrangled in harmless strife
about the water, who should be first to draw it and reach

the ship, for both their need and the wonderful breeze urged

that they sail on, and there even now do Myrmidon youths
shoulder brimming jugs and with nimble swift feet
contend with one another for victory in the race.

Be gracious, prince, brood of the blessed, and may these songs
be sweeter year by year to men. And now I have come
to your labors' illustrious end, for no adventure again
beset you as from Aegina you voyaged home. No winds
of hurricane opposed, but tranquilly you skirted
Cecropian land, Euboean Aulis, and Locrian towns
and happily stepped upon the beach at Pagasae.

IV. 1769
–1781

HERODAS

The Procuress

CHARACTERS

Metriche: the wife or mistress of Mandris

Gyllis: an old woman

Threissa: a slave

M: Threissa, someone's knocking at the door.
Go see if it's one of ours come from the farm.

T: Who's at the door?
               G: It's me.   T: Who's you? Afraid
to come closer?   G: Look, I'm already in!

T: But who are you?   G: Gyllis, mother of
Philaenion. Tell Metriche I'm here.
Call her.   M: Who is it?   T: Gyllis.   M: Gyllis!
Scat, you slave! What Fate persuaded you
to visit us? Is this an epiphany
of goddess to man? It's five months, no six,
I think, since anyone's seen you even in
a dream, by the Fates, coming to the door!

G: I live far off, my child, and the mud in the lane
comes up to the knees. I'm feeble as a fly.
Old age has got me and is my shadow now.

M: Don't exaggerate your age. . . . Gyllis.
You still like to squeeze the men, I'm sure.

G: Joke! That's what you younger women do.
But jokes like this won't warm you up like a man.
How long, my child, has it been that you've tossed and turned
in your bed alone? Ten months since Mandris sailed
for Egypt—he's sent not an alphabet letter to you.

Doesn't he drink from a new cup and hasn't
he forgotten you? The goddess's home
is there, and everything there can possibly be,
Egypt has: gymnasiums and wealth,
a lovely climate, goddesses and glory,
philosophers and gold, little boys,
precinct of sibling gods, a good king,
the museum, wine, every nice thing
you'd want, women, as many, by Kore, bride
of Hades, as heaven boasts it holds of stars,
and lovely as the goddesses that rushed
to Paris for judgment — may they forgive me!
What kind of life is this, warming the chair,
poor girl? Your youthful charms will be but ash.
Look around, cheer up, change your ways for a while.
A ship's not safe with a single anchor . . . If this
comes . . . . no one raise
us . . . . savage storm
. . . .
                              no one knows
. . . .
                              unstable for men
. . . .
                                    But haven't you got
someone on the side?   M: Certainly not.

G: Then listen to what I'm dying to tell you.
   Gryllus, son of Metaline, Pataikos'
   daughter, five times victor in the games:
   as a boy at Pytho, twice at Corinth, the down
   just blooming upon his cheeks; at Pisa twice
   he took the men in a boxing match, and he's rich —
   beautifully so — he doesn't lift a straw
   from the ground — for Cythereia an untouched seal.
   Seeing you at Mise's procession down,
   his innards seethed, his heart was stung mad,
   and neither night nor day did he leave my house,

dear child, but wept and wailed to me and claimed
that he was dying of love. Metriche,
my pet, grant the goddess this single sin.
Dedicate yourself lest old age
cast her glance and take you unawares.
Double profit! He'll be more generous
than you think. Consider it. Listen
to me. I care for you, by the Fates, I do!

M: Gyllis, your white hair blunts your wits.
By Mandris' voyage home, by dear Demeter,
I'd not have listened to this from another woman.
I'd have taught her to sing a lame song lame
and consider my doorsill hostile to her.
Don't come to me again, my friend, with a tale
like this! Tell your young a tale befitting
old crones. Let Metriche, daughter
of Pytheas, warm her chair. No one mocks
my Mandris. These aren't the words, they say, that Gyllis
wants to hear. Threissa, wipe clean
the black shell. Pour three-sixths of unmixed
with a dollop of water and give it to her to drink.

G: Thank you, no.   M: Here, Gyllis, drink up.

G: I didn't come to tempt you, but on a holy . . .

M: On a *what*? Gyllis!

G: Whatever . . . . . . my child . . . . .
sweet. By Demeter, Metriche, Gyllis
has never drunk sweeter wine than this.
Goodbye, my dear, and take care of yourself.
May Myrtale and Sime keep young
as long as there is breath left in Gyllis.

III

The Schoolmaster

CHARACTERS

Metrotime: mother of Kottalos

Kottalos: Metrotime's errant son

Lampriskos: the schoolmaster

M: Lampriskos, the dear Muses allow you
  enjoyment of life upon condition that you
  cudgel this boy across the back until
  his wicked soul just hovers upon his lips.
  He's gambled away the roof above our heads
  playing spin-the-coin. Knucklebones
  are not enough, Lampriskos. It's worse
  than that by far! Where the schoolhouse is—
  the cruel thirtieth demands tuition
  even if I wail like Nannakos—
  he probably couldn't say. The gambling house,
  where thugs and runaway slaves hang out, that
  he knows well and can point the way to another.
  His wretched tablet that I'm worn out waxing
  every month lies abandoned by
  the bedpost close against the wall, except
  when he glares at it as though it were Hades and writes—
  nothing any good and wipes it clean.
  His dice lie more gleaming by far in
  his bags and mesh carryalls than the flask
  we use day in, day out for oil. He can't
  recognize the letter *a,* not even
  if one shouts it five times to him.
  His father the day before yesterday

was teaching him to spell the name "Maron,"
and this fine scholar wrote the throw "Simon."
I call myself an idiot that I didn't
teach him to pasture asses rather than reading
books—I'd have support for my old age.
Whenever his father or I ask him to
recite—just as you'd ask a little child—
his old father failing in hearing and sight,
then he strains as though through a pierced jug:
"Hunter Apollo." Your poor granny, I say—
and she's illiterate—could recite that,
or any Phrygian you'd meet. But if we dare
to grumble anymore, for three whole days
he doesn't know our door—he's pillaging
his granny, whose cupboard's bare, or on the roof
he spreads his legs and crouches like an ape.
Can you imagine how my insides writhe
when I see his wickedness? It's not so much
him, but every tile that's broken—like
a wafer—and winter's coming—costs me
an obol and a half. I weep for every
single tile I have to pay for.
In all the apartments they're saying, "This is the work
of Kottalos, Metrotime's son."
I dare not open my mouth to deny it.
Look at his back—all scales! It comes of wasting
his blunted life in the woods. You'd think that he
was some Delian fisherman, potting with weels.
He knows his festive sevenths and twentieths better
than the astrologists. He can calculate
the holidays—even in his sleep.
But, Lampriskos, if you hope for good success
in life and to chance upon the better things,
give him not less. . . .   L: Metrotime, stop—
he'll get no less. Where's Euthies?
Where's Kottalos? Where's Phillos? Quick, lift

Kottalos, shoulder high. Expose him to
Akeses' moon. I approve your conduct, I do!
Knucklebones are not enough, palms up
with your chums. You've got to go to the gambling den
and play spin-the-coin with those thugs?
I'll make you more decorous than a young girl
who disturbs not even a straw—if that's what you want!
Where's my sharp whip, my oxtail scourge,
with which I maim fettered rapscallions and such?
Hand it here before I choke on my bile.

K: By the Muses, Lampriskos, I beg you,
and by your beard and little Kottalos' life,
not with the oxtail! Maim with the other!

L: You're so wicked, Kottalos, that no one
would praise you, even if you were for sale, or in
the country where the mice would eat iron.

K: How many lashes, Lampriskos, will I get?

L: Don't ask me. Ask your mother how many.

K: Ai, ai! How many, you two?   M: As I wish to live,
all that your wicked hide can possibly take.

K: Stop! Lampriskos, enough!   L: You
stop your bad behavior.   K: I won't do a thing,
I swear by the dear Muses, Lampriskos.

L: You, what a lot of tongue you've got to wag,
I'll gag you with the mouse if you grumble more.

K: Look, I've shut up. Don't kill me, please!

L: Kokkalos, let him go.   M: Don't stop now,
Lampriskos, flog on till sunset.

L: But . . . .

M: He's more full of tricks than the Hydra by far.
You've got to him—even over his book,
the cipher! Twenty more if he's going to read
better than even Clio the Muse herself.

K: Nyah— L: May you happen to coat your tongue with honey.

M: On second thought, I'll ask the old man,
Lampriskos, once I get home.
I'll bring him fettered so that the revered Muses
whom he's insulted can see him jumping up
and down with both feet bound together.

IV

Women at the Temple

CHARACTERS

Kynno: a woman making a sacrifice

Phile: a woman accompanying Kynno

Kokkale: probably a slave

Kydilla: a slave

Neokoras: the custodian of the temple

Ky: May you rejoice, Paeon lord, who rule
Tricca and inhabit sweet Cos
and Epidaurus, and may Coronis who gave
you birth and Apollo rejoice and Hygeia
whose right hand you touch and those whose
honored altars these are, and may
Panake and Epio and Ieso
rejoice and those who sacked Laomedon's house
and walls, Machaon and Podaleirius,
healers of savage illnesses, and all
the gods and goddesses who share your hearth,
Paeon father. Graciously accept
this cock I sacrifice, a little dessert.
He was the herald of my household walls.
Our well is neither ready nor deep or else
we'd have offered an ox or a sow of crackling skin
and not a cock for the healing of illnesses
that you wiped away, O Lord, with the stretching forth
of your gentle hands. Kokkale, put the dish
on Hygeia's right.   Phi: Ah, what lovely statues,
Kynno dear! What sculptor cut this stone,
and who set it up in dedication here?

Ky: The sons of Praxiteles. Don't you see
the letters on the base? Euthies,
Prexon's son, set it up.   Phi: May Paeon
bless them and Euthies too for lovely works.

Ky: Phile, look at that girl gazing up there
at the apple. Wouldn't you say that she'd just faint
dead away if she couldn't have it?

Phi: But, Kynno, that old man . . .   Ky: By the Fates,
that little boy is throttling his fox-goose.
If we couldn't see close up that it's a stone,
you'd swear that it could speak. The time will come
when men will learn to put life into dead stone.

Phi: Look at this statue here of Batale,
daughter of Myttes, Kynno, how she steps.
If someone's not seen Batale but sees
this statue, she won't miss the real thing.

Ky: Come with me, Phile, and I'll show you
something lovelier than you've seen in all
your life. Kydilla, go call the custodian.
Do you hear me, girl—gaping and gawking like that?
My god, she pays no heed to what I say
but stands staring at me—worse than a crab!
Go on, I say, and call the custodian.
Glutton! As hopeless in the temple as you are
at home—everywhere you go the same!
Kydilla, I call this god to witness how
you burn me up though I don't want to burst.
I call him to witness, I say. The day will come
when you'll have cause to scratch that head of yours.

Phi: Kynno, don't be so easily upset
by everything. She's just a slave, and slaves
you know, haven't got much between the ears.

Ky: She's soft and getting shoved more and more.
But wait—the door is just open, the curtain

undone.   Phi: Don't you see, Kynno dear,
what works of art they are? You'd say Athena
had carved these lovely things—bless the Lady.
This naked boy—if I scratch him, Kynno dear,
won't I leave a welt? For his flesh lies
upon him, pulsing like warm warm water
in the picture. As for his silver fire tongs—
wouldn't Myllos or Pataikiskos,
the son of Lamprion, pop out their eyes,
supposing them really made of genuine silver?
The ox and the man leading it and the girl
and this hook-nosed man with the bristly hair—
don't they look as real as the living day?
If I didn't think it unbecoming a woman,
I'd have screamed for fear that the bull harm me—the way
he looks, Kynno, out of the side of his eye.

Ky: The workmanship of Apelles from Ephesus
is accurate in all he painted, Phile.
You can't say, "The man saw one, rejected
another." Whatever came to his mind he was quick
and eager to try. Anyone who's looked
at his work without the proper appreciation
ought to be hung by the feet in a fuller's shop.

Neo: Ladies, your sacrifice was correctly performed
and propitious too. No one has pleased Paeon
more than you. Ië, Ië, Paeëon.
Be gracious for these lovely sacrifices
to these women, their husbands, and all their kin.
Ië, Ië, Paeëon, may these things be.

Ky: May they be, O greatest one, and may
we come in good health to sacrifice
again with husbands and young. Kokkale,
be sure to carve a drumstick off and put
a scone in the serpent's box, auspiciously,
and drench the barley tarts with honey. We'll eat
the rest at home . . . .

Friends in Private

CHARACTERS

Metro: A woman

Koritto: another woman, friend of Metro

K: Do sit down, Metro. Get up and set
   the lady a chair. Must I do everything
   myself? Slut! Do you do nothing without
   being told? I've got a stone, not a slave,
   a corpse in the house. But when I measure out
   the barley, you count the grains, and if any spills,
   the walls can't withstand your puffs and pouts.
   Now you wipe it off and shine it up,
   you thief? Be grateful we've got a guest — or else
   you'd have had a taste of the flat of my hand!

M: Koritto dear, we wear the same yoke.
   I snarl day and night and bark like a dog
   at these idiot slaves. But what I've come to you
   about — get out from underfoot, make
   yourselves scarce, you blockheads, tongues
   and idleness — I ask you — don't lie,
   Koritto dear, who stitched it up for you,
   your scarlet dildo?   K: Where in the world did you
   see that, Metro?   M: Nossis, Erinna's daughter,
   had it the other day. What a lovely gift!

K: Nossis? Who gave it to her?   M: You won't let on
   if I tell?   K: By these sweet eyes, Metro dear,
   no one will hear from Koritto's lips a word
   that you say.   M: Euboule, Bitas' wife, it was
   who gave it to her and said nobody'd know.

K: Women! That one will be the death of me yet!
I gave it to her because she begged for it.
Metro, I hadn't used it yet myself!
She presents it as though it were something she'd found
        and to those
she shouldn't. Many good-byes to a friend like that!
Let her look for another friend in place of me!
To have lent to Nossis my property to whom
I don't think—forgive me, Adrasteia,
if I grumble too much—if I had a thousand, I'd not
give her a single one that was rotten with age.

M: Don't, Koritto, get your dander up
if you hear some foolish talk. A woman's that nice
puts up with everything. I'm to blame—
I babble too much. I ought to cut out my tongue.
But about that that I mentioned just now to you—
who was it that stitched it up? Tell a friend.
Why do you look at me with a smile like that?
Aren't I Metro, your oldest friend? Why
this delicacy? I beg you, Koritto, don't lie—
tell me who stitched it up. K: Why do you beg?
Kerdon stitched it. K: Which Kerdon, please?
For there are two Kerdons. The gray-eyed one,
the neighbor of Kylaithis' Myrtaline?
He couldn't make a plectrum for a lyre!
There's another near Hermodoros' apartment house
just off the square. He was someone once, but now
he's old. Kylaithis of blessed memory
did it with him. May her kin remember her.

K: Neither one of these, as you say, Metro.
This one's Chian perhaps or Erythraean,
little and bald. The image of Prexinos.
Alike as two figs. Except when he talks.
Then you know it's Kerdon, not Prexinos.

246

He works for a profit at home and keeps it quiet—
there's a tax collector lurking at every door.
But his work, what work! You'd think Athena's hands
had done it, not Kerdon's. Metro, he came out
with two. I thought I'd pop out my eyes when I saw.
No man—now we're alone—ever had one
so long and stiff as these. Not only that—
they were smooth as sleep and their little straps as soft
as wool—not great leather thongs. You couldn't find
another cobbler more well disposed to women.

M: Why didn't you take them both?   K: What didn't I do,
Metro? What enticement didn't I try? I kissed,
I stroked his bald pate, I poured him out
a sweet drink, called him Daddy. My body
was the one and only thing I didn't give.

M: If that's what he asked, you should have given it.

K: Yes, but one can't act unsuitably.
Bitas' wife, Euboule, was right there.
She grinds our millstone day and night and makes
it slog. She's too tight to pay out
four obols to sharpen up her own.

M: How did he know the way to your house,
Korrito dear? Don't tell me any lies.

K: Artemis, Kondas' wife, sent him here,
pointing out to him the tanner's house.

M: Artemis is on to anything new,
especially when it comes to pandering.
But if you couldn't wangle the two of them yourself,
you should have asked who ordered the other one.

K: I did, but he swore he couldn't tell me.

. . . .

M: You've told me where I must go. I'm off now
to Artemis to learn who this Kerdon is.

247

Wish me well, Koritto. Someone's starved
and it's time for me . . .   K: Close the door.
Then count the chickens. See they're all there.
Throw them some darnel. . . . There's no doubt
that chicken thieves would take the hen from your lap.

ARATUS

Selections from *Phaenomena*

Proem

From Zeus let us begin, him we mortals never
leave unnamed. Full of Zeus are all the streets
and all the markets of men. Full of Zeus is the sea
and the harbor. Everywhere we all have need of Zeus.
For we are his race, and in his kindness he gives
favorable signs to men and urges his peoples to work,
making them mindful of livelihood. He tells them when
the clod is best for the ox and hoe and when the seasons
are ripe for planting trees and all manner of seeds,
for he it was himself who fixed the signs in heaven
and set aside the constellations and marked for the years
what stars should most of all signify to men
the seasons so that all things might grow unfailingly.
Men worship him for this, always, first, and last.
Hail, father, mighty wonder, blessing to mankind,
to you and to the former race. Hail, Muses,
all the gentle ones. In answer to my prayer
give signs to me, as it is right, to sing the stars.

(*ll.* 1–18)

Beneath both the feet of Boötes you may see
the virgin who holds in her hand the gleaming sheaf of
    wheat.
Whether the daughter of Astraeus, who, men say,
was primeval sire of the stars, or child of some other,
may her course be smooth. But another tale runs among
men. They say that truly she dwelt once on earth
and came face to face with men and that never
did she disdain the ancient tribes of women and men,

but mingled and sat with them, immortal though she was.
Men called her Justice then. But she, assembling the elders,
in the marketplace or in the wide-wayed streets,
would sing, urging on them judgments fair to the people.
Not yet did the men of that time know dismal strife
or blaming dissension or the harsh din of the battle cry.
They lived simply. The cruel sea lay far from them
and not yet did ships bring sustenance from afar,
but oxen and the plow and the lady herself of the peoples,
Justice, bestower of gifts, provided the myriad all.
She lived here while earth nourished the Golden race,
but with the Silver race she mingled only a little,
and not readily, for she missed the ways of the men
of old. But still she was here in the time of that Silver race.
She'd come at evening from the echoing hills, alone,
nor would she mingle nor speak gently to anyone.
But when she had filled the high hills with crowds of men,
then she would threaten them, rebuking their evil ways,
and say that she'd never appear again at their prayers.
"How inferior a race the sires of the Golden Age left
behind them. But you will leave a worse breed.
Truly wars and the cruel shedding of blood will be
the lot of mankind and evil affliction will lie
upon them." So she spoke and went to the hills and left
all the people behind, who gazed after her still.
But when even they were dead and there next was born
a race of Bronze, men more deadly than those before,
the first to forge the evil sword of the highwayman
and first too to feed on the flesh of the plowing ox,
then did Justice come to hate that race of men
and take her flight toward heaven. She dwells there now
where still during the night there appears to mortal men
the Virgin, standing near Boötes seen from afar.

(*ll.* 96–136)

Weather Signs

Take as a sign of the rising wind the swelling sea
and the beaches that boom far and loud and the crags of the sea,
when they echo though the weather is fine, and take also
as a sign the mountain's steep moaning peaks and crests,
and when to the dry land the heron in scattered flight
comes from the sea with many a shrill, screaming cry
and is storm-tossed by the wind that rouses the flats of the sea,
and when the petrels fly about in fine weather
and suddenly wheel round to face the rising winds.
Many times the wild ducks and the sea-wheeling gulls
beat their wings on the dry shore or a cloud rests
on its side on the mountain peaks. And now withered hairs
in the down of the white thistles are sign of the wind, whenever
many float on the dumb sea, before and behind.

From where the summer's thunder and lightning flashes come,
look just there for the gales to come on. And when
down through the black night the shooting stars fall
frequently and their paths are white behind them,
expect the wind to come on the same road as they.
But if other shooting stars come opposite these
and others from other parts, then be on your guard
against winds of every sort. These are hard to judge
and blow in ways difficult for men to predict.

But when from the East and from the South the lightning flashes,
and again from the West and now from the North, then the sailor
fears on the sea that here the deep will take him,
and here also the rain from the sky. For such lightnings
herald rain. Often before the rains come,
clouds, very like fleece, appear, or a double rainbow
makes a sash over the wide sky or a star
has a darkening ring that looks like a circled threshing floor.

Many times the birds of the lake or those of the sea
insatiably dive and dip themselves in their own waters;

or around the lake for a long time swallows dart
and strike just so with their breasts the rippling mere; or the more
unfortunate tribes, a feast for water snakes, just there
from the water, fathers of the tadpoles, rumble and croak;
or the lonely tree frog murmurs his morning song;
or elsewhere the cawing crow by the jutting shore stalks
on the dry land when the roaring storm comes on or
dips in the river entirely to the shoulders his head,
or even dives down and covers himself completely
or swaggers much beside the water cawing coarsely.
    And oxen now before the rain gaze heavenward
and sniff the air, and ants from their hollow lairs bring up
with haste all their eggs, and centipedes in swarms
are seen creeping up the walls, and those wandering worms
men call the entrails of the black earth, and hens,
with cock, pluck themselves and often cluck with note
like the plop of water dropping on water. And then at times
generations of crows and jackdaw tribes become a sign
of coming rain from Zeus when they appear in flocks
and shriek like hawks. And crows imitate with voice
the lordly drops of falling rain or sometimes crowing
twice with husky voice they flap and whir their wings,
and household ducks and jackdaws beneath the roof
seek the eaves and clap their wings or toward the sea
the loud shrilling heron seeks his way. Of these
do not fail to heed a thing when on guard
for rain, nor if more than formerly the midges bite
and lust for blood and snuff accumulates about
the nozzle of the lamp upon a misty night.
    Nor if in winter's season there rises the light of lamps,
steady at times, but then again sparks leap
like light bubbles, and if from the spot itself rays
gleam, nor if in spreading heat of summertime
the island birds are born in crowds, nor fail to heed
the pot or tripod on the fire when many sparks
surround them, nor when in ash of blazing coal there burn
specks like millet seeds, but consider also these

when on the look for rain. If a misty cloud stretches
along a high hillside's base and yet its peaks
gleam clear, then you will be beneath fair sky.
Fair sky too will you have when by the flat of the sea
appears a cloud close to the ground that does not rise
but is pressed down there like a long flat stone.

When the sky is fair, look for storm, and from the storm
for calm. Look to the Manger that the Crab wheels by
when first it is cleared beneath of all its mist, for the Manger
is cleared when the tempest wanes. The steady flame of lamps
and the owl hooting softly at night are a sign of storm
abating, and when with many a soft and varying note
the crow caws, and the rooks, alone, call twice their lonely
song but then cry out often and loud and long.
Fuller then in flocks, when they take thought of their roost,
they are filled with voice. One would think that they rejoice,
hearing how they call with shrill sounding cries
around the leaves of the trees, and sometimes on the trees,
when first they roost, then wheel about and clap their wings.

Cranes too before a calm will wing their way
all in single path nor be blown back beneath
fair sky. But then from the stars pure light is dimmed
when no banked clouds obscure nor other dark nor moon
run by beneath but suddenly themselves grow weak,
let this be no longer sign of calm for you; expect
a storm, and when some clouds stay in a single place,
and of others, some pass by and some follow behind.

Cackling geese that scurry for feed are a great sign
of storm, and the nine-generation crow singing at night,
and jackdaws calling late, and the finch piping at dawn,
and all the birds in flight from the sea, the robin and wren
diving into the hollow clefts and jackdaw tribes
that come from the parched pastureland to their late roost.
Nor do the tawny bees, when a storm is coming on,
go far to cull their wax but wheel there close by
their honey and works. Nor on high do cranes in long
lines take the same paths but wheel and turn back.

And when in windless weather delicate spider webs
are drifting and flames from the lamp flicker and dim, or fire
in fair weather and lamps are hard to kindle, expect
a storm. Why tell to you all the signs there are
for men? Ugly clotted ash is a sign of snow.
And the lamps a sign of snow when spots like millet seeds
surround its burning wick; the live coal, of hail
when the coal shines but is inside like a light mist
within the blazing fire. Oaks burdened with acorns
and the black mastic trees are not untried. Often
the miller peers on all sides lest the summer slip
from his hand. Holm oaks with frequent acorn crops
in measure foretell a heavy storm to come. May they
not be burdened exceedingly and everywhere,
but far from drought may the plowlands bear their sheaves of wheat.
　　Three times the mastic buds, three times it bears its fruit.
Each crop in turn gives sign to sow the seed, for men
divide in three the seeding time, the middle and both
ends. The first fruit heralds the first crop;
the middle, the middle; the last, the last crop of all.
The loveliest fruit that the blooming mastic bears foretells
the richest crop from the plow; a meager yield of fruit,
the meanest crop; and the moderate, moderate yield of grain.
Just so, three times, the stalk of the squill gives bloom
to signify a harvest of like abundance. All
the signs the plowman marked in the mastic fruit, all
these he can detect in the blossoming white of the squill.
　　But when in autumn many wasps swarm everywhere
even before the Pleiades set in the west, one can
foretell a coming storm, its swirl like the swarm of wasps.
From sows and ewes and she-goats, whenever they mate,
female with male, and then in turn are mounted again,
as from the wasps, one can foretell a mighty storm.
When the she-goats, the ewes, and the sows are late to mate,
the poor man is glad because they signify to him,
not very warmly clad, a winter that is mild.

The timely plowman takes heart in timely flights of cranes;
the late in late. Just so do winters follow cranes—
early when they come in flocks and early, but when
they come late and not in flocks and over a longer time,
not many at once, winter's delay helps later crops.
    If oxen and sheep after the laden harvest time
root in the earth and turn their heads to the north wind,
surely then the Pleiades will bring as they set
a winter of storms. May they not dig too much for then
winter is fierce and friend to neither trees nor tilth.
May the snow be deep on the spreading fields and on the grass
not yet mature or tall, so that an anxious man
can take joy in his prosperity. May the stars
above be always the same, and let no comets come—
not one nor two nor more, for many comets mean
a drought. Nor on the mainland does the farmer rejoice
when flocks of birds from the islands fill his fields of wheat
when summer comes, but for his harvest is filled with fear.
lest vexed with drought it come with empty spears and chaff.
    The goatherd man takes joy in the birds themselves when they come
in measure, expecting thereafter a season of much milk.
So do men wander and toil and earn their keep
in this way and that. All are ready to see the signs
at their feet and straightway to make them their own.
    By their sheep do shepherds detect a storm whenever they
with unusual haste run to their pasture, some of them
apart from the flock, now rams, now little lambs, play
beside the way, butting their horns, or whenever, some here,
some there, they leap, with all four feet, but the older ones,
with horns, keep two feet on the ground, when apart
from the flock in the evening they move unwillingly and crop
the grass on every side though urged with many a stone.
From oxen cowherds and plowmen learn of a stirring storm
whenever the oxen lick with their tongues around the hooves
of their forefeet, or stretch themselves out in their stalls
on their right sides. Then the ancient plowman expects

to delay his sowing. And when the cattle gather and low
incessantly as they go to the stall at the ox-loosing hour,
the calves loathe to leave the meadow give sign that soon
they will not take in stormless weather their fill of food.
Nor do goats greedy for the thorny oak predict
sunny skies, nor sows that rage over their beds.
     And when the lonely wolf howls long and loud
or when with scant regard for farming men he descends
to cultivated fields, as though he craved some lair
near to men, seeking shelter there, expect
a storm when the third dawn comes circling round. So too
by previous signs you can detect the wind to come
or storm or rain, on the very same day or the next day
or on the third day toward dawn. But neither were mice
when they squeaked and skipped like dancers beneath fair skies
rather more than was their wont unmarked by men of old,
nor dogs. For the dog digs with both his paws when he
suspects that a storm is coming on. And those mice
then prophesy a storm. And from the sea the crab
creeps toward land when a storm is about to burst.
And mice in the daytime toss their straw with their feet
and long to build their nests when signs of rain appear.
     Make light of none of these. It's good to look for sign
on sign. When two go the same way, the hope
is more. Take courage in a third. You can always count
the signs of the passing year—if ever such a dawn
appears at the rising or setting of a particular star
as the sign foretells. It would profit you much to mark
the last four days of the waning month and first four
of the new, for they hold together the ends of the meeting months
when the sky for eight nights is more treacherous
for want of the bright-eyed moon. Study all
the natural signs together throughout the year, for then
you will never predict the weather extemporaneously.

(*ll.* 909–1154)

MOSCHUS

Europa

Once Cypris sent to Europa a sweet dream.
It was the third watch of night when dawn stands near.
when sleep that is more sweet than honey besets the lids,
looses the limbs, and fetters the eyes with soft bonds,
and when the tribe of true dreams goes pasturing forth.
Then slumbering in the roofed room of her royal home
Phoenix' daughter, a virgin still, Europa the girl,
thought that two continents were battling for her,
Asia and the opposite coast. They were women in shape.
Of these one was of foreign mien. The other was like
a native in form. The latter embraced the girl the more
and said that she had given her birth and had brought her up.
The other laid violent hands upon the girl
and dragged her, not unwilling, off, and said that fate
decreed Europa her gift from aegis-bearing Zeus.
The girl leapt up from her covered couch, much afraid,
with pounding heart, for she saw her vision a waking dream,
and she sat silent for a long time and kept both
the women still before her fluttering wakeful eyes.
At last the maiden raised her trembling voice in fear:
    "Which of the heavenly ones sent me visions like these?
What sort of dreams as I lay on my covered couch in my room
slumbering so very sweetly so terrified me?
Who was the foreign woman whom I saw as I slept?
What a longing for her clutched at my heart and how joyously
did she embrace me as though she'd seen her own child.
But may the blessed ones make this dream propitious for me."
    She spoke and leapt up and looked for her dear friends,
girls of her own age, companions of good stock—
she used to play with them when she began the dance
or when she bathed herself in the river torrent's stream

or when from the meadow she'd pluck the lilies of sweet breath.
These came straightway to her and each girl had in her hand
a basket for gathering buds, and then to the meadow they went
beside the sea where they so often gathered in crowds
to take their joy in the blooming rose and the sound of the sea.
Europa herself came carrying a basket of gold,
a sight to see, a marvelous thing, the work of Hephaestus,
which he gave to Libya when she went to Poseidon's bed,
and she bestowed it upon the exceedingly lovely Telephaasa,
who was of kindred blood, and then to the blameless Europa
her mother Telephaasa made it a most distinguished gift.
Upon it were fashioned many a curious and glittering scene.
Among them was Inachian Io, wrought in gold,
while she was still a calf, not yet a woman in form,
and she went back and forth over the briny paths,
using her feet like a swimmer. The sea was enameled blue.
High upon the two brows of the seaside cliffs
men stood about in crowds to see the seafaring cow,
and there was Cronian Zeus touching with gentle hand
the heifer, Inachus' daughter, beside the seven-mouthed Nile,
and from the lovely-horned cow he made her a woman again.
Of silver was fashioned the flowing stream of the Nile and the calf
of bronze and of pure gold was wrought Zeus himself,
and all about beneath the basket's rounded rim
was fashioned Hermes and next to him there lay stretched
Argus surpassing all in never-sleeping eyes,
and, murdered, from his crimson blood there sprang up
the peacock all aglow with the colored fan of its tail,
which it spread just as though it were a swift ship
and covered all around the golden basket's lip.
Such was the basket of the exceedingly lovely Europa.

When the girls came to the meadow, all alive with bloom,
they took their delight in this bud and that. One
would pluck the fragrant narcissus, another the hyacinth,
another the violet, another the creeping thyme.
Many a blossom swelled in the meadows fostered by spring.

They picked the fragrant down of the yellow crocus cup,
and rivaled one another in blooms. The princess herself
culled with her hands the glorious rose with its color of flame
and shone as among the Graces, Aphrodite, the daughter of foam.
But not for long was she destined to cheer with the blossoms her heart
nor to preserve unsullied her maiden's virgin sash.
For the son of Cronus, as soon as he saw the princess, was struck
in his heart and laid low by the arrows, unforeseen,
of Cypris, who alone has the power to subdue Zeus.
He hoped to avert the wrath of Hera, his jealous wife,
and to deceive the tender mind of the virgin girl,
so he hid his godlike form and put on the form of a bull,
not the sort that's fed in the stalls nor the kind that splits
the sod, drawing the well-bent plow, nor of the sort
that feeds at the head of the flock, nor was he even such
that, bound beneath the yoke, draws the well-laden cart.
The rest of his hide was all tawny to see except
that a circle of silver gleamed in the midst of his noble brow,
and his eyes were gray-green beneath and lightninged desire,
and equal to one another his horns rose up from his head
like crescents of the horned moon were its rim split in two.
He came to the meadow and took care not to frighten the girls
when he appeared. They all longed to come near,
to touch the lovely bull. His ambrosial odor that came
from afar surpassed even the pleasant meadows' scent.
He took his stand before the blameless Europa's feet,
and licked her neck and quite enchanted the young girl.
She touched him all around and gently with her hands
wiped much foam from his mouth, and then she kissed the bull.
And he mooed as sweetly as honey. You'd say that you'd heard
the sweet echoing tone of a sounding Mygdonian flute.
He knelt before her feet and gave Europa a look
as he lowered his neck and nodded to show her his broad back.
The princess spoke to her long-haired maiden friends and said,

  "Come here, my dear friends of my own age, so that
sitting upon this bull we may take our joy. For all

of us he'll spread his back and take us—so gentle is he,
so kind and sweet to see. He's not like other bulls
at all. His mind, like one fitting for human kind,
plays over him and he lacks only the power of speech."

   She spoke and sat down upon his back with a smile. The others
intended the same, but suddenly the bull leapt up—
he'd got whom he meant—and swiftly he made his way to the sea.
Europa turned back and kept calling her dear friends.
She'd stretch out her hands, but they couldn't reach to catch her.
Treading upon the shore like a dolphin he ran forth
and keeping his hooves dry he skimmed the wide waves.
And then the sea grew smooth and calmed as he came on,
and whales gamboled about before the feet of Zeus,
and the joyful dolphin tumbled over the surge from the depths,
and the Nereids rose up from under the sea, and they all
on the backs of the whales sat and ranged themselves in rows.
The rumbling Earth-shaker himself over the sea
directed the waves and led over the briny path
his beloved brother, and there were gathered all around
the Tritons, flautists of the sea, who sound loud
and deep. On their long conch shells they played the marriage song.
But Europa sat on the back of the bull and kept hold
with one hand of his long horn. Her other hand
drew up the crimson fold of her robe that the water might not—
unspeakably—wet the dress as it trailed in the foaming sea.
Billowing deep at the shoulder, Europa's full robe,
like the sail of a ship, made light work of carrying her.
But when she was far off the coast of her fatherland
and could see no sea-beat coast not sheer mountain peak,
and there was only air above the boundless sea
beneath, she gazed about her and raised her voice like this:

   "Where do you take me, bull-god? Who are you? How
with your swing-feet can you cross the cruel paths of the sea?
Aren't you afraid? The sea is for ships to run upon,
fleet and swift. Bulls are afraid of the briny path.
Where will you get sweet drink? What food will come from the deep?

What god are you?—for you do what a god can do.
Neither do briny dolphins on land nor bulls at all
on the sea range in rows, but you on land and sea
without a tremor dart about and your hooves are oars,
and soon above the gray-green mists, high aloft,
and quick as swift-winged birds you'll take your flight.
Alas, how very unlucky I am! I left the home
of my father to go following after this bull, and I take
a strange voyage and go wandering alone.
But may you, Earth-shaker, lord of the hoar sea,
meet me propitiously. It is you whom I hope to see
steering this voyage straight and conducting me, for not
without a god do I go over the watery waves."
So she spoke and the beautifully horned bull replied,

    "Take courage, my maiden girl. Don't fear the swell of the sea.
Zeus himself am I, and if close by I look
like a bull—well, I can look like what I choose.
Desire for you drove me to mark out so much sea
in the guise of a bull. Crete soon will welcome you.
She was my own nurse and she will be the scene
of your bridal too. From me you'll bear renowned sons,
all of them scepter-bearing kings for men on earth."

    So he spoke and it happened just as he'd said. Crete
appeared and Zeus took back again his own shape.
He loosed her maiden sash and the Hours prepared his bed.
She who had been a maid became the bride of Zeus
and to Cronus' son bore sons, straightway a mother become.

BION

Lament for Adonis

I weep for Adonis, "The lovely Adonis is dead."
"Dead the lovely Adonis," the Loves weep too.

No longer in crimson cover, Cypris, sleep.
Arise in dark robes, and beat your breasts
and say to all, "The lovely Adonis is dead."

I weep for Adonis. The Loves weep too.

The lovely Adonis lies in the hills, his thigh
struck with the tusk, white against white,
and Cypris grieves as he breathes his delicate last.
His black blood drips down his snowy flesh,
his eyes are numb beneath his brows, and the rose
flees from his lips. The kiss dies too. Cypris
will have it never again. The kiss of the dead
is enough, but Adonis knows not that she's kissed him dead.

I weep for Adonis. The Loves weep too.

Savage the wound that Adonis has in his thigh.
Cythereia bears a greater wound in her heart.
His own hounds howl for that boy. The Oread
nymphs bewail him too, and Aphrodite
unbraids her hair, and through the oak woods
she wails, distraught, disheveled, unsandaled, and the wild
brambles tear and cull her sacred blood.
Shrilling through the long glens she goes,
calling her Assyrian lord, her child.
The black blood spouted about his navel.
His chest was crimsoned from his thighs. His breasts,
white as snow before, were scarlet now.

Alas for Cythereia. The Loves wail too.

She lost her lovely man. She lost her sacred
beauty, the beauty she had while Adonis lived.
Her beauty died with Adonis. "Alas for Cypris,"
all the mountains say, and the oaks, "For Adonis woe,"
and the rivers weep for Aphrodite's grief,
and the springs in the hills shed tears for Adonis,
and the blossoms blush red from grief. Cythera
through all its vales, through every glen, sings,
"Alas for Cythereia. The lovely Adonis is dead."

And Echo replies, "The lovely Adonis is dead."
Who would not have wept for Cypris' dreadful
love? When she saw Adonis' fatal wound,
when she saw the crimson blood around his wasting
thigh, spreading her arms, she cried, "Wait,
Adonis, allow me to touch you one last time.
I want to embrace you, press my lips to yours.

"Adonis, stay, kiss me one last time.
Kiss me just so long as the kiss lives.
Until you breathe your life away into
my mouth, your breath into my heart, your sweet
kiss I'll milk. I'll drain your love. I'll keep
this kiss as I do Adonis himself since you
abandon me and go to far-off Acheron,
to its grim and hateful king, while I, alas
a goddess, must live and cannot follow you.
Persephone, take my spouse. You're stronger than I.
All that is lovely comes to you, but I
am ill-fated. I have insatiable grief,
and I weep for Adonis who's dead to me. I'm afraid
of you. You die, O thrice-desired. Like a dream
my love has fluttered away, and Cythereia
is widowed now. Bereft are the Loves in her house.
Her embroidered sash is lost too. Oh, why
were you so bold? Why did you hunt? Why,
being fair, were you so mad to wrestle the beast?"

So did Cypris lament. The Loves wailed too.
Alas Cythereia, the lovely Adonis is dead.

The Paphian sheds as many tears as Adonis
shed blood and every drop becomes a bud;
the blood bears roses; the tears, anemones.

I weep for Adonis, "The lovely Adonis is dead."

No longer in the oak thickets mourn your man,
Cypris. The lonely leaves make no bed
for Adonis. Let Adonis, now dead, share
your bed, Cythereia. He is a lovely corpse,
a lovely corpse, just as though he slept.
Lay him in soft coverlets in which
he spent the night in sacred sleep with you.
On the golden couch lay the disheveled Adonis.
Cover him with garlands and flowers. As he
died, so also all the blossoms withered.
Sprinkle him with Syrian ointments and myrrh.
Let all the perfumes die. Your perfume is dead.
Delicate Adonis lies in robes
of purple. Around him the Loves moan and wail.
They cut their hair for Adonis. One
cast arrows, another a bow, a quiver, a feather.
One loosed Adonis' sandal. One bore water
in a golden pitcher, another washed his thighs.
One, behind, fanned the lad with his wings.

"Alas, Cythereia," the Loves wail too.

Hymen has quenched every lamp at the door
and scattered the bridal wreath. No longer
does he sing the wedding song but more
"Woe for Adonis." The Graces weep for the son
of Cinyras, "Lovely Adonis is dead." More
shrilly they cry "Woe" than they sing the Paean.
Even the Fates weep and wail, "Adonis,"

and sing a spell to bring him back, but he
can't hear them. It's not that he's not willing
but that the Maiden will not let him go.

Cease your grieving today, Cythereia, cease
beating your breasts. You must wail again,
weep again, come another year.

PSEUDO-MOSCHUS

Lament for Bion

Sing me "Woe," you glades and Dorian water,
and weep, you rivers, for the charming Bion.
Now, orchards, grieve; now, groves, lament.
Now, blossoms, breathe with darkened clusters,
and, roses and anemones, flush with grief.
Now, hyacinth, speak your letters and say the more
"Woe" with your petals; the lovely singer is dead.

Begin, Sicilian Muses, begin the dirge.

Nightingales that mourn in the thick leaves,
tell the Sicilian springs of Arethusa
that Bion the cowherd is dead and that with him
music also is dead and the Dorian song.

Begin, Sicilian Muses, begin the dirge.

Mourn, Strymonian swans, beside the waters
and with shrill tongues sing your mournful ode,
and tell Oeagrus' daughters, tell to all
the Bistonian nymphs, the Dorian Orpheus is dead.

Begin, Sicilian Muses, begin the dirge.

He, beloved of the herds, no longer sings.
No longer beneath the oaks does he sit and sing,
but in Pluto's house he chants the Lethaean strain.
The mountains are voiceless. The cows beside the bulls
wander and moan and are reluctant to pasture.

Begin, Sicilian Muses, begin the dirge.

Apollo himself, Bion, wept for your death.
Satyrs grieve and the black-robed Priapi.
The Pans mourn for your song and through the wood

275

the springs lament and their waters turn to tears.
On the rocks Echo grieves that she is stilled
and no longer mimics your lips. For your death
trees cast their fruit and blossoms withered.
From goats no milk flowed nor honey from hives —
grieved, it died in the comb, for no longer,
now your honey is dead, need it be gathered.

Begin, Sicilian Muses, begin the dirge.

Not so by the shores of the sea did the Siren weep,
nor ever so on the crags did the nightingale sing;
Not so on the long hills did the swallow mourn,
nor so in the dark blue waves did the Ceryl shrill;
nor so did Ceyx cry for the Halcyon's woe,
nor so in the dells of dawn for Morning's son
did Memnon's bird flutter and keen about
the tomb as when they grieved for Bion dead.

Begin, Sicilian Muses, begin the dirge.

The nightingales and all the swallows — he'd taught
them to speak and they delighted him — sat
on stumps and sang antiphonally and wailed,

"Lament, you mourning birds, and so will we."

Begin, Sicilian Muses, begin the dirge.

Who will make music upon your pipe, O thrice-
desired? Who will place lips upon your reeds?
Who will be so bold, for your lips and your breath
live yet, and the sound of your song is pasturing still
in those stalks. Shall I give your pipe to Pan?
Perhaps even he will fear to press
his lips to it lest he come after you.

Begin, Sicilian Muses, begin the dirge.

Galataea laments your song. You once
delighted her when she sat with you upon

the shore of the sea—you didn't sing like the Cyclops.
Lovely Galataea rejected him, but you
she looked upon more sweetly than upon
the sea. Now she's forgotten the wave and sits
on the lonely sand and pastures your cows still.

Begin, Sicilian Muses, begin the dirge.

All the gifts of the Muses have died with you,
O cowherd, lovely maiden kisses, lips
of boys. The Loves disheveled wail about
your tomb, the Cypris loves you much more than the kiss
she gave Adonis but yesterday when he died.
This is for you a second grief, most shrill
of rivers, this, Meles, a new grief.
Homer perished before, Calliope's sweet
mouth, and you, they say, mourned your son
with many floods of tears. You filled the sea
with your sound. And now you weep a second son
and waste away with grief anew. Both
were beloved of springs. One drank at Pegasus' fount.
The other got Arethusa's draft. Homer
sang of Tyndareus' lovely daughter and Thetis'
mighty son and Atreus' son Menelaus.
But that one sang not wars, not tears, but Pan.
A cowherd, he piped and tended his cattle with song
and fashioned pipes and milked the sweet calf
and taught the kisses of boys and cherished Love
in his breast and provoked the passion of Aphrodite.

Begin, Sicilian Muses, begin the dirge.

Every famous city mourns you, Bion,
every town. Ascra mourns you more
than Hesiod. Boeotian woods long not so much
for Pindar. Not so much did lovely Lesbos
grieve for Alcaeus. Not so much did Teos
lament her bard. Paros longs more

for you than for Archilochus. Mitylene
keens your song instead of Sappho's still.
. . . .
Among the Syracusans a Theocritus . . .
But I sing a song of Ausonian grief—no
stranger to pastoral song, my legacy is
the Dorian Muse you taught, your portion to me.
You left others your wealth but me your song.

Begin, Sicilian Muses, begin the dirge.

Alas, the mallows, when in the garden they die,
and the fresh parsley and springing curl of anise,
they live again and grow another year.
But we men, tall and strong and wise,
when once we die, deaf in the hollow earth,
we sleep a sleep from which there is no waking.
And you will lie in the earth cloaked in silence.
The Nymphs allow the frog to sing forever.
No matter. It's not a pretty song he sings.

Begin, Sicilian Muses, begin the dirge.

Poison, Bion, came to your lips.
Poison you ate. Could it touch such lips and not
turn sweet? What mortal so savage as to mix
and give the drug at your call? Song went cold.

Begin, Sicilian Muses, begin the dirge.

Justice comes to all. But I in my grief
weep and lament your death. If I'd been able
like Orpheus once to descend to Tartarus, as once
Odysseus, and Achilles before him, I'd have gone
to Pluto's house to see you, and, if you sang
to Pluto, to hear what you sang. But come, shrill
to the Maid a sweet Sicilian bucolic song,
for she's Sicilian and played on Aetna's shores,

278

and she knows the Dorian song. Your tune will have
reward, and as once she gave to Orpheus because
he played so sweetly his Eurydice again,
so you, Bion, she'll send to the hills. If I
were able to pipe, in Pluto's house I'd sing.

FROM *THE GREEK ANTHOLOGY*

Antipater of Sidon

XIII (7.464)

Artemeias, surely when you from the nether world's bark
    set foot upon Cocytus' chthonic shore,
bearing in your arms your infant, newly dead,
    the youthful Dorian women pitied you
in Hades and asked about your death. And you, your cheeks
    ravaged with tears, gave them this grievous reply:
"My friends, I gave birth to twins; one I left behind
    with Euphron, my husband; the other I bring to the dead."

XVII (7.209)

Here beside the threshing floor, O hardworking ant,
    I've made you a grave mound from the thirsting sod,
that even in death you may enjoy Demeter's furrow
    of grain, laid in a chamber the plow upturned.

XXV (7.241)

Myriad times, Ptolemy, your father, myriad times
    your mother, defiled their abundant hair in grief.
Much did your tutor mourn and gathered with warrior hands
    the dark dust to pour over his head.
Mighty Egypt plucked out her hair, and the broad home
    of Europa groaned aloud. The Moon herself,
darkened by grief, abandoned the stars and her heavenly paths,
    for you perished by a pestilence that was
Lord of the Feast for the whole land before you took
    in your young hand your father's ancestral scepter.
Night did not receive you from night, for such princes
    not Hades leads to hell but Zeus to Olympus.

XXVIII (7.353)

This is the barrow of grizzled Maronis, on which you see
    yourself a drinking cup carved on the stone.
She took her wine straight, babbled forever, and grieves
    for neither her children nor their destitute father.
This single thing she mourns even beneath her mound,
    that the wine god's cup on her tomb is empty of wine.

I (6.14)

To Pan three brothers hung up these tools of the trade:
    Damis his snare for trapping mountain beasts,
Cleitor these nets for catching fish; Pigres
    this unbroken collar for fettering flying birds.
One from the woods, one from the air, and one from the sea
    never came home with empty flaxen nets.

XXII (7.172)

I, who used to ward off the starlings and that snatcher
    of seed, the high-flying Bistonian crane,
was stretching the well-twisted thongs of my leather sling, I
    Alcimenes, keeping off a cloud of birds,
when a dipsas viper wounded me about the ankles;
    injecting my flesh with bitter bile from her bite,
she deprived me of sunlight. See how gazing at creatures of air,
    I did not know the bane that crept at my feet.

XIII (7.23)

Let the four-clustered ivy flourish about you, Anacreon,
    and the delicate blossoms of crimson-colored meadows,
and let the springs of snowy-white milk bubble up,
    and fragrant-sweet wine pour forth from the earth,
so that your ashes and bones may take their joy, if truly
    any delight there is that touches the dead.

A. Tell me, woman, your parents, your name, your land.   B. Calliteles
    begat me; Praxo, my name; Samos, my land.
A. Who put up this tomb?   B. Theocritus who took
    my virginity. I was a maiden still.
A. How did you die?   B. In the pangs of labor.   A. Tell me,
    what age had you reached?   B. Twice eleven years.
A. Childless?   B. Stranger, no. I left behind Calliteles,
    three years old, a little baby still.
A. May he reach a most blessed and hoary old age.   B. And may
    Fortune steer your course with fair wind.

V (6.174)

To Pallas, three girls, all of an age, skilled as the spider
    at spinning delicate webs, made dedication:
Demo, her well-braided basket; Arsinoe, her spindle,
    worker of well-spun yarn; and Bacchylis,
her well-wrought comb, nightingale among spinsters,
    with which she parted the woven threads of the warp,
for they chose, each one, O stranger, to live an honorable life,
    earning their own keep by the work of their hands.

Anyte

IX (7.208)

This tomb Damis built for his courageous horse
    who died when murderous Ares pierced his breast,
and the black blood bubbled through his tough hide,
    and he soaked the earth's clod with his awful gore.

XI (7.202)

No longer, as before, will you wake at dawn and flap
    your rapid wings to rouse me from my bed,
for while you slept, the fox crept up; he took
    your neck in his claws and neatly he killed you.

XII (7.215)

No longer shall I exult in the floating seas and arch
    my neck, rising from out of the deep, nor leap
and snort about the beautifully painted bows of the ship,
    taking delight in my own figurehead,
for a wave of the purple-dark seas thrust me ashore,
    and I lie here along a narrow beach.

XIII (6.312)

The children, billy goat, have put crimson reins
    on you, and a muzzle on your shaggy mouth.
They race you like a horse around the god's shrine
    that he may watch them in their infant joy.

XX (7.190)

For her locust, nightingale of the fields, and her cricket that slept
    in the oaks, Myro, the little girl, has made
a single tomb, shedding childish tears, for Death,
    inexorable, has taken her two pets.

V (7.486)

Often on this her daughter's tomb did Cleina grieve
    and call out for her dear short-lived child,
summoning up the soul of Philaenis, who before
    her marriage crossed the pallid Acheron.

Asclepiades

VI (5.203)

Lysidice dedicated to you, Cypris,
　　her spur, the golden goad of her shapely leg,
with which she trained many a horse upon its back,
　　nor reddened ever her thighs, so lightly she rode,
for she finished the course without the spur and therefore hung
　　her weapon of gold upon your temple door.

XV (12.46)

I am not yet twenty-two and I am tired of living.
　　O Loves, why this torture? Why set me ablaze?
For if I die, what will you do? Clearly, Loves,
　　silly boys, you'll play at dice as before.

XXVIII (7.11)

This is the sweet work of Erinna, not much, of course,
　　for I was only a girl of nineteen years,
but of more power than that of many others. Had death
　　not come so soon, who would have had my name?

Dioscorides

XXXIX (7.166)

Lamisca, who breathed her last in lamentable pangs of labor,
　　the daughter of Eupolis and Nicarete,
with her twin babes, a Samian by birth, is buried beside
　　the Nile on Libyan shores, twenty years old.
But, maidens, bring to the girl the gifts of the newly delivered
　　and shed warm tears on her cold tomb.

XL (7.167)

Call me Polyxena, the wife of Archelaus,
　　daughter of Theodectes and Demarete.
I was a mother too as far as my labor went,
　　but my baby died before it was twenty days old,
and I died at eighteen years, briefly a mother,
　　briefly a bride, in all, briefly alive.

X (12.37)

Eros, that bane of men, molded soft as marrow
　　the buttocks of Sosarchus, the Amphipolitan,
as a joke, hoping to irritate Zeus, because his thighs
　　were much more honey-sweet than Ganymede's.

I (5.56)

They drive me mad, those rosy lips, forever prattling,
　　soul-dissolving gates of a mouth like nectar,
and eyes that flash like lightning beneath luxuriant brows,

nets and snares of my innermost heart and soul,
and milky breasts, beautifully paired, desirable,
    well formed, and more delightful than any bud.
But why do I show bones to dogs? Midas' reeds
    are witness to the fate of tattletales.

Diotimus

IV (7.261)

What use to suffer in labor, give birth to children, if she
   who gives them birth is to see her child dead?
For his mother heaped this grave mound for young Bianor,
   but the mother ought to have had this from her child.

V (7.475)

Polyaenus' daughter, Scyllis, came to the wide gates,
   grieving for her bridegroom, Evagoras,
the son of Hegemachus. She was to sit at his hearth.
   The widow did not return to her father's house.
Poor girl, within three months she died, miserably,
   in a fatal wasting away in grief of her soul.
For both of them this melancholy memorial
   of their love stands beside the well-worn road.

Erinna

I (7.710)

Stele and my Sirens and mournful pitcher that hold
    the little ash of Hades, tell those who pass by
my tomb to greet me, whether citizens
    or from another town, and say that I
was buried here, still a bride, and that my father
    called me Baucis, that I was born in Tenos,
that they may know. And tell them too that my companion
    Erinna engraved this word upon my tomb.

II (7.712)

I am the grave of Baucis the bride. Passing by
    my stele, say to Hades beneath the earth,
"You are grudging, Hades. The lovely letters you see
    will tell the very cruel fate of Baucis:
how her bridegroom's father lighted the girl's funeral pyre
    with the same torches that blazed for the wedding song,
and you, Hymenaeus, exchanged the melodious marriage hymn
    for the mournful sound of threnodies sung for the dead."

Leonidas of Tarentum

VII (6.204)

To Pallas, Theris, cunning of hand, dedicated
  his unbent cubit rule and his taut saw
with its curved grip, his shining ax and his bright plane,
  his rotating bore, when he abandoned his craft.

LXXIII (7.478)

Whoever then are you? Whose wretched bones are these
  still here in a broken coffin beside the road?
Your simple monument and grave are constantly scraped
  by the axle and wheel of the traveler's wayfaring cart.
Soon the wagons will grind your ribs down to powder,
  poor wretch, and no one will shed a tear for you.

LIX (7.67)

Gloomy minister of Hades who sail this stream
  of Acheron in your barge of murky blue,
even though your gruesome boat is loaded down
  with corpses, take me, Diogenes the Dog.
My baggage is a purse, a leather oil flask,
  my old cloak, and the obol that ferries the dead.
All that I acquired in life I bring to Hades
  as I come. I leave nothing beneath the sun.

LVI (6.305)

To Gluttony and Guzzling, that fastidious gourmet,
  stinking Dorieus made the following gifts:
round-bellied cauldrons for boiling made in Larisa, and pots,

and a cup with wide-gaping lip, and a flesh hook,
well-bent and beautifully wrought, all of bronze,
    and his cheese grater, and ladle for stirring soup.
So now accept these mean gifts from a mean donor,
    and never, Gluttony, grant him temperance.

XX (7.295)

Theris, thrice-old, who got his living from
    his lucky weels, who swam the sea more
than a gull, a preyer on fishes, a hauler of nets, who dived
    to clefts in the rocks, no sailor on many-oared ships,
Arcturus did not destroy, nor did a storm drive
    to their end the many decades of his years,
but he died in his reed hut, naturally, quenched
    like a lamp by the extraordinary length of his life.
It was not his children who erected this tomb nor was it his wife,
    but rather the guild of his fellow spearers of fish.

XV (7.652)

Thundering sea, why in savage storm did you plunge
    headlong into the deep Teleutagoras,
son of Timares, as he sailed his little ship, cargo
    and all, drowning him in your greedy wash?
Now terns and fish-devouring gulls grieve for him,
    who lies somewhere dead on a broad beach,
and Timares, seeing his son's bewept but empty tomb,
    weeps the more for his child Teleutagoras.

XLV (6.309)

His ball, beautifully leaved, and his noisy boxwood rattle,
    and the knucklebones he was so crazy for,
and his whistling top Philocles hung up to Hermes,
    for these were the toys of his boyhood's innocent play.

LV (6.298)

A wallet, the hide of a goat, tough and untanned, a stick
    for walking with, an oil flask without
a scraper, a dog-skin purse without a penny in it,
    a hat to shade his unholy head: these
were the spoils of Sochares that Hunger hung up upon
    a tamarisk bush as a trophy for her when he died.

XXI (7.198)

If the tombstone placed over me is small to see and close
    to the ground, O passerby, nevertheless,
give praise to Philaenis, sir. For me, her singing insect,
    who used to walk on thistles and thorns, she loved
for two years, a grasshopper, and she buried me,
    for her delight in my melodious twang.
Nor did she disown me dead but built this tiny tomb,
    a monument to my many-strophied songs.

XXXVII (6.302)

Get out of my hut, you stealthy vermin! Leonidas'
    meager meal bin doesn't run to feeding mice!
The old man makes do with salt and a crumb or two.
    From my father I learned to accept a life like this.
So why do you mine this corner for dainties, you little gourmet,
    where you'll not taste even the scraps from my meal?
Get off to other houses. Go—my stores are scant—
    to where you'll plunder more generous supply.

XVI (7.654)

Forever brigands and pirates, the Cretans are never just.
    Whoever has known a Cretan to be just?
And so Cretans they were who shoved me into the sea

as I sailed with my pathetic little cargo,
poor Timolytus. Now sea gulls keen for me,
and there is no Timolytus in this tomb.

LXXII (7.726)

Old Platthis often thrust away her morning's sleep
  and her evening's too, to ward off poverty.
At the threshold of her hoary old age she used
  to sing a tune to her spindle and friendly distaff,
and beside the loom until the dawn she would weave with the Graces
  the long course back and forth of Athena,
or, shriveled herself, would spin on shriveled knee thread
  sufficient for the loom, a lovely woman.
At eighty years she saw the waters of Acheron,
  beautiful and beautifully weaving Platthis.

Meleager

XV (12.47)

Still in his mother's lap the baby Love played
    at dice in the morning and shot my soul away.

XLIX (5.157)

Love fed Heliodora's fingernail and made
    it sharp, for her scratch goes right down to the heart.

XLVII (5.148)

I say that my sweetly prattling Heliodora will someday
    in stories surpass with her graces the Graces themselves.

XIII (7.196)

Shrilling cicada, drunk on drops of dew, you sing
    the country song that makes the wildwood talk,
and, perched on petals, your legs like little saws, you rub
    your sunburnt skin, ringing music like
the lyre's. But sing some new delight for woodland nymphs,
    striking up a song antiphonal
to Pan, that I may have relief from Love and catch
    a noonday nap beneath the plane tree's shade.

LXV (7.207)

I was a quick-footed, long-eared hare, just snatched from my mother's
    breast while still a babe, when Phanion
of the sweet flesh adored and cherished me in her lap
    and fed me upon the flowers of spring. No longer

did I pine for my mother but died from a surfeit of dining, for I
    got fat on many a feast. She buried my corpse
close to her couch so that in her dreams she could always see
    my little grave just there beside her bed.

XXXVIII (5.178)

Sell it, though it sleeps still at its mother's breast!
    Sell it! Why should I rear such a saucy thing?
It's pug-nosed and winged and scratches lightly with its nails
    and laughs even when it's crying. Besides
it can't be nursed, it babbles constantly. Sharp-eyed,
    savage, not even his mother can tame it. A monster!
And so it shall be sold. If a merchant sailing off
    wants to buy a baby, here's the place!
But look, it begs, all in tears. Well, never mind,
    I'll not sell. You can be Zenophila's.

LIII (5.214)

I foster a Love fond of playing ball. It throws
    to you, Heliodora, my quivering heart.
Agree to play with Passion, for if you cast me
    from you, he'll frown upon this flouting of sport.

XLVIII (5.155)

Within my heart Love himself made Heliodora,
    that sweetly prattling girl, soul of my soul.

XXI (12.132a)

Did I not tell you, my soul, "By Cypris, you will be caught,
    O luckless in love, if you fly again and again
to the mistletoe?" Didn't I tell you? The snare has got you.
    Why gasp in your bonds? Love has fettered your wings

and set you on fire. When you faint, he sprinkles you with myrrh,
and gives you when you thirst hot tears to drink.

XIV (5.57)

If you burn my scorched soul too often, Love, she'll fly
away. She too, you cruel child, has wings.

XXV (5.156)

Love-prone Asclepias with eyes like a summer's day
persuades us all to make the voyage of love.

XVI (12.48)

I'm down. Step on my neck, you savage god, with your heel.
    I know how heavy you are. I also know
your flaming bolts. But if you torch my heart, you'll not
    kindle it, for it's already ash.

XXXIII (5.151)

Mosquitoes, shameless and shrill of voice, sucking the blood
    of men, winged monsters of the night,
let Zenophila sleep a little in peace, I beg,
    and feed on the flesh of my limbs instead.
But why do I cry out in vain? Even beasts,
    savage and wild, enjoy the warmth of her flesh.
I give you warning now, you evil creatures. Don't be
    so bold, or you'll know the jealous might of my hands.

XXXIV (5.152)

Mosquito, may you fly, a swift courier for me
    and whisper, touching the tip of Zenophila's ear,
"Sleepless, he waits for you, but you forget your loves

and sleep." Then, dear singer, fly away.
    Speak softly to her. Don't wake her lover to hurt her
        because he's struck jealous of me. But if
    you bring me the girl, I'll cover you with a lion's skin,
        mosquito, and give you a club to hold in your hand.

XLVI (5.147)

I'll weave in the white violet. I'll weave in
    the tender narcissus with myrtle berries and leaves.
I'll weave in the laughing lilies too and the sweet crocus,
    the purple hyacinth, and the rose, that lover
of love, so that the wreath on Heliodora's brow
    will scatter its buds on her lovely fragrant curls.

XXXV (5.171)

The cup takes its sweet joy and tells how it touches
    the prattling lips of Zenophila, in love
with love. Blessed cup! Would that she'd put her lips
    to mine and drink down my soul at a single draft.

XXXVI (5.174)

You're sleeping, Zenophila, my tender bloom. I wish
    that I were a wingless sleep to come beneath
your eyelids. Then not even he who charms the eyes
    of Zeus but only I would have you.

XLII (5.136)

Pour and say again and again and yet again,
    "Heliodora's." Mix that sweet name
with the wine and put on me that garland drenched with myrrh,
    though it's yesterday's, a memory of her.
Look, the rose, lover of love, weeps because
    he sees her elsewhere and not at this breast of mine.

XLIII (5.137)

Pour for Heliodora Persuasion and pour for Cypris
    Heliodora; again, for the same, the Grace
of sweet speech, for I call her one goddess and mix
    her desirable name in the straight wine that I drink.

LVI (7.476)

Tears beneath the earth, Heliodora, I give
    to you in Hades, the relic of my love.
Tears, sad tears. On your tomb, much bewept, I pour
    remembrance of my longing and of my love.
Pitiably, I, Meleager, lament for you,
    beloved even in death, an empty tribute
to Acheron. Where is the blossom of my desire? Hades
    has taken and dust defiled her full bloom.
I beg you, nourishing earth, take gently in your arms
    and to your breast her whom all bewail.

LI (5.163)

Flower-feasting bee, why do you touch upon
    Heliodora's flesh and abandon the buds
of spring? Do you say that she's got the goad of Love that is
    both bitter and sweet to the heart? Yes, I think
that this is what you say. Go back to your garden again,
    lover of love. This is no news you bring.

XLIV (5.141)

Yes, I'd rather hear Heliodora's voice
    in my ear than the harp of Leto's son, by Love!

XXXI (5.144)

Now the white violet blooms and narcissus that loves
    the rain and lilies haunting the hills. Now she,

Love's own love, among blossoms the blossom of spring,
    Zenophila, Persuasion's rose, is in bloom.
Meadows, why do sparkle and laugh for your buds? This girl
    is lovelier than those fragrant blossoms by far.

Tymnes

V (7.211)

The stone says that it covers here the white dog
    from Malta, Eumelus' most faithful guard.
They called him Bull while he lived, but now the quiet paths
    of night contain that creature's barking voice.

Mnasalcas

Say, stranger, that this is the tomb of the mare Aethyia.
    Her feet were fleet as the wind. Though the dry land
bore her, most light of limb, often she'd skim, like a bird,
    the long course and speed as far as the ships.

Bassus

5.125

I'm not planning to turn into gold. Somebody else
    can become a bull or melodious swan upon
the shore. I'll leave tricks like that to Zeus. Instead
    of putting on wings, I'll give Corinna two cents.

Crinagoras

5.119

You toss now to the left; you toss now to the right,
  Crinagoras, upon your empty bed.
Unless charming Gemella lies there beside you,
  you'll get in your rest no sleep, only exhaustion.

Philodemus

5.132

O foot, O leg, O thighs for which I rightly died,
    O buttocks, O cunt, O flanks, O shoulders, O breasts,
O delicate neck, O arms, O eyes that drive me mad,
    O most accomplished movement, O excellent kisses
done with the tongue, O little cries that excite me!
    If she is Italian and if her name is Flora,
and if she is no singer of Sappho, well, Perseus
    was in love with Indian Andromeda.

5.115

I fell in love with Demo of Paphos. No big surprise.
    And, second, with Demo of Samos. No big deal.
Then, third, with Demo of Naxos. It was no longer a joke.
    Fourth, with Demo of Argos. The Fates themselves,
I suppose, have named me Philodemus, "lover of Demos,"
    as I always have some hot desire for Demo.

5.123

O two-horned moon, you love the parties that last all night,
    so shine through the lattice work and cast your light
upon golden Callistion. No one begrudges a goddess
    her seeing the secrets of love. You bless us both,
I know, O moon, Callistion and me, for once
    Endymion set your very soul ablaze.

5.131

Xanthippe's strumming, her chatter, her speaking eye, her song,
    and the fire just now begun will scorch you,
my soul; from what, or when, or how I do not know,
    but, my unlucky heart, when you smolder, you will.

5.112

I've been in love. Who hasn't? I went out and got drunk.
    Who hasn't? I was out of my mind. Who did it?
Some god, no doubt. Well, let it go. White hairs come
    in place of the black. It's a sign of the age of sense.
When it was time to play, I played. Now that it isn't,
    I'll try to put my mind to better things.

5.120

In the middle of the night I slipped away from my husband
    and, drenched with the heavy rain, I came to you.
Now, are we going to sit and do nothing, or are
    we going to sleep, without talking, as lovers ought?

5.121

Philaenion is small and swart, but her hair curls more
    than parsley, and her flesh is more tender than down.
Her voice has more magic than Aphrodite's sash.
    She offers me all and often spares me her begging.
May I love such a Philaenion until I find,
    O golden Cypris, another more perfect than she.

Rufinus

5.87

Melissias denies her love, but her body screams
 that it's been struck by a whole quiver of arrows.
Her step is unsteady. She catches her breath in uneven gasps.
 There are dark purple hollows beneath her eyes. But, Loves,
by your fair-wreathed mother, Cytherea, burn the faithless girl
 until she cries aloud and says, "I burn."

5.73

Dear God, I didn't know that Cytherea was bathing,
 letting her hair fall through her hands and down
her back. Pity me, mistress, and don't put a curse
 on my eyes because they've seen your immortal form.
Now I know. It's Rhodoclea, not Cypris, I see.
 But that beauty! You've seduced a goddess, it seems.

5.69

When Pallas and golden-sandaled Hera saw Maeonis,
 they both made this heartfelt cry. We will not undress
again. One shepherd's judgment's enough. It wouldn't do
 to lose a second time in a contest of form.

5.62

Time has not quenched your beauty. Much of your bygone prime
 survives. Your charms have not aged, nor has
the loveliness left those gleaming apples of yours or your rose.
 How many did that divine blossom burn
to ashes before . . . .
 . . . .

5.88

Lamplighter, if you can't set two equally
    ablaze, quench or transfer the flame in one.

5.74

Rhodoclea, I send you this wreath which I wove with my own hands
    from beautiful flowers. There is the lily there
and the petals of the rose, the anemone, covered
    with dew, the tender narcissus and violet,
gleaming dark blue. Put it on and stop being proud.
    Both you and the garland, my girl, blossom and fade.

5.60

The silver-footed girl was bathing, letting the water
    moisten the golden apples that were her breasts.
Their skin was smoother than curdled milk. Her rounded buttocks,
    their flesh more fluid than water, rolled and tossed
when she walked. She'd spread her hand to cover swelling Eurotas —
    not all of it but only as much as she could.

A TECHNOPAIGNION

Wings

See me, the lord of deep-bosomed earth, who turned Acmonides upside down
and don't be afraid that someone so small should have
such a shaggy beard, for I was born when Necessity
ruled and kept apart by grievous command
all creatures that crept or flew
through air
or in Chaos.
The swift-winged child of Cypris
and Ares, the warrior god, I am not called,
for I ruled not by force but by gentle Persuasion,
and earth and the depths of the sea and brazen heaven
yielded to me, and I took their ancient scepter and gave judgment to gods.

MAPS

GLOSSARY OF PROPER NAMES

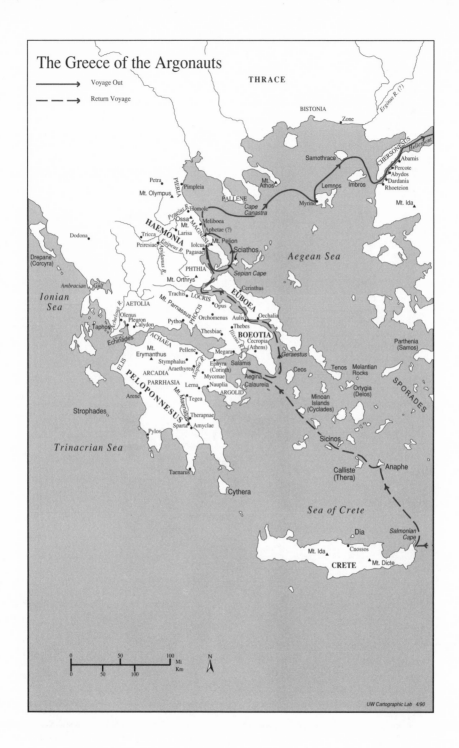

The Greece of the Argonauts

→ Voyage Out

⇢ Return Voyage

THRACE

BISTONIA

Zone

Erginus R. (?)

Samothrace

Hellespont

CHERSONESUS

Abarnis

Percote

Abydos

Dardania

Rhoeteion

Mt. Athos

Lemnos

Imbros

Mt. Ida

Petra

Pimpleia

PIERIA

Mt. Olympus

PALLENE

Cape Canastra

Myrine

Homole

Peneius R.

HAEMONIA

Ossa

Meliboea

MAGNESIA

Larisa

Aphetae (?)

Dodona

Tricca

Peiresiae

Enipeus R.

Iolcus

Apidanus R.

Pagasae

Mt. Pelion

Sciathos

Aegean Sea

Drepane (Corcyra)

PHTHIA

Sepian Cape

Mt. Orthrys

Ambracian Gulf

Cerinthus

Ionian Sea

Trachis

LOCRIS

EUBOEA

Mt. Parnassus

Opus

Achelous R.

AETOLIA

PHOCIS

Aulis

Oechalia

Olenus

Pleuron

Calydon

Pytho

Orchomenus

Parthenia (Samos)

Taphos

Thesbiae

Thebes

Geraestus

Echinades

ACHAEA

BOEOTIA

Cecropia (Athens)

Tenos

Melantian Rocks

SPORADES

Mt. Erymanthus

Pellene

Cephissus R.

Megara

Salamis

Ceos

Stymphalus

Araethyrea

Ephyra (Corinth)

Aegina

ELIS

ARCADIA

Mycenae

Calaureia

Ortygia (Delos)

PARRHASIA

Lerna

Nauplia

PELOPONNESUS

Arene

Mt. Maenalus

Tegea

ARGOLID

Minoan Islands (Cyclades)

Strophades

Therapnae

Sicinos

Pylos

Sparta

Amyclae

Taenarus

Trinacrian Sea

Calliste (Thera)

Anaphe

Cythera

Sea of Crete

Dia

Salmonian Cape

Mt. Ida

Cnossos

Mt. Dicte

CRETE

0   50   100   Mi
0   50   100   Km

N

UW Cartographic Lab 4/90

The Voyage of the Argonauts

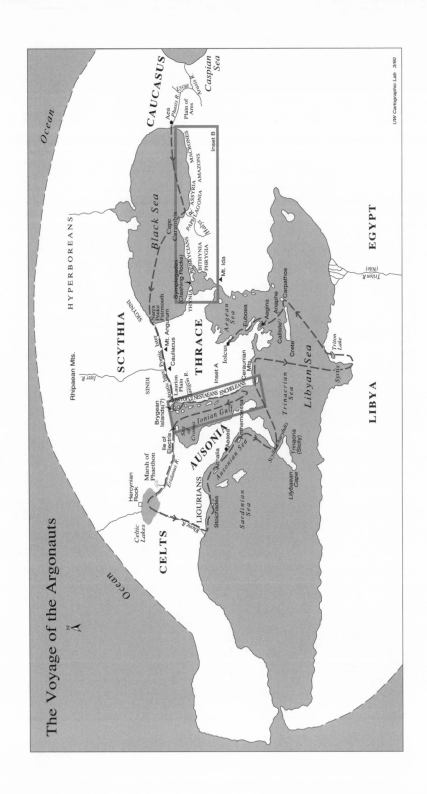

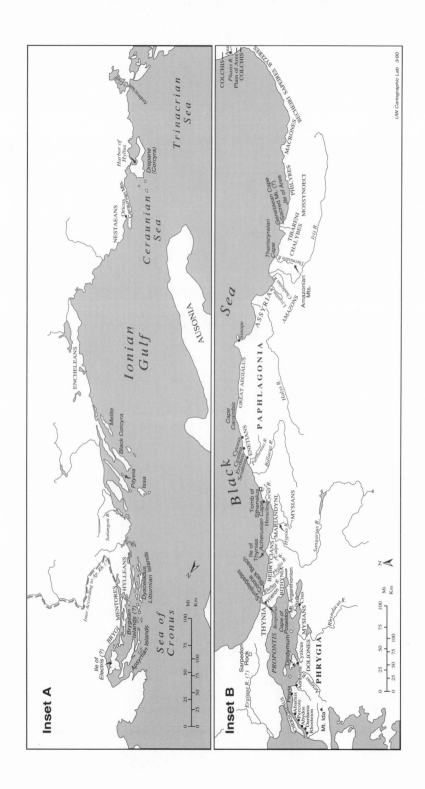

Inset A

Ister According to Ap Rh II

Ile of
Electris (?)
Ida
BRYGI
MENTORES
HYLLEANS
Brygean
Islands (?)
Apsyrtian Islands
Dyscelladus
Liburnian Islands
Salangon R.
N
Mi
Km
0   25   50   75   100
0   25   50   75   100

ENCHELEANS

NESTAEANS

Amantes R.

Harbor of
Hyllus
Oricum Mts.
Ceraunian Mts.
Drepane
(Corcyra)

*Ceraunian
Sea*

*Trinacrian
Sea*

Melite
Black Corcyra
Piyeia
Issa

*Ionian
Gulf*

*Sea of
Cronus*

AUSONIA

Inset B

Sarpedon
Erginus R.
Thynias (?)
Rock
Calpe Beach
Strophades
Acherusian
Black Beach
THYNIA
Cius
PROPONTIS
BITHYNIA
Bosporus
Cape of
Posidon
Mt. Arganthonon
Dindymum
Cyzicus
Adrastela
MYSIANS
DOLIONES
Rhyndacus R.
PHRYGIA
Phrygia
Aesepus R.
Abarnis
Percote
Abydos
Dardania
Rhoeteion
Mt. Ida
CHERSONESUS

N
Mi
Km
0   25   50   75   100
0   25   50   75   100

Priolas
Rhebas R.
Hypius R.
Lillaeus R.
Sagaris R.
Hypius R.
MARIANDYNI
BEBRYCIANS
Sangarius R.
MYSIANS

Ile of
Thynias
Tomb of
Sthenelus
Heraclea
Cape
Acheron R.

Cromna
Cytorus
Erythini
Sesamus
Cape
Carambis
ENETIANS
GREAT AEGIALUS
PAPHLAGONIA
Sinope
Halys R.
Parthenius R.
Billaeus R.

ASSYRIA
AMAZONS
Amazonian
Mts.
Lycastus R.
Chadisia R.
Thermodon R.
Iris R.

*Black
Sea*

Theriscyrean
Cape
Genetaean Cape
Sacred Mt.
Ile of Ares
Plain of Ares
TIBARENI
CHALYBES
MOSSYNOECI
PHILYRES
MACRONES
BECHEIRI
SAPEIRES
BYZERES
Phasis R.
COLCHIS
COLCHIS

UW Cartographic Lab 3/90

GLOSSARY
Of Proper Names

This glossary includes the names of the poets contained in this volume. It does not include the names of nonmythological persons who may be assumed to be purely fictional.

Abantes: A people of Epirus, in northwestern Greece. They lived in the Ceraunian Mountains.

Abantian: Epithet of Euboea.

Abarnis: A city of the Troad, on the coast of the Hellespont in northwestern Asia Minor.

Abas: 1. An Argive, the reputed father of Idmon, who was actually fathered by Apollo. 2. A Euboean, the father of Canethus and grandfather of the Argonaut Canthus.

Abydos: A city of the Troad, on the coast of the Hellespont in northwestern Asia Minor.

Acacallis: A daughter of Minos.

Acastus: An Argonaut, son of Pelias.

Achaea: 1. A district of Greece in the northern Peloponnesus. 2. An area of Thessaly in northern Greece.

Achaeans: 1. The people of Achaea. 2. Often used as a name for the Greeks in general.

Acharnae: In *Idyll* VII probably not the Attic deme but a place on Cos.

Achelous: 1. A river between Acarnania and Aetolia in western Greece. 2. A river god.

Acheron: 1. A river of the underworld. 2. A river of Bithynia, thought to be an entrance to the underworld.

Acherusian headland: A promontory near the river Acheron in Bithynia.

Achilles: Son of the Argonaut Peleus; the greatest fighter of the Greeks during the Trojan War.

Acis: A river in Sicily, famous for its cold water.

Acmonian grove: A wood near the river Thermodon in Assyria where the Amazon race was conceived by Ares and Harmonia.

Acmonides: Son of Acmon, i.e., Heaven.

Actaeon: Son of Aristaeus, who for seeing Artemis bathing was turned into a stag and torn to pieces by his own hounds.

Actor: 1. A Locrian, father of the Argonaut Menoetius and grandfather of Achilles' friend Patroclus. 2. A Locrian, father of Irus. 3. Father of Sthenelus.

Admetus: King of Pherae in Thessaly in northern Greece. An Argonaut.

Adon: Adonis.

Adonis: A handsome youth with whom Aphrodite fell in love. Despite her warnings he persisted in hunting and was killed by a boar. Originally a dying-rising fertility god. His rites were popular in Greece from the fifth century on.

Adrasteia: 1. A nymph, the nurse of Zeus. 2. A city on the southern coast of the Propontis.

Adrastus: Purified Tydeus when he fled from Calydon to Argos after committing a murder, gave him his daughter in marriage.

Adresteia: A goddess who punished excess of any kind.

Aea: A city of Colchis.

Aeacus: A son of Zeus, father of the Argonauts Telamon and Peleus.

Aeaea: Circe's island off the coast of Italy.

Aeaean: Of Aea or Aeaea.

Aeetes: King of the Colchians and keeper of the golden fleece. Father of Medea.

Aegaeon: A giant said to be buried by Poseidon under an island in the Propontis.

Aegaeus: 1. Apparently a river of Corcyra. 2. Father of the nymph Melite.

Aegean Sea: The sea between Greece and Asia Minor.

Aegialus: 1. Another name for Achaea, a province of Greece in the northern Peloponnesus. 2. The coast of Paphlagonia on the southern shore of the Black Sea.

Aegilus: A deme of Attica on the Greek mainland, but in *Idyll* I possibly a deme of Cos.

Aegina: An island near Attica in central Greece.

Aegle: One of the Hesperides, nymphs who live in Atlas' garden.

Aenete: Mother of Cyzicus, king of the Doliones.

Aeneus: Father of Cyzicus, king of the Doliones.

Aeolids: A people of the western Peloponnesus, descendants of Aeolus, the father of Cretheus and Athamas.

Aeolus: 1. King of the winds. 2. A son of Zeus, father of Cretheus and Athamas. 3. In the *Hymn to Demeter,* father of Canace, mother of Triopas.

Aesepus: A river near the Hellespont in Asia Minor.

Aeson: Son of Cretheus and father of Jason. King of Iolcus in Thessaly in northern Greece. Deposed and killed by his half-brother Pelias while Jason was on his Argonautic expedition.

Aesonis: A city of Magnesia in northeastern Greece.

Aethalia: An island on the west coast of Italy, now Elba.

Aethalides: Son of Hermes, the Argonauts' herald.

Aetna: Volcanic mountain in Sicily.

Aetolian: Of Aetolia, a district in central Greece.

Agamemnon: Greek hero of the Trojan War.

Agamestor: A local hero of the Boeotians, a people of central Greece.

Agenor: 1. Father of Cadmus and Europa. King of Phoenicia. 2. Father of Phineus, the blind seer.

Agesilaus: A name for Hades. Means "leader of the peoples."

Ajax: Greek hero of the Trojan War.

Akeses: The pilot of Neleus, king of Pylos, who always waited for the full moon, so "Akeses' moon" means the time for action.

Alae Araphenides: An Attic deme between Marathon and Brauron with a temple of Artemis.

Alcaeus: A lyric poet of the late seventh–early sixth century B.C. of Mitylene on Lesbos.

Alcimede: Mother of Jason.

Alcinous: King of the Phaeacians, whom Apollonius places on the island of Drepane (Corcyra).

Alcmena: Mother of Heracles and Iphicles. Wife of Amphitryon but ravished by Zeus, who was the true father of Heracles.

Alcon: Father of the Argonaut Phalerus.

Aleus: Father of the Argonauts Amphidamas and Cepheus.

Aloeus: Father of Otus and Ephialtes, giants who tried to conquer the gods of Olympus.

Alope: A city of Thessaly in northern Greece.

Amarantian: Colchian. Epithet of the river Phasis, because its source was in the Amarantine mountains. The Amarantes were a people of Colchis.

Armarantine mountains: Located in Colchis at the eastern end of the Black Sea.

Amazons: A race of women warriors who lived on the southern shore of the Black Sea.

Ambracia: A province of northwestern Greece.

Amnisus: A river of Crete.

Amphidamas: An Argonaut, son of Aleus.

Amphion: 1. An Argonaut, son of Hyperasius. 2. Son of Zeus and Antiope; rebuilt Thebes with his brother Zethus.

Amphipolitan: Of Amphipolis, a town of Macedonia, northern Greece.

Amphithemis: Also called Garamas; son of Apollo and Acacallis; father of the Libyan Caphaurus.

Amphitrite: A sea goddess; wife of Poseidon.

Amphitryon: Heracles' mortal father.

Amphrysus: A river in Thessaly where Apollo tended the flocks of Admetus.

Ampycus: Father of the Argonaut Mopsus the seer.

Amyclae: A city of Laconia in the Peloponnesus.

Amycus: King of the Bebrycians, a people of the southern shore of the Black Sea near the Bosporus.

Amymone: 1. A spring at Argos in the northern Peloponnesus. 2. Daughter of Danaus and mother of Nauplius, an ancestor of the Argonaut Nauplius.

Amyntas: In *Idyll* VII probably a real person but otherwise unknown.

Amyrus: A river of Thessaly in northern Greece.

Anacreon: A lyric poet born in Teos in Lydia, Asia Minor, ca. 570 B.C.

Anaphe: An island of the Sporades, an island chain southeast of the Cyclades in the Aegean Sea.

Anapus: A river of Sicily near Syracuse.

Anaurus: A river of Thessaly, northern Greece.

Ancaeus: 1. Son of Lycurgus. 2. Son of Poseidon. Both are Argonauts.

Anchiale: A nymph, mother of the Dactyls of Crete.

Anchises: Lover of Aphrodite. Father of Aeneas.

Andromeda: Daughter of the Ethiopian king Cepheus and of Cassiopeia. Exposed to a sea monster and rescued by Perseus.

Angurum: A mountain in Scythia, to the north of Greece.

Anthemoeisian lake: A lake in Bithynia, a land on the eastern shore of the Propontis.

Anthemoessa: The island of the Sirens in the Tyrrhenian Sea off the west coast of Italy.

Antianeira: Mother of the Argonauts Erytus and Echion.

Anticleia: Mother of Odysseus.

Antigenes: In Idyll VII probably a real person but otherwise unknown.

Antiope: 1. Daughter of Asopus; mother of Amphion and Zethus. In another version she was the daughter of Nycteus, who tried to kill her when he discovered she was pregnant by Zeus. 2. A queen of the Amazons.

Antipater of Sidon: Epigrammatist of the *Greek Anthology*. Fl. ca. 130 B.C.

Anvil of Tiryns: Heracles. Tiryns was a city in the Peloponnesus.

Anyte: A woman poet of Tegea in Arcadia. Fl. ca. 300 B.C.

Aonian: Boeotian.

Apelles: Famous Greek painter. Fourth century B.C.

Aphareus: Father of the Argonaut Idas, thus the epithet Aphareian for Idas. He was also the father of Lynceus.

Apheidas: A hero of Arcadia, a district in the central Peloponnesus.

Aphrodite: Goddess of love.

Apidaneans: The Arcadians, a people of the central Peloponnesus.

Apidanus: A river of Thessaly in northern Greece.

Apis: A name of the Peloponnesus.

Apollo: Son of Zeus and Leto. God of light, music, and healing.

Apollonius of Rhodes: Poet and grammarian. Fl. 222–181 B.C. Pupil of Callimachus. Taught rhetoric in Rhodes. Returned to Alexandria and succeeded Zenodotus as chief librarian there. Author of the *Argonautica.*

Apsyrtians: People of the Apsyrtides, islands in the Adriatic; they are supposed to be named after Medea's brother Apsyrtus.

Apsyrtus: Son of Aeetes. Brother of Medea.

Araethyrea: Hometown of the Argonaut Phlias in the eastern Peloponnesus.

Aratus: 1. Lived at Soli in Cilicia, Asia Minor. Fl. 270 B.C. Spent the latter part of his life at the court of Antigonus Gonatas in Macedonia. Author of the *Phaenomena,* an astronomical poem, which was translated by Cicero into Latin. 2. A friend of Theocritus, mentioned in *Idylls* VI and VII. Probably not the same as the poet Aratus of Soli.

Araxis: A river of Colchis on the eastern end of the Black Sea.

Arcadia: A province in the Peloponnesus associated especially with Pan. The Arcadians were known for their backward ways.

Archilochus: Iambic and elegiac poet, born on Paros ca. 700 B.C.

Arcturus: A very large and bright star in the constellation Boötes. Its rising marks the beginning of autumn.

Areius: An Argonaut, son of Bias.

Arene: A city of Messenia in the southern Peloponnesus.

Ares: God of war.

Arestor: Father of the Argonaut Argus.

Arete: Wife of Alcinous, king of the Phaeacians.

Arethusa: A fountain on the island of Ortygia at Syracuse. Originally a Nereid nymph, in pursuit of whom the river Alpheus dived underground.

Aretus: One of the Bebrycians.

Arganthonian mountain: A mountain of Bithynia on the eastern end of the Propontis.

Arges: One of the Cyclopes.

Argive: 1. Of Argos, a city of Argolis in the Peloponnesus. 2. Commonly used for the Greeks in general.

Argo: A ship of the Argonauts, built by Argus (the son of Arestor) with the goddess Athena's help.

Argonauts: The crew of the Argo: Jason and his companions.

Argos: City in the northeast Peloponnesus. Sometimes refers to a larger surrounding district, or used for Greece in general.

Argus: 1. Son of Arestor, an Argonaut. 2. The guardian with eyes all over his body whom Hera out of her jealousy set to watch Io. Hermes beguiled him to sleep and so slew him. From his blood arose the peacock, with a hundred eyes on its tail. 3. A son of Phrixus, one of four who joined the Argonauts at the isle of Ares in the western Black Sea.

Ariadne: Daughter of King Minos of Crete. She supplied Theseus with the thread that led him out of the labyrinth. Later Theseus abandoned her on the island of Dia.

Aristaeus: Son of Apollo and the nymph Cyrene. Father of Actaeon. Founder of bee-keeping.

Aristis: In *Idyll* VII probably a real poet of Cos.

Arsinoa: Wife and Sister of Ptolemy II Philadelphus of Egypt.

Artaceus: One of the Doliones.

Artacie: A spring near Cyzicus, on the southern shore of the Propontis.

Artemis: Goddess of the hunt, childbirth, the moon. In *Idyll* I she seems to be identified with Hecate.

Asbystian: The Asbystes were a people in Cyrenaica (Libya), North Africa.

Asclepiades: An epigrammatist of the *Greek Anthology.* Contemporary of Theocritus. Third century B.C.

Ascra: A town in Boeotia, central Greece. Birthplace of the poet Hesiod.

Asia: The continent.

Asopus: 1. A river of the Peloponnesus. 2. Father of Sinope, who tricked Zeus into letting her keep her virginity. 3. Father of Corcyra, whom Poseidon loved.

Assyria: A country in Asia Minor on the southern shore of the Black Sea.

Asterion: An Argonaut, son of Cometes.

Asterius: An Argonaut, son of Hyperasius.

Asterodeia: A nymph who was mother of Apsyrtus by Aeetes.

Astraeus: Father of the stars.

Astypalaea: Mother of the Argonaut Ancaeus, the son of Poseidon.

Atalanta: A maiden of Arcadia who took an important part in the Calydonian boar hunt. Meleager gave her the head and hide of the boar as a prize. By some accounts an Argonaut, but Apollonius has Jason refuse her request to join the expedition.

Athamantian plain: A plain in Phthia in central Greece, named for Athamas.

Athamas: Son of Aeolus; father of Phrixus and Helle. King of Orchomenus in Boeotia, central Greece.

Athena: Goddess of wisdom and protectress of heroes.

Athos: A mountain in northern Greece.

Atlas: A Titan who was said to support the sky on his shoulders.

Atreus: Father of Agamemnon and Menelaus.

Attic isle: Salamis, an island off the coast of Attica, central Greece.

Augeias: An Argonaut, son of Helios.

Aulion: A cave of Paphlagonia on the southern shore of the Black Sea.

Aulis: A city of Boeotia in central Greece.

Ausonian: Italian.

Autesion: Father of Theras, who gave his name to one of the Cyclades, Thera.

Autolycus: One of three brothers, sons of Deimachus and former companions of Heracles, who joined the Argonauts in Assyria.

Azanian: Of Azania in Arcadia in the Peloponnesus.

Azilis: A place of uncertain location in Libya where Battus and the people from Thera dwelt for six years before founding Cyrene.

Bacchiadae: A family of Ephyra (Corinth) on the Peloponnesus who settled on the island of the Phaeacians.

Basileus: One of the Doliones.

Bassus: An epigrammatist of the *Greek Anthology*. First century A.D.

Battus: I. Founder of the Greek colony Cyrene in Libya, North Africa, birthplace of the poet Callimachus. His real name was Aristotle. "Battus" was thought to mean "stutterer," but probably meant "king." 2. Father of the poet Callimachus (Epigram XXXV). Epigram XXI is in his voice. Battus' father was Callimachus the general.

Baucis: A friend of the poet Erinna.

Bear: The constellation.

Bearded One: Pan.

Bebrycia: An area on the southern shore of the Black Sea near the Bosporus; same as Bithynia. The Bebrycians were known as a warlike people; their king Amycus forced strangers to fight with him.

Becheiri: People of the southeastern shore of the Black Sea near Colchis.

Bellerophon: Corinthian hero. Owner of the winged horse Pegasus.

Berecynthian: Name of a mountain range in Phrygia, Asia Minor.

Berenice: Wife of Ptolemy I Soter and mother of Ptolemy II Philadelphus of Egypt. Deified after her death.

Bias: Father of Talaus and Areius, two Argonauts from Argolis in the Peloponnesus.

Billaeus: A river of Paphlagonia on the southern shore of the Black Sea.

Bion: Bucolic poet of Smyrna in Asia Minor. Fl. 100 B.C. Spent last years of his life in Sicily, where he was poisoned.

Bistonian: Thracian.

Bithynian: Of Bithynia, an area on the southern shore of the Black Sea near the Bosporus.

Black Beach: A promontory in Bithynia near the river Rhebas.

Blemyes: A tribe that lived on the eastern bank of the Nile on the southern border of Egypt. They were subject to the Ethiopians.

Blessed Ones: The gods.

Boedromius: An epithet of Apollo. Means "running to a cry for help."

Boeotia: A province of central Greece, northwest of Attica.

Boötes: The northern constellation containing the bright star Arcturus. He appears to be driving the Great Bear.

Boreas: The north or northeast wind; father of the Argonauts Zetes and Calais.

Bosporus: The narrow strait between the Propontis and the Black Sea where the Clashing Rocks were located.

Bourina: A spring southwest of the town of Cos.

Brimo: A name of Hecate.

Britomartis: Also called Dictyna, a Cretan goddess sometimes identified with Artemis.

Brontes: One of the Cyclopes.

Brygean islands: Off the coast of Illyria on the northern Adriatic Sea.

Brygi: People of Illyria on the northern Adriatic Sea.

Butes: An Argonaut, son of Teleon.

Byblis: A spring in Miletus, a city of Caria, Asia Minor.

Byzeres: A people of the southeastern shore of the Black Sea near Colchis.

Cadmeians: Descendants of Cadmus. A name for Thebans.

Cadmus: Founder of Thebes and brother of Europa. Father of Autonoë (*Bath of Pallas*), Polydorus, Ino, Semele.

Caeneus: Father of the Argonaut Coronus.

Caeratus: A river near Cnossus in Crete.

Calais: An Argonaut, son of Boreas and brother of Zetes.

Calaureia: An island in the Saronic Gulf off Corinth in central Greece.

Callichorus: 1. A well at Eleusis in central Greece. 2. A river of Paphlagonia on the southern shore of the Black Sea.

Callimachus: Born in Cyrene, North Africa. Lived and worked in Alexandria. Cataloger of the great library there from ca. 260 B.C. until his death in ca. 240 B.C. Wrote poetry of many genres, including hymns, epigrams, and aetiological works.

Calliope: The Muse of epic poetry; mother of the Argonaut Orpheus.

Calliste: An island in the Aegean Sea later known as Thera.

Calpe: A river of Bithynia, on the southern shore of the Black Sea near the Bosporus.

Calydna: The name of several Aegean islands. The one in *Idyll* I may be Calymnos, northwest of Cos.

Calydon: A city in Aetolia in western Greece; home of the Argonaut Meleager.

Calypso: Daughter of Atlas with whom Odysseus spent seven years on the island of Ogygia.

Canace: The mother of Triopas by Poseidon.

Canastra: A headland of the Chalcidice Peninsula on the northern coast of the Aegean.

Canethus: Father of the Argonaut Canthus.

Canthus: An Argonaut.

Caphaurus: A Libyan who killed the Argonaut Canthus.

Carambis: A headland in Paphlagonia on the southern shore of the Black Sea.

Carnean: The feast of Apollo Carneius.

Carneius: An epithet of Apollo in many Dorian states, for example, Sparta, Thera, Cyrene.

Carpathus: An Aegean island to the east of Crete.

Caspian Sea: An inland sea in central Asia Minor. Visualized by Apollonius as a gulf of the river Ocean, which encircled the earth.

Castalia: A spring on Mount Parnassus sacred to Apollo and the Muses.

Castor: 1. Argonaut from Lacedaemon in the Peloponnesus. One of the Dioscuri, twin sons of Zeus (Polydeuces was his twin); brother of Helen. He was a famous horse-trainer. 2. Son of Hippalus. Not known outside *Idyll* **XXIV**. Apparently not the twin of Polydeuces.

Caucasus: The mountain range, near Colchis, which separates Europe from Asia. The Titan Prometheus was chained there as punishment for giving fire to men.

Cauliacus: A rock in the Balkans visible from the river Ister on its supposed passage from the Black Sea to the Adriatic.

Cayster: A river in Lydia, Asia Minor.

Cecropia: A name for Attica, a district in central Greece.

Cecrops: An early mythological king of Athens.

Celadon: A river apparently between Pylos and Arcadia in the Peloponnesus.

Celts: People of western Europe, especially those living along the rivers Eridanus (Po) and Rhone.

Centaurs: A race of half-horse, half-man creatures, known for their savagery; they lived in Magnesia in northern Greece.

Ceos: An island of the Cyclades in the Aegean Sea.

Cephalus: The husband of Procris and son of Deioneus.

Cepheus: An Argonaut, son of Aleus.

Ceraunian Mountains: Mountains lying to the north of Epirus in northwestern Greece.

Ceraunian Sea: The Adriatic off the northwest coast of Italy.

Cerinthus: City of Euboea, the long island off the coast of central Greece.

Cerossus: An island off the coast of Illyria in the Adriatic.

Ceryl: A seabird, perhaps the tern or sea swallow.

Ceryneian: Of Mount Ceryneia between Arcadia and Achaea in the Peloponnesus where Heracles took the hind.

Ceyx: Husband of Alcyone. Changed with her into a seabird.

Chadesians: A tribe of Amazons living on the southern shore of the Black Sea.

Chalciope: Daughter of Aeetes. Sister of Medea.

Chalcodonian peak: A mountain in Thessaly in northern Greece.

Chalybes: A people of the southern shore of the Black Sea, known for their metallurgy.

Chaos: The shapeless mass out of which the universe was made.

Chariclo: Wife of Everes and mother of Teiresias.

Charybdis: A sea monster, visualized as a whirlpool opposite Scylla at the entrance to the straits between Italy and Sicily.

Chersonese: A peninsula of Thrace that forms the northern coast of the Hellespont.

Chesian: Of Chesion, a cape on the island of Samos in the Aegean.

Chian: Of Chios, an island in the Aegean. "Chian bard" is a name for Homer, since he is sometimes said to have been born on Chios.

Cheiron: The famous centaur, half man, half horse, who reared several Greek heroes, including Jason and Achilles.

Chromis of Libya: Not known to be a real person. His Libyan origin would suggest that he was a singer of pastoral songs and probably therefore a Greek.

Chytus: A harbor of Cyzicus on the southern shore of the Propontis.

Cian, or Cianian: From Cius.

Cimmerians: A people living north of the Black Sea.

Cinyras: Mythical King of Assyria or Cyprus; father of Myrrha, and by her of Adonis.

Circaean plain: A plain near Colchis on the eastern end of the Black Sea.

Circe: An enchantress, daughter of the sun, sister of Aeetes; lived on the island of Aeaea. Later visited by Odysseus.

Cissaetha: The name of a goat in *Idyll* I. Probably connected with the word for ivy, on which goats feed.

Cius: 1. A city of Mysia on the western end of the Propontis. 2. A river in the same area.

Clarius: Epithet of Apollo, from Claros.

Claros: A sanctuary of Apollo in Ionia on the western shore of Asia Minor.

Clashing Rocks: The rocks at the northern mouth of the Bosporus. See Cyanean rocks.

Cleite: 1. Wife of Cyzicus, king of the Doliones, whom the Argonauts killed by mistake on their way through the Propontis. 2. A spring named after Cleite, who hanged herself in grief for her husband.

Cleombrotus: A pupil of Plato.

Cleopatra: Wife of the blind seer Phineus.

Clio: The Muse of history.

Clymene: Maternal grandmother of Jason.

Clytia: In *Idyll* VII a mythical ancestor of Phrasidamus and Antigenes but otherwise unknown. Said to have married Eurypylus, son of Poseidon.

Clytius: An Argonaut, son of Eurytus.

Clytonaeus: Father of the Argonaut Nauplius.

Cnidus: A city in Caria, Asia Minor.

Cnossus: A city of Crete, famous as the seat of King Minos.

Cocytus: A river of the underworld.

Coeus: A Titan, father of Leto.

Colchis: A country on the eastern shore of the Black Sea. Ruled by Aeetes.

Colone: A rock of Bithynia, on the western end of the Black Sea near the Bosporus.

Comatas: According to one account, a herdsman who sacrificed animals from his master's flock to the Muses. His master therefore shut him up in a chest and two months later found him alive and the chest filled with honeycomb. This happened at Mount Thalamus near Thurii in southern Italy.

Cometes: Father of the Argonaut Asterion.

Concord: Personified goddess for whom the Argonauts built a shrine on the island of Thynias off the coast of Bithynia in the Black Sea.

Corcyra: 1. Daughter of Asopus, whom Poseidon carried away and settled on an island in the Adriatic. 2. The island named for the girl Corcyra which Apollonius calls Corcyra the Black. Modern-day Corcyra is referred to in the *Argonautica* as Drepane.

Corinth: A city in central Greece.

Coroneia: A city of Boeotia in central Greece.

Coronis: Mother of Asclepius by Apollo, killed by Artemis for infidelity.

Coronus: An Argonaut, the son of Caeneus.

Corycian: Of Corcyrus: 1. A mountain, city, or cave in Cilicia, Asia Minor. Famous for saffron. 2. A cave of Mount Parnassus in central Greece, inhabited by nymphs.

Cos: An island in the Aegean. A center of the cult of Asclepius.

Crab: The constellation Cancer.

Crannon: A place in Thessaly in northern Greece.

Crataeis: A name of Hecate.

Creion: The hill to which Eumedes took the Palladium.

Crete: A large island in the Mediterranean, center of the prehistoric Minoan civilization. The Cretans had reputations as liars and pirates.

Cretheus: Grandfather of Jason and brother of Athamas.

Crinagoras: Epigrammatist of the *Greek Anthology.* First century B.C.–first century A.D.

Crobialus: A city of Paphlagonia on the southern shore of the Black Sea.

Cromna: A city of Paphlagonia on the southern shore of the Black Sea.

Cronian Sea: The northern part of the Adriatic Sea.

Cronus: A Titan, the father of Zeus.

Ctimene: A city in Thessaly in northern Greece, home of the Argonaut Eurydamas.

Ctimenus: Father of the Argonaut Eurydamas.

Curalius: A river of Boeotia near Coroneia, central Greece.

Curetes: 1. The armed deities who reared Zeus in a cave on Mount Ida in Crete. 2. A people of Acarnania in western Greece.

Cyanean rocks: Also called the Symplegades or the Plegades. The Clashing Rocks at the northern mouth of the Bosporus. Once the Argo passed safely through the rocks, they never clashed again but became firmly rooted.

Cyclopes: Three giants who forged Zeus' weapons — lightning and thunder.

Cydonia: A town on the north coast of Crete.

Cyllenus: One of the Dactyls.

Cynthian: Of Cynthus, a mountain on the island of Delos in the Aegean.

Cypris: A name for Aphrodite, also called the Cyprian goddess.

Cyre: A stream in Cyrene. It runs underground for a distance and reappears at the temple of Apollo as the Fountain of Apollo.

Cyrene: 1. Daughter of Hypseus. A nymph beloved of Apollo; mother of Aristaeus. 2. A city in Libya, North Africa, named for the nymph.

Cyrnus: Corsica, an island in the Mediterranean.

Cytaean: Colchian, after the city Cytae, birthplace of Medea.

Cythera: An island off the south coast of the Peloponnesus, sacred to Aphrodite.

Cytherea, or Cythereia: Aphrodite, from the island Cythera.

Cytissorus: A son of Phrixus.

Cytorus: A city of Paphlagonia on the southern shore of the Black Sea.

Cyzicus: 1. King of the Doliones, a people of the southern coast of the Propontis. 2. The city ruled by Cyzicus.

Dactyls: Minor deities who had their origin in Crete on Mount Ida, but were associates of the Great Mother goddess in Asia Minor. They were skilled in metalworking, medicine, and sorcery.

Daira: Hecate.

Danaans or Danai: A name for the Greeks.

Danae: Mother of the hero Perseus. Her father Acrisius placed her and the child in a box, which he cast into the sea.

Danaus: Brother of Aegyptus, father of the fifty Danaids, and founder of Argos. An ancestor of the Greeks. Apollonius connects him with the Argonaut Nauplius.

Daphnis: A Sicilian cowherd, beloved of a nymph, to whom he swore eternal fidelity. In *Idyll* I he seems to be dying of love for a mortal girl who pursues him, but the story behind the *Idyll* is obscure.

Dardania: A city of the Hellespont.

Dascylus: 1. Father of Lycus, king of the Mariandyni. 2. Son of Lycus.

Deileon: One of the three sons of Deimachus, former companions of Heracles, who joined the Argonauts in Assyria.

Deimachus: Father of Deileon, Autolycus, and Phlogion, who joined the Argonauts in Assyria.

Deioneus: Father of Cephalus.

Delian: Of Delos.

Delos: An island in the Cyclades, sacred as the birthplace of Apollo and Artemis. Also called Ortygia.

Delphians: People who live at Delphi, the famous sanctuary of Apollo in Phocis, central Greece.

Delphyne: A dragon of Parnassus in central Greece, killed by the young Apollo. This monster is also known as the Python.

Demeter: Goddess of agriculture. Mother of Persephone, who was carried off by Hades.

Deo: A name for Demeter.

Deucalion: Son of Prometheus, who brought the Greeks civilized institutions such as cities and temples. In another story, Deucalion and his wife alone survived the great flood and repeopled the earth with stones that they threw over their shoulders.

Dia: An old name for the island of Naxos in the Aegean, where Ariadne was abandoned by Theseus.

Dictaean: Of Mount Dicte, in Crete, where Zeus was supposedly reared. Other stories say he grew up in a cave on Mount Ida in Crete.

Dictaeon: Mountain on Crete named for the nymph Dictyna.

Dicte: A mountain on Crete. Some stories say that Zeus was reared there in a cave.

Dictyna: A Cretan goddess, also called Britomartis. An associate of Artemis and sometimes identified with her.

Dindymum: Mountain on a peninsula in the southern Propontis, near the city of Cyzicus. The Argonauts made a shrine there to the mother of the gods, Rhea.

Diogenes the Dog: The Cynic philosopher born in Sinope of Pontus, Asia Minor. Later lived in Athens. Known for his sour disposition and acid tongue. The term Cynic comes from the Greek word for dog and reflects the Greeks' contempt for the school's style of life.

Diomedes: One of the major warriors in the *Iliad.* In Book 5.330ff. Diomedes wounds Aphrodite and drives her from the battlefield.

Dione: Mother of Aphrodite, but in *Idyll* VII she seems to be Aphrodite herself.

Dionysus: The god of wine.

Dioscorides: Epigrammatist of the *Greek Anthology.* Late third century B.C. Probably lived in Alexandria.

Diotimus: Nothing is known of this poet but he probably wrote in the third century B.C.

Dipsacus: A Bithynian, son of the river Phyllis and a nymph. He gave shelter to Phrixus on his journey toward Colchis with the golden ram.

Dodona: Zeus' oracle in northwestern Greece. There the priests interpreted Zeus' will from the sound of the wind in a grove of oak trees.

Dodonian oak: A beam in the keel of the Argo, brought by Athena from Zeus' sacred groves in Dodona. This beam gave Argo the power of speech.

Doeantian plain: A plain on the southern coast of the Black Sea in Assyria inhabited by the Amazons.

Doeas: A hero for whom the Doeantian plain was named.

Dog Star: The star Sirius.

Doliche: Either Euboea, an island east of central Greece, or Icaros, an island off Lycia, Asia Minor.

Doliones: A people of the southern coast of the Propontis, ruled by Cyzicus. They welcomed the Argonauts but later fought them by mistake.

Dolopian: Of the hero Dolops. An epithet of the city Ctimene in Thessaly.

Dolops: A hero whose tomb the Argonauts visited on the coast of Magnesia in northern Greece.

Dorian: Refers to a tribe of Greeks who settled in Corinth, Sparta, and much of the Peloponnesus. They were distinguished by their dialect, which featured broad *a*'s.

Dotium: A place in Thessaly, northern Greece.

Drepane: The island of the Phaeacians off the coast of northwestern Greece. The name means "sickle isle." The island was later known as Corcyra.

Dryopians: An impious people punished by Heracles. He killed Theiodamas, a Dryopian, and took his son Hylas to be a servant.

Dysceladus: One of the Liburnian islands in the Adriatic Sea off the coast of Illyria.

Earth: A goddess, considered to be the mother of many mythological figures.

Earth-born: See giants.

Earth-shaker: Poseidon, the god of earthquakes.

Echetus: A wicked king of Epirus, northwest Greece. He poked out his daughter's eyes when he learned of her lover Aechmodicus.

Echinades: Islands at the mouth of the Achelous River in Aetolia in central Greece.

Echion: An Argonaut, son of Hermes.

Echo: A wood nymph, echo personified.

Edonian hills: Named for the Edoni, a Thracian tribe south of the range of Rhodope in northern Greece.

Egypt: The country in eastern North Africa.

Eidyia: Wife of Aeetes, King of Colchis.

Eilatides: "Son of Eilatus," the Argonaut Polyphemus.

Eilatus: Father of the Argonaut Polyphemus.

Eileithyia: Goddess of childbirth.

Elare: The mother of the giant Tityos, who tried to rape Leto. Leto's son Apollo killed Tityos.

Eleans: People of Elis, a district in the northern Peloponnesus. They were ruled by the Argonaut Augeias.

Electra: Daughter of the Titan Atlas. The isle of Electra is Samothrace in the northern Aegean.

Electris: An island located by Apollonius at the mouth of the Eridanus (Po) in the northern Adriatic Sea.

Electryon: A king of Mycenae whose sons fought raiders called the Teleboae or Taphians.

Eleusis: City in central Greece, where the Mysteries were celebrated. Sacred to Demeter.

Elysian field: Home of the heroes in the underworld.

Encheleans: An Illyrian people living in the Ceraunian Mountains in northwestern Greece.

Endymion: The beautiful sleeping youth with whom the Moon fell in love. He was a shepherd of Latmus, a mountain in Caria in Asia Minor.

Eneteian: Paphlagonian, of the land on the southern shore of the Black Sea.

Enipeus: A river of Thessaly in northern Greece.

Enna: A city of Sicily.

Enyalius: Epithet of Ares, means "warlike."

Enyo: A Greek goddess of battle. Companion of Ares.

Ephesus: A city of Lydia, Asia Minor.

Ephyra: An old name for Corinth, a city in the Peloponnesus near the isthmus.

Epidaurus: A town in the central Peloponnesus. A center of the cult of Asclepius.

Epio: "Gentle one." A daughter of Asclepius.

Erato: Muse of amorous poetry.

Erechtheus: A mythical king of Athens.

Erginus: 1. An Argonaut, son of Poseidon. 2. A river in Thrace in northern Greece.

Eribotes: An Argonaut, son of Teleon.

Eridanus: The river Po in northern Italy.

Erinna: A woman poet of either Theos or Lesbos. An ancient source gives her *floruit* as 353–52 B.C.

Erinys: A Fury or spirit of vengeance.

Eros: Son of Aphrodite. Cupid.

Erymanthian marsh: A marsh in Arcadia in the Peloponnesus.

Erysichthon: Son of Triopas. In most versions of the tale he is old enough to have a grown daughter.

Erytheis: One of the Hesperides, nymphs who live in Atlas' garden.

Erythini: A town in Paphlagonia on the southern shore of the Black Sea.

Erythraean: From Erythraea, a town in Aetolia or Boeotia, central Greece.

Erytus: An Argonaut, son of Hermes.

Eryx: A mountain in Sicily sacred to Aphrodite.

Etesian winds: Winds that blow in the Aegean every year for forty days from the rising of Sirius.

Ethiopia: A country in Africa, south of Egypt.

Ethiopians: 1. A people of Africa, south of Egypt. 2. In the *Argonautica,* people who live on the farthest edges of the world, either on the western or the eastern shores of the river Ocean.

Euboea: A long island off the east coast of central Greece.

Eucritus: In *Idyll* VII probably a real person but otherwise unknown.

Eumedes: Suspected by the Argives of intending to betray the Palladium (a carved image of Pallas, originally at Troy) to the Heracleidae, Eumedes took it to the hill called Creion.

Eumolpus: This figure (in *Idyll* XXIV) is otherwise unknown.

Eunice: A nymph.

Euphemus: An Argonaut, son of Poseidon.

Eupolemeia: Mother of the Argonaut Aethalides.

Euripus: The strait between the island of Euboea and the mainland of Greece.

Europa: 1. Daughter of Agenor, king of Phoenicia. Zeus, in the form of a bull, carried her off to Crete. 2. Daughter of Tityos; mother of the Argonaut Euphemus.

Europe: The continent.

Eurotas: A river in Laconia, the southern Peloponnesus.

Eurydamas: An Argonaut, son of Ctimenus.

Eurydice: Orpheus' wife. See Orpheus.

Eurymedon: A name of the hero Perseus.

Eurymenae: A city in Thessaly in northern Greece.

Eurynome: A daughter of Ocean. She and her husband Ophion ruled Olympus but were cast out by Cronus and Rhea.

Eurypylus: 1. Prehistoric king of Libya. 2. Another name for the sea god Triton, the son of Poseidon.

Eurystheus: King of Mycenae for whom Heracles accomplished his twelve labors.

Eurytion: An Argonaut, son of Irus.

Eurytus: A famous archer and king of Oechalia of Euboea, Greece. Father of the Argonauts Clytius and Iphitus.

Eusorus: Father of Aenete and grandfather of Cyzicus, king of the Doliones.

Everes: Father of the seer Teiresias.

Fair Mouth: A mouth of the Ister (Danube) River in the Black Sea.

Fair Harbor: The harbor at Cyzicus on the southern shore of the Propontis.

Far-Archer: Epithet of Apollo.

Fates: In *Argonautica* I a translation of Keres, the death spirits.

Floating Islands: The Strophades, islands in the Ionian Sea.

Furies: The Erinyes, spirits of vengeance.

Galatea: 1. One of the Nereids, daughter of Nereus and Doris, a nymph of the sea. 2. The name of a work by Callimachus that apparently dealt with the Nereid Galatea.

Ganymede: Cupbearer to Zeus, who, enamored of his beauty, had carried him off to heaven.

Garamas: Another name for Amphithemis, a Libyan hero and son of Apollo.

Genetaean promontory: A cape near the land of the Tibareni on the southern shore of the Black Sea.

Gephyrus: One of the Doliones.

Geraestus: A promontory of the island of Euboea off central Greece.

Giants: Earth-born men of a wild and savage nature.

Glaucus: A sea god.

Golgi: A place in Cypris, seat of Aphrodite.

Gorgon: In the *Argonautica,* Medusa, one of three Gorgon sisters. Medusa was decapitated by Perseus.

Gortynian: Of Gortyn, a city in Crete.

Graces: Lovely sisters, usually three in number and of divine, though variously given, parentage. They are commonly associated with Aphrodite.

Graucenii: Scythians who lived on the shore of the Ister River to the north of Greece.

Gyrton: A city of Thessaly in northern Greece.

Hades: The underworld, home of the dead; also the god thereof, Death.

Haemonia: A name for Thessaly.

Haemonian rock: The site of a sanctuary of Poseidon on the Peneus River in Thessaly in northern Greece.

Haemus: A mountain range in Thessaly, northern Greece.

Hagnias: Father of Tiphys, the pilot of the Argo.

Halcyon: A half-mythical seabird, often identified with the European kingfisher.

Haleis: The name of a deme on Cos but in *Idyll* VII probably the name of a stream within the deme.

Haliartus: A town in Boeotia, central Greece.

Halicarnassian: Of the city Halicarnassus in Caria, Asia Minor.

Halys: A river of Paphlagonia on the southern shore of the Black Sea.

Hamadryad: An oak tree nymph.

Harmonia: 1. A nymph, mother of the Amazon race by Ares. 2. Wife of the Theban king Cadmus.

Harpalycus (of Panopeus): Not known outside *Idyll XXIV*.

Harpies: Female monsters with bird bodies and human heads.

Hebrus: Chief river of Thrace in northern Greece.

Hecale: An impoverished old woman of noble descent in whose hut Theseus took refuge from a storm when on his way to subdue the bull at Marathon. Also the title of Callimachus' epyllion on this story.

Hecate: A goddess of the night, the underworld, magic, crossroads, graves. Sometimes identified with Artemis or the moon. Accompanied by dogs of the Styx and spirits of the dead. Protectress of enchantresses, including Medea.

Hector: Son of Hecuba and Priam. Chief Trojan hero of the Trojan War.

Hecuba: Wife of Priam, king of Troy. Mother of Hector.

Helen: Wife of the Greek hero Menelaus. Consort of the Trojan Paris. The most beautiful woman in the world and the cause of the Trojan War.

Helice: 1. Also known as Callisto. Daughter of Lycaon and mother of the twins Pan and Arcas. Arcas' tomb seems to have been on Mount Maenalus in Arcadia. 2. The constellation the Great Bear.

Helicon: A mountain in Boeotia, central Greece. Sacred to Apollo and the Muses.

Helios: The sun god.

Hellas: Greece.

Helle: Sister of Phrixus. The two children escaped their wicked stepmother on the back of a golden ram sent by Zeus, but Helle fell into the sea at the narrow strait called the Hellespont.

Hellespont: The strait between the Aegean and the Propontis, named for Phrixus' sister Helle.

Hephaestus: A fire god. Son of Hera, husband of Aphrodite. Portrayed as a lame smithy.

Hera: The wife and sister of Zeus. The goddess of marriage.

Heracleitus: In Epigram II a poet and friend of Callimachus, not the Ionian philosopher. The "nightingales" in the epigram are his poems.

Heracles: The great hero of Greece, known especially for his twelve labors. Son of Zeus and Alcmena.

Hercynian rock: A rock or mountain in the land of the Celts (probably in Germany).

Hermes: The messenger of the gods, son of Maia and Zeus.

Herodas: Poet, probably of third century B.C., perhaps of Cos. Wrote mimes.

Hesiod: Poet of Boeotia. Seventh century B.C. Wrote a *Theogony* and the *Works and Days*, which Aratus' *Phaenomena* resembles.

Hespere: One of the Hesperides, nymphs who live in Atlas' garden.

Hesperides: Nymphs whose name means "daughters of the west". They are usually located in the far west, but Apollonius places them in Libya, where they guard the golden apples of immortality with the help of the serpent Ladon.

Hesperus: The evening star.

Hestia: Goddess of the family hearth.

Hië Paeëon: "Hail, healer." Hië (spelled ië in Herodas IV) is a cry of joy but suggests in its sound the Greek word for "shoot" (an arrow) as well.

Himera: The name of two rivers in Sicily; also the name of a town on one of these rivers.

Hippo: Queen of the Amazons. Probably the same as Hippolyte.

Hippodameia: Daughter of Oenomaus and wife of Pelops, who won her from her father in a chariot race.

Hippolyte: A queen of the Amazons. The capture of her girdle was one of Heracles' labors.

Hippotas: Father of Aeolus, king of the winds.

Hippuris: One of the Sporades, islands in the southern Aegean.

Homer: The poet of the *Iliad* and the *Odyssey*. Fl. 750 B.C.

Homole: The name of a mountain in Thessaly, northern Greece, on the north of the Ossa range; also a town in the area. Theocritus in *Idyll* VII probably means the town.

Hours: Goddesses of the seasons.

Hyacinthus: One of the Doliones.

Hyantian: Boeotian.

Hydra: A many-headed venomous monster of Lerna in Argolis. It was killed by Heracles.

Hyetis: A spring in Miletus of Caria, Asia Minor.

Hygeia: "Health." A daughter or the wife of Asclepius.

Hylaeus: A centaur who insulted Atalanta and was shot by her.

Hylas: Son of Theiodamas. He was reared by Heracles and became his squire. He originally belonged to the local mythology of the Ciani, a people on the southern shore of the Propontis, Asia Minor.

Hylleans: Phaeacians led by Heracles' son Hyllus, who established a colony in the northern Adriatic, or Cronian, Sea.

Hyllus: 1. Son of Heracles and the Phaeacian nymph Melite. 2. A harbor on the Phaeacian island Drepane (Corcyra).

Hymen or Hymenaeus: The god of marriage.

Hyperasius: Father of the Argonauts Asterius and Amphion.

Hyperboreans: People living in the far North, favorites of Apollo.

Hypius: A river of Bithynia on the southern shore of the Black Sea near the Hellespont.

Hypseus: Father of Cyrene, the nymph with whom Apollo fell in love when he saw her wrestling with a lion.

Hypsipyle: Queen of Lemnos, an island in the northern Aegean.

Iapetus: A giant. Father of Prometheus.

Iasius: Father of the famous runner Atalanta.

Icmaeus: Epithet of Zeus as god of rain.

Ida: 1. A mountain near Troy where Paris judged three goddesses in a beauty contest. 2. A mountain on Crete where, in some versions, Zeus was reared in a cave. (Other versions locate the cave on Mount Dicte.)

Idalium: A place on Cyprus, seat of Aphrodite.

Idas: An Argonaut, son of Aphareus.

Idmon: An Argonaut, son of Apollo, who taught him the art of divination.

Ieso: "Healing one." A daughter of Asclepius.

Ilissus: A river of Attica in central Greece.

Illyrian: Of Illyria, the northwestern part of the Balkan Peninsula.

Imbrasus: A river on the island of Samos in the Aegean.

Imbros: An island in the northern Aegean Sea.

Inachus: Father of Io. King of Argos.

Indian: Of India. In Philodemus 5.132 this seems to be an exaggeration of Andromeda's exotic origin. She is usually said to be the daughter of an Ethiopian king. In the *Argonautica* "Indians" refers to the people living east and south of the Indus River, the eastern boundary of Alexander's empire.

Inopus: A spring in Delos which was supposed to have a subterranean connection with Egypt.

Io: Daughter of Inachus, King of Argos. Hera turned her into a cow when she discovered Zeus' lust for the girl.

Iolcian tomb: The tomb of Pelias in Iolcus.

Iolcus: A town in Thessaly, northern Greece.

Ionian Sea: The sea between Greece and Italy.

Ionians: The Greek inhabitants of Asia Minor.

Iphias: A priestess of Artemis at Iolcus.

Iphicles: The mortal twin of Heracles. Son of Amphitryon and Alcmena.

Iphiclus: 1. An Argonaut, uncle of Jason. 2. An Argonaut from Aetolia, son of Thestius.

Iphinoe: A woman of Lemnos, the herald of Queen Hypsipyle.

Iphitus: 1. An Argonaut, son of Eurytus. 2. An Argonaut, son of Naubolus.

Iris: 1. The rainbow goddess and messenger of Hera. 2. A river of Assyria on the southern shore of the Black Sea.

Irus: Father of the Argonaut Eurytion.

Ismenus: A river of Boeotia in central Greece. On its bank near Thebes there was a sanctuary of Apollo.

Issa: One of the Liburnian islands in the Adriatic Sea off the coast of Illyria.

Ister: A river of Thrace in the Balkan Peninsula, now the Danube. Contrary to the geography of Apollonius, the Danube does not open into the Adriatic.

Isthmian: Of the isthmus of Corinth, between the Peloponnesus and central Greece. The Isthmian Games were in honor of Poseidon.

Italy: A country in southern Europe.

Itone: City in Thessaly.

Itonian: An epithet of Athena, because of her cult at Itone.

Itymoneus: 1. One of the Doliones. 2. One of the Bebrycians.

Ixion: King of the Lapiths in Thessaly. For insulting Hera he was bound to a perpetually revolving wheel in Hades.

Jason: The son of Aeson. Leader of the Argonauts.

Kids: The constellation.

Kore: A name for Persephone, the daughter of Demeter who was abducted by Hades.

Labdacus: Son of Polydorus. Grandson of Cadmus of Thebes.

Lacedaemon: Sparta, both the city and the surrounding territory, in Laconia, southeastern Peloponnesus.

Lacereia: A city of Thessaly in northern Greece.

Ladon: The dragon who lived with the Hesperides and guarded the golden apples.

Lampeia: A district in Arcadia in the central Peloponnesus.

Lampetia: The elder daughter of Helios who tended his cattle.

Lamprion: Father of Pataikiskos in Herodas IV.

Laocoon: An Argonaut, the illegitimate brother of Oeneus and guardian of Meleager.

Laomedon: Legendary king of Troy.

Lapiths: A savage mountain race living near Mount Olympus in Thessaly. Famous for their battle with the Centaurs.

Larisa: A city of Thessaly in northern Greece.

Latmian: Refers to Latmus, a mountain in Caria, Asia Minor, where Selene (the Moon) lulled Endymion to sleep.

Laurium: A plain near the basin of the Ister (Danube) River, inhabited by the Sindi.

Leda: Mother of the Argonauts Castor and Polydeuces.

Lemnos: An island in the northern Aegean inhabited by women who had killed their husbands and sons. The island was sacred to Hephaestus, the smith god.

Leodocus: An Argonaut, son of Bias.

Leonidas of Tarentum: Epigrammatist of the *Greek Anthology.* Of Tarentum in southern Italy, third century B.C.

Lerna: A lake in Argolis in the Peloponnesus. Famous as the home of the Lernaean Hydra.

Lernus: 1. The son of Proetus; Lernus and Proetus are ancestors of the Argonaut Nauplius. 2. The reputed father of the Argonaut Palaemonius, whose father was actually Hephaestus.

Lesbos: An island in the Aegean where the poet Sappho lived.

Lethaean: Of the river Lethe in the underworld. Drinking of its water caused complete forgetfulness.

Leto: Daughter of the Titan Coeus; mother of Apollo and Artemis.

Liburnian islands: Islands off the coast of Illyria in the Adriatic Sea. Issa, Dysceladus, and Pityeia.

Libya: 1. A country in North Africa. 2. A nymph, wife of Triton.

Ligyans: People living in Liguria, the area around the mouth of the Rhone River.

Ligystian islands: A chain of islands northwest of Corsica off the coast of Liguria. Also called Stoechades.

Lilybean point: A promontory in western Sicily.

Limnae: Perhaps in Athens but more probably in Laconia, the Peloponnesus.

Linus: Son of Apollo and tutor of Heracles, who killed him with a blow of the lyre.

Lipara: The largest of the Aeolian islands north of Sicily.

Locrian: Of Locris, a district in central Greece.

Loves: The Erotes or Cupids.

Lusa: A place in Arcadia, the Peloponnesus.

Lycaean range: In Arcadia, the Peloponnesus.

Lycaon: Father of Helice; king of Arcadia, in the central Peloponnesus.

Lycastians: A tribe of Amazons living in Assyria on the southern shore of the Black Sea.

Lycia: A district in southern Asia Minor.

Lycidas: In *Idyll* VII a mysterious figure often thought to be a known poet in disguise. Sometimes thought to be Pan. The name, however, is common even outside bucolic poetry, and he may be a real person of that name otherwise unknown.

Lycope: In *Idyll* VII probably not the town in Aetolia but a place on Cos.

Lycopeus: In *Idyll* VII probably a real person otherwise unknown.

Lycoreian: Epithet of Apollo, from Lycoreia, a town on Mount Parnassus above Delphi.

Lycoreus: A servant of Amycus, king of the Bebrycians.

Lyctian: Of Lyctus, a town in Crete.

Lycurgus: An Arcadian who sent his son Ancaeus to join the Argonauts.

Lycus: 1. King of the Mariandyni, a people on the southern shore of the Black Sea neighboring the Bebrycians. 2. A river of Bithynia on the southern shore of the Black Sea, in the land of the Mariandyni. 3. A river of Colchis at the eastern end of the Black Sea.

Lygdamis: A king of the Cimmerians.

Lynceus: An Argonaut, son of Aphareus, known for his excellent vision.

Lyra: A place in Paphlagonia on the southern shore of the Black Sea where Orpheus dedicated his lyre to Apollo.

Lyrceian: Epithet of the city Argos in the eastern Peloponnesus.

Machaon: Son of Asclepius. A physician.

Macrians: A people of Greek origin living south of the Propontis in the mountains near Cyzicus. They were at war with the Doliones.

Macris: 1. The island of the Phaeacians, also called Drepane or Phaeacia, which is probably Corcyra. 2. Daughter of Aristaeus who nursed the baby Dionysus in Euboea. Pursued by Hera, she took refuge in a cave on Drepane.

Macrones: A people of the southern shore of the Black Sea near Colchis.

Maenalian: Of Mount Maenalus in Arcadia.

Maenalus: A mountain in Arcadia, sacred to Pan.

Magnesia: 1. A district in Thessaly in northern Greece. 2. A district in Caria in Asia Minor.

Maia: The mother of the messenger god Hermes.

Maid or Maiden: Persephone.

Malis: A nymph.

Malta: The island at the western end of the Mediterranean.

Manger: The cluster Praesepe in the constellation Cancer.

Mariandyni: A people of Bithynia on the southern shore of the Black Sea. They were enemies of King Amycus and the Bebrycians.

Medea: An enchantress. Daughter of King Aeetes of Colchis.

Megabrontes: One of the Doliones.

Megalossaces: One of the Doliones.

Megarians: Colonists from Megara in central Greece who settled on the southern coast of the Black Sea in the land of the Mariandyni.

Melampus: Brother of Bias.

Melanippe: An Amazon who was kidnapped by Heracles and ransomed by her sister Hippolyte.

Melantian rocks: Rocks near the island Calliste (Thera) in the Aegean Sea.

Melas: A son of Phrixus.

Meleager: 1. An Argonaut, son of Oeneus. 2. A poet fl. ca. 100 B.C., born in Gadara in Palestine. Educated at Tyre of Phoenicia. Spent his later life on the island of Cos. Compiled after 93 B.C. an anthology of epigrams of which 134 were his own.

Meles: A river near Smyrna in Ionia, Asia Minor, where Homer is sometimes said to have been born.

Meliboea: A city of Magnesia in northern Greece.

Melie: A nymph, mother of Amycus, king of the Bebrycians.

Meligunis: A name for the island Lipara.

Melissae: Priestesses of Delphi. The name means "bees."

Melite: A nymph, mother of Hyllus by Heracles. 2. An island in the Adriatic Sea.

Meliteius: A mountain on Corcyra, named for the nymph Melite.

Memnon: Son of Dawn and Tithonus. His tomb was visited every year by birds called Memnonidae, descendants of Memnon.

Menelaus: Son of Atreus, brother of Agamemnon, and husband of Helen.

Menetes: Father of Antianeira.

Menoetius: An Argonaut, son of Actor.

Mentores: A people of Illyria on the east coast of the Adriatic.

Merops: Father of Cleite.

Midas: A king of Phrygia whose touch turned everything into gold. Because he preferred Pan's piping to Apollo's, Apollo gave him ass's ears. Midas hid them from everyone except his barber, who entrusted the secret to a hole in the ground. Later, reeds that covered the place revealed the secret when shaken by the wind.

Midea: A town in Argolis in the Peloponnesus.

Miletus: A city in Caria, Asia Minor.

Mimas: 1. One of the giants slain at Phlegra. 2. A mountain in Ionia, opposite the island of Chios, Asia Minor. 3. A Bebrycian.

Minoan: 1. Of Minos. 2. Of Crete.

Minos: King of Crete, son of Zeus and father of Ariadne.

Minyae or Minyans: 1. The descendants of Minyas. 2. By extension, the Argonauts, many of whom were descendants of Minyas.

Minyas: Son of Aeolus; founder of Orchomenus in Boeotia.

Mise: Originally perhaps a Phrygian deity. Introduced into Eleusinian myth of Demeter and Kore. She persuaded Demeter to break her fast of mourning for Kore.

Mitylene: A town of Lesbos, an island in the Aegean, where the poet Sappho was born, ca. 612 B.C.

Mnasalcas: An epigrammatist of the *Greek Anthology*. Probably of Sicyon and of the third century B.C.

Mopsus: Son of Ampycus; a seer and one of the Argonauts.

Morning Mist: Egypt.

Moschus: Lived in Syracuse. Fl. ca. 150 B.C. Author of the *Europa*.

Mossynoeci: A people of the southern shore of the Black Sea.

Mount of Bears: Arcton, a peak near Cyzicus on the southern shore of the Propontis.

Munychia: A harbor of Athens, where Artemis had a temple.

Muses: Daughters of Zeus and Memory; patronesses of all the arts.

Museum: The Mouseion at Alexandria. A famous seat of learning, it included the famous library, observatories, laboratories, dining halls, a park, and a zoo.

Mycenae: A city of Argolis in the Peloponnesus, ruled by Eurystheus.

Mygdoni: Neighbors of the Mariandyni.

Mygdonian: Phrygian. The flute was supposed to have come with the worship of Dionysus from Phrygia in Asia Minor.

Myllos: In Herodas III the name may imply "fool."

Myndus: A town on the coast of Caria, Asia Minor.

Myrine: A city on the island Lemnos.

Myrmidon: Father of Eupolemeia and grandfather of the Argonaut Aethalides.

Myrmidons: Inhabitants of Aegina, an island in the Saronic Gulf between Argolis and Attica.

Myrtilus: Oenomaus' charioteer during the race in which Pelops won Oenomaus' daughter Hippodameia. In one version Pelops bribed Myrtilus to sabotage his master's chariot, but when Myrtilus asked for his reward, Pelops pushed him off a cliff. As he fell he cursed Pelops' descendants, among whom were Atreus and Agamemnon.

Myrtle-hill: Myrtyssa in Cyrene.

Myrtosian peak: A mountain near Cyrene in Libya.

Mysia: A country in Asia Minor.

Naiads: River nymphs.

Nannakos: A mythical Phrygian king before Deucalion. Foresaw the flood and called together his people to try to appease the gods with tears.

Narex: A mouth of the river Ister (Danube), opening on the Black Sea.

Nasamon: A Libyan, brother of Caphaurus.

Naubolus: 1. An ancestor of the Argonaut Nauplius. 2. Father of the Argonaut Iphitus.

Nauplius: 1. Son of Poseidon; ancestor of the Argonaut Nauplius. 2. An Argonaut, son of Clytonaeus.

Nausithous: King of the Phaeacians before Alcinous.

Naxos: An Aegean island. See Dia.

Neleus: Son of Codrus, founder of Miletus. King of Pylos, a city in southern Peloponnesus, and father of Pero and the Argonaut Periclymenus.

Nemesis: Anger or Indignation, personified in the *Bath of Pallas*.

Nepeian plain: The plain by the city Adrasteia on the southern shore of the Propontis.

Nereids: Daughters of Nereus. Sea nymphs.

Nereus: A sea god, sometimes called "the old man of the sea."

Nestaeans: A people of Illyria. Some lived on the more northerly shores of the Adriatic, where Apollonius thought the Ister (Danube) had a mouth. Others lived toward the south, in the Ceraunian Mountains opposite Drepane (Corcyra).

Nestian land: The northeastern shores of the Adriatic.

Nicias: A physician and poet, friend of Theocritus.

Nicippe: A priestess in the *Hymn to Demeter.*

Nile: The great river of Egypt.

Nisaeans: See Megarians. Nisa is the port of Megara, a city in central Greece.

Nomius: "Of shepherds," an epithet of Apollo.

Nycheia: A nymph.

Nycteus: A brother of the king of Thebes. Father of Antiope.

Nymphaea: The island of Calypso. It was located somewhere in the southern Adriatic, perhaps near Drepane (Corcyra).

Nysa: A town in Caria, Asia Minor.

Nyseian: "Of Nysa," an epithet of Dionysus.

Oaxus: A river or town of Crete.

Ocean or Oceanus: One of the Titans, envisioned as a river flowing around the earth and seas.

Odysseus: The hero of Homer's *Odyssey.*

Oeagrus: Father of Orpheus. King of Thrace in northern Greece.

Oechalia: A city of Euboea in central Greece.

Oecus: A town of Caria in Asia Minor.

Oedipus: King of Thebes, who blinded himself upon discovering that he had killed his own father and married his own mother.

Oeneus: King of Calydon in Aetolia, who neglected to sacrifice to Artemis. In revenge she sent the Calydonian boar to ravage his lands. Father of the Argonauts Meleager and Laocoon.

Oenoe: 1. A nymph who rescued and married Thoas, the father of Hypsipyle. 2. An island in the Cyclades named for the nymph Oenoe, later called Sicinus after her son by Thoas.

Oenomaus: Father of Hippodameia. See also Myrtilus.

Ogygian: An epithet of Thebes, after its mythical king Ogyges.

Oileus: An Argonaut from Locris in central Greece.

Olenian: Of Olenus, a city of Aetolia in central Greece.

Olympus: A mountain in Macedonia, northern Greece, where the gods live.

Onchestus: A city of Boeotia in central Greece.

Ophion: A god who ruled Olympus in ancient times but was cast out with his wife, Eurynome, by Rhea and Cronus.

Opus: A city of Locris in central Greece.

Orchomenus: 1. Son of Minyas and king of the town Orchomenus. 2. A town in Boeotia.

Oread: Of the mountains.

Oreides: A Bebrycian.

Oreithyia: Daughter of the Athenian king Erechtheus. She was carried off by Boreas, the North Wind, and became the mother of the Argonauts Zetes and Calais.

Oricus: A city of Epirus in northern Greece.

Orion: 1. A mythical hunter of great beauty. Slain by Artemis because he outraged her while she was hunting. 2. The constellation, important for navigation.

Ormenidae: In Callimachus' *Hymn to Demeter*, the sons of Ormenus.

Ornytus: 1. A Bebrycian. 2. Grandfather of the Argonaut Iphitus.

Oromedon: Presumably a mountain on the south coast of Cos.

Orpheus: A bard and one of the Argonauts. Son of Oeagrus and the Muse Calliope. Famous for bringing his wife Eurydice back from the underworld.

Ortygia: A name for Delos, the island where Leto gave birth to Apollo and Artemis.

Ossa: A mountain in Thessaly, northern Greece, said to be one of the mountains piled on Olympus by the giants Otus and Ephialtes.

Othrys: A mountain in Thessaly, northern Greece.

Otrere: A queen of the Amazons.

Otus: A gigantic son of Poseidon who fell in love with Artemis and was slain by her.

Pactolus: A river of Lydia in Asia Minor.

Paean: Hymn, song, or chant to Apollo.

Paeëon: Either Apollo the "Healer" or the hymn to him as such. In *Argonautica* IV Paeëon is the physician of the gods. Again, probably an epithet of Apollo.

Paeon: Apollo the "Healer."

Pagasae: The port of Iolcus in Thessaly in northern Greece, where the Argonauts began their voyage.

Palaemonius: An Argonaut, son of Hephaestus. His reputed father was Lernus.

Pallas: A name for Athena.

Pallatid Rocks: The hill of Creion, named from the Palladium (a carved image of Pallas).

Pallene: A promontory of the Chalcidice Peninsula in the northern Aegean Sea.

Pan: A rustic deity of shepherds. Usually portrayed as partly human in form but with the horns, ears, and legs of a goat. Plays the pipes, which he is sometimes said to have invented.

Panaceia: All-healing.

Panake: "Healer of all." A daughter of Asclepius.

Panopeus: A town in Phocis, central Greece.

Paphian: Aphrodite. Of Paphos, a city on the island of Cyprus in the eastern Mediterranean.

Paphlagonians: Inhabitants of Paphlagonia on the southern shore of the Black Sea. They are descendants of Pelops.

Paraebius: A friend of Phineus in the *Argonautica*.

Parian: Parian marble, from the island Paros in the Aegean. The best quality Parian was snow-white in color.

Paris: Son of Priam who stole Helen from Menelaus and so caused the Trojan War. In Herodas I the reference is to the beauty contest in which he chose Aphrodite because she promised him the most beautiful woman in the world.

Parnassus: A mountain in Phocis, central Greece, sacred to Apollo and the Muses.

Paros: An island in the Aegean, birthplace of the poet Archilochus, born ca. 700 B.C.

Parrhasian: Of Parrhasia, a district in Arcadia in the central Peloponnesus.

Parthenia: A name of the island of Samos on the Aegean coast of Asia Minor.

Parthenius: A river of Paphlagonia in Asia Minor.

Pasiphaë: Daughter of Helios, wife of Minos, mother of Ariadne and of the Minotaur, born from her union with a great bull sent by Poseidon.

Pataikiskos: In Herodas IV the name may imply "thief."

Patroclus: Greek hero of the Trojan War. Achilles' best friend.

Pegae: A spring in Mysia on the southern coast of the Propontis. The word simply means "spring."

Pegasus: Bellerophon's winged horse. A blow from his hoof created the fountain Hippocrene on Mount Helicon in Boeotia, central Greece.

Peiresiae: 1. A city of Thessaly in northern Greece. 2. A city on the coast of Magnesia in northern Greece. These two may be the same city.

Peirithous: King of the Lapiths.

Pelasgian: 1. Of the people of Thessaly in northern Greece. 2. Of the Macrians, a people of the Propontis who lived in the mountains near Cyzicus. They were emigrants from Greece. 3. Used as a name for the Greeks in general.

Pelasgus: A legendary ancestor of the Arcadians. Said to have been born of the earth. The Pelasgi were supposed to have been the earliest inhabitants of Greece.

Peleus: An Argonaut, son of Aeacus. He was the father of Achilles.

Pelian: Of Mount Pelion in Thessaly in northern Greece.

Pelias: King of Iolcus in northern Greece. Half-brother of Aeson and uncle of Jason, whom he sent for the golden fleece. While Jason was away, he killed Aeson. In revenge Medea persuaded his daughters to cut him in pieces and boil him in a cauldron on the pretext of restoring his youth.

Pelion: A mountain in Thessaly, northern Greece.

Pellene: A city of Achaea in the northern Peloponnesus.

Pelles: Grandfather of the Argonauts Asterius and Amphion and founder of the city Pellene.

348

Pelopeia: Daughter of Pelias.

Pelopidae: Descendants of Pelops, a mythical king of Phrygia.

Pelops: Founder of the house of Atreus. Son of Tantalus, father of Atreus and Thyestes, grandfather of Agamemnon and Menelaus. He was said to be the ancestor of the Paphlagonians, a people of the Black Sea. See also Myrtilus.

Peneus or Peneius: The chief river of Thessaly in northern Greece.

Percosian: Of Percote.

Percote: A city in the Troad in Asia Minor.

Perge: A city in Pamphylia, Asia Minor.

Periclymenus: An Argonaut, son of Neleus, and a favorite of Poseidon.

Perimede: No enchantress of this name is otherwise known. It may be just another name for Medea.

Pero: Daughter of Neleus; mother of the Argonauts Areius, Talaus, and Leodocus.

Perse: Wife of Helios and mother of the witch Circe.

Persephone: Daughter of Demeter. Carried off to the underworld by Hades. Also called Kore.

Perses: Father of Hecate.

Perseus: Son of Zeus and Danae and a hero of Argolis in the Peloponnesus. He killed the gorgon Medusa and rescued the princess Andromeda from a sea monster.

Peuce: An island at the mouth of the Ister (Danube) in the Black Sea.

Phaeacians: The people of the island Drepane (Corcyra) off the coast of northwestern Greece, known for their luxuries and their expertise in sailing. Their king was Alcinous.

Phaethon: 1. Another name for Apsyrtus. The word means "the shining one." 2. The son of Helios. He convinced his father to let him drive the sun chariot for a day but lost control of the horses and was hurled to earth by a lightning bolt from Zeus.

Phaethusa: A daughter of Helios and guardian of his sheep.

Phalerus: An Argonaut, son of Alcon.

Phasis: A river in Colchis falling into the Black Sea. It had its source in the Amarantine Mountains.

Pherae: A city in Thessaly in northern Greece ruled by the Argonaut Admetus. There Artemis was worshipped as Hecate.

Philammon: A musician. Son of Apollo.

Philetas: Coan poet and scholar, tutor to the young Ptolemy Philadelphus.

Philinus: This was the name of a famous Coan runner, but the man named in *Idyll* II is probably not literally the same. He is probably not the Philinus in *Idyll* VII either.

Philodemus: Epigrammatist of the *Greek Anthology*. First century B.C. Of Gadara in Palestine.

Philyra: 1. A daughter of Ocean; the mother of the centaur Cheiron by the Titan Cronus. 2. An island in the eastern part of the Black Sea where Philyra lived.

Philyres: A people of the Black Sea living on the island of Philyra or the neighboring coast.

Phineus: A blind seer, son of Agenor, living on the coast of the Black Sea near the Bosporus. He was tormented by the Harpies for revealing the will of Zeus to men.

Phlegra: A district in Macedonia. Site of the battle between the gods and the giants.

Phlias: An Argonaut, son of the wine god Dionysus.

Phlogius: 1. One of the Doliones. 2. One of the three sons of Deimachus, former companions of Heracles who joined the Argonauts in Assyria.

Phocians: People of Phocis, a district in central Greece that includes Apollo's oracle at Delphi (Pytho).

Phocus: A son of Aeacus, killed by his brothers the Argonauts Telamon and Peleus.

Phoebus: A name of Apollo.

Phoenicia: A country in Asia Minor.

Phoenix: Father of Europa (in Moschus).

Pholus: A centaur who lived on Mount Pholus in Arcadia. He entertained Heracles with a cask of wine presented to the centaurs by Dionysus.

Phorcys: A sea god, father of the monster Scylla.

Phrasidamus: In *Idyll* VII probably a real person but otherwise unknown.

Phrixus: A son of Nephele and Athamas, king of Orchomenus. Phrixus' stepmother, Ino, tried to kill him and his sister Helle. They escaped on the back of a golden ram sent by Zeus. Phrixus flew all the way to Colchis, but Helle fell into the sea.

Phrontis: One of the sons of Phrixus who were traveling from Colchis to Orchomenus to claim their inheritance when they were shipwrecked and rescued by the Argonauts.

Phrygia: A country in Asia Minor. In *Idyll* XV the name of a slave girl probably from Phrygia.

Phrygian: Of Phrygia, but in the *Bath of Pallas* it refers to Paris.

Phthia: A city of Thessaly in northern Greece, home of the Argonaut Pelius.

Phylace: A city of Thessaly.

Phylacus: Maternal grandfather of Jason.

Phylleian mountain: A peak in Thessaly in northern Greece.

Phyllis: A river in Bithynia on the southern shore of the Black Sea.

Physadeia: A spring at Argos in the Peloponessus.

Pieria: A district of Thrace in northern Greece ruled by the Argonaut Orpheus. It was also thought to be the home of the Muses.

Pierides: A name of the Muses.

Pimpleian: Of Pimpleia, a mountain in Thrace in northern Greece where Orpheus was born.

Pindar: The great choral poet of the late sixth–early fifth centuries B.C. He was born in Thebes in Boeotia, central Greece.

Pindus: A mountain in Thessaly, northern Greece.

Pisa: A town in Elis, the Peloponnesus. The site of the Olympian Games.

Pitane: A place on the river Eurotas in Laconia, the Peloponnesus, with a temple of Artemis.

Pityeia: 1. A city of the Troad in Asia Minor. 2. One of the Liburnian islands in the Adriatic Sea.

Plato: The fourth-century Athenian philosopher.

Pleiades: The constellation. It sets in winter and rises in summer.

Pleistus: A river of Pytho (Delphi), the sanctuary of Apollo in central Greece.

Pluto: God of the underworld.

Podaleirius: Son of Asclepius. A physician.

Polydeuces: An Argonaut from Lacedaemon in the Peloponnesus, brother of Castor. Both were sons of Zeus and were worshiped as the Dioscuroi.

Polyphemus: 1. One of the Cyclopes, one-eyed, cannibalistic giants. 2. An Argonaut, son of Eilatus.

Polyxo: The aged nurse of Hypsipyle, queen of Lemnos in the northern Aegean.

Pontus: The Black Sea. Also called the Euxine Sea.

Poseidon: God of the sea and earthquakes, brother of Zeus and Hades.

Posideian headland: A cape on the eastern end of the Propontis.

Praxiteles: Famous Greek sculptor of the fourth century B.C.

Priapus: A rustic deity of fertility. Represented as a grotesque human with a huge and erect phallus. He was a guardian of gardens, a kind of scarecrow, to warn off thieves but also to bring good luck.

Priolas: Brother of Lycus, king of the Mariandyni.

Proetus: Son of Nauplius, the ancestor of the Argonaut Nauplius.

Prometheus: A Titan who stole fire from the Olympians and gave it to men. Zeus punished him by chaining him to a rock in the Caucasus Mountains east of the Black Sea and sending an eagle every day to devour his liver.

Promeus: One of the Doliones.

Propontis: The sea at the head of the Hellespont in Asia Minor.

Prytaneia: The city chambers.

Pseudo-Moschus: A pupil of Bion who came from southern Italy but is otherwise unknown. Author of the *Lament for Bion*.

Ptelea: This is probably a place in Cos, but it is not certain.

Pterelaus: King of Taphos, an island in the Ionian Sea. Vanquished by Amphitryon with the help of Pterelaus' daughter, who pulled out the golden hair that was the source of his strength.

Ptolemy: 1. In *Idyll* XV, Ptolemy II Phildelphus, reigned 285–46 B.C. 2. In Antipater of Sidon 7.241 probably Ptolemy Philometer, reigned 180–ca. 145 B.C., whose son Eupator died in or about 150 B.C. There were full eclipses of the moon visible in Egypt in both July and December of 150 B.C.

Pylos: A city of Messenia in the southern Peloponnesus.

Pyrrhus: Son of Achilles. Also called Neoptolemus.

Pytho: Delphi, the seat of Apollo's oracle in Phocis, central Greece.

Pyxa: A town on Cos.

Ram's Bed: A place in Colchis near the grove that contained the golden fleece.

Rhamnus: A place in Attica, central Greece.

Rhea: A Titaness, the wife of Cronus and mother of Zeus. She was identified by the Greeks with Cybele, the Great Mother goddess of Asia Minor.

Rhebas: A river of Bithynia on the southern shore of the Black Sea. Its mouth is close to the Bosporus.

Rhipaean Mountains: Mountains in the land of the Hyperboreans in the far north.

Rhodanus: The river Rhone.

Rhodope: A mountain range in Thrace, northern Greece.

Rhoecus: A centaur who insulted Atalanta and was slain by her.

Rhoeteian shore: A cape on the coast of Asia Minor at the Hellespont.

Rhyndacus: A river of Phrygia in northern Asia Minor.

Rufinus: Epigrammatist of the *Greek Anthology.* Second century A.D.?

Sacred Rock: A rock near Cyzicus where the Argonauts landed by mistake.

Salangon: A river in Illyria on the western side of the Balkan Peninsula.

Salmone's point: A headland on the eastern end of Crete.

Samos: An island in the Aegean, off the coast of Ephesus in Asia Minor.

Samothrace: An island in the northern Aegean.

Sangarius: A river flowing through Bithynia on the southern coast of the Black Sea.

Sapeires: A people on the southern shore of the Black Sea close to Colchis.

Sappho: One of the greatest of the lyric poets. Born ca. 612 B.C. in Mitylene on the island of Lesbos in the Aegean.

Sardinian sea: The part of the Mediterranean immediately west of Sardinia and Corsica.

Sardis: A city in Lydia, Asia Minor.

Sarpedonian rock: A rock in Thrace, the area immediately north of the Aegean Sea.

Satyrs: Wild companions of Dionysus, usually represented with long, pointed ears, the stumps of horns, tails, hairy bodies, and erect phalluses.

Sauromatae: A people of Scythia, a vaguely defined area north of Thrace. The name was also applied to a people living north and east of the Black Sea.

Sciathos: An island near Magnesia in northern Greece.

Scylla: A sea monster living in a underground cave, visualized as a rock at the entrance to the straits between Italy and Sicily, opposite Charybdis.

Scythian: 1. The Scyths were nomadic tribes to the north of the Black and Caspian seas. They were famous as horsemen. 2. In Apollonius, people living north of Thrace.

Sepian point: A cape in Magnesia in northern Greece.

Serbonian lake: A lake in lower Egypt where the monster Typhaon was buried by Zeus (in other versions he is located under Mount Aetna on Sicily).

Sesamus: A city of Paphlagonia on the southern shore of the Black Sea.

Sesostris: A mythical king of Egypt.

Sicanians: Sicilians.

Sicelidas: The epigrammatist of the *Greek Anthology* commonly called Asclepiades.

Sicily: The large island in the Mediterranean at the foot of Italy.

Sicinus: 1. Son of Thoas, the former king of Lemnos. 2. An island in the Aegean Sea, also called Oenoe.

Sigynni: A people living on the river Ister (Danube).

Simichidas: Probably to be identified with Theocritus himself in *Idyll* VII.

Simois: A river near Troy, Asia Minor.

Sindi: A people living on the river Ister (Danube).

Sinope: Daughter of Asopus, brought to Assyria on the southern shore of the Black Sea by Zeus.

Sintian: An epithet of the island Lemnos in the northern Aegean. The Sintians were the former inhabitants of the island who received Hephaestus when he was cast out of Olympus.

Siphaean: An epithet of the Thespians, inhabitants of the city Thespiae in Boeotia in central Greece. Siphaea was a place-name in the area of Thespiae.

Sirens: Daughters of the river Achelous and the Muse Terpsichore. Birdlike women who sang so sweetly that they lured sailors aground on the island Anthemoessa and destroyed them.

Sirius: The Dog Star.

Soli: A city of Cilicia in Asia Minor. Birthplace of the poet Aratus.

Sparta: A city of Laconia, the Peloponnesus.

Sphodris: One of the Doliones.

Sporades: Islands in the Aegean Sea, east of the Cyclades.

Spring of the Horse: A spring on Mount Helicon, in Boeotia.

Springs of the Hours: See Hours.

Steropes: One of the Cyclopes.

Sthenelus: A companion of Heracles on his expedition against the Amazons. Sthenelus was killed, and his tomb was built in Paphlagonia on the southern shore of the Black Sea.

Stoechades: Islands northwest of Corsica and Sardinia, close to the European coast.

Straits of the Cow: The Bosporus. The "cow" is Io.

Strymonian: Of the river Strymon in Thrace, northern Greece.

Stymphaean: Of Stymphaea in Epirus, northern Greece.

Stymphalian lake: A lake in Arcadia in the central Peloponnesus inhabited by great birds with bronze feathers. The birds were killed by Heracles as his sixth labor.

Styx: A river of Hades, the underworld. Any god who swore by the river Styx was unable to break his oath.

Syracusans: The people of the city of Syracuse on Sicily, a Doric settlement.

Syria: A country in Asia Minor.

Syrtis: A gulf on the coast of Libya in northern Africa.

Taenarus: 1. A city of Laconia in the Peloponnesus. 2. A promontory on the southern Peloponnesus. An entrance to the underworld was thought to be there.

Talaus: An Argonaut, son of Bias.

Talos: A bronze giant who guarded Crete

Taphians: Inhabitants of islands off the coast of Acarnania in central Greece. They had a reputation as pirates. They were sometimes called Teleboae.

Tartarus: The underworld.

Taurian: Of the Tauri, a people of Scythian descent, near the Crimea. They worshipped Artemis with human sacrifice.

Taygeton: A mountain near Sparta in Laconia, the Peloponnesus.

Tegea: A city of Arcadia in the central Peloponnesus.

Teiresias: The famous Greek seer of Thebes who foretold Oedipus' fate. He was blinded in his youth for having seen Athena bathing.

Telamon: A hero especially associated with Heracles in the expeditions against the Amazons and against Troy. He was also one of the Argonauts; son of Aeacus and brother of Peleus.

Teleboae: See Taphians.

Telecles: One of the Doliones.

Telemus: A seer who lived among the Cyclopes and prophesied the blinding of Polyphemus by Odysseus.

Teleon: 1. Father of the Argonaut Butes. 2. Father of the Argonaut Eribotes.

Telephaasa: Mother of Europa (in Moschus' *Europa*).

Tenos: An island in the Aegean.

Teos: A town in Lydia, Asia Minor, where the poet Anacreon was born ca. 570 B.C.

Terpsichore: The Muse of dancing; wife of Achelous and mother of the Sirens.

Tethys: The wife of Oceanus.

Teucrian: Trojan.

Thebe: 1. A nymph, daughter of Triton, who gave her name to the city of Thebes in Egypt. 2. The city Thebes in Boeotia in central Greece.

Thebes: 1. A city of Boeotia, central Greece. It was originally founded as Cadmeia by Cadmus, but Amphion and Zethus built its walls and renamed it. 2. A city in Egypt.

Theiodamas: King of the Dryopians, central Greece; father of Hylas, Heracles' squire.

Themis: A goddess of justice and prophecy. A Titaness, mother of the Seasons and the Fates.

Themiscyra: A town in Assyria on the southern shore of the Black Sea where a tribe of Amazons lived.

Themiscyreian headland: A promontory neighboring the town Themiscyra.

Theocritus: Born in Syracuse. Lived in Alexandria and probably Cos. Fl. 280 B.C. Creator of pastoral poetry. Also wrote epyllia and epigrams.

Thera: An island in the Aegean, also a city on the island.

Therapnaean: Of Therapnae, a city in Laconia in the Peloponnesus. This name was applied to Polydeuces because Castor and Polydeuces had their sanctuary and tomb in the city.

Theras: A descendant of the Argonaut Euphemus who left Sparta to found a colony on one of the Cyclades, Calliste (Thera), to which he gave his name.

Thermodon: A river of Assyria on the southern shore of the Black Sea.

Theseus: King of Athens, sometimes counted among the Argonauts. With Ariadne's help he slew the Minotaur. When he left Crete, he took Ariadne with him but abandoned her on the island of Dia (Naxos).

Thespiae: A town in Boeotia, central Greece.

Thestius: Father of the Argonaut Iphiclus from Aetolia.

Thetis: A sea goddess; mother of Achilles and wife of the Argonaut Peleus.

Thoas: Father of Hypsipyle and former king of the Lemnians. He was the only man to escape the massacre of the Lemnian men.

Thrace: The area immediately north of the Aegean Sea, bordering on northern Greece to the west and forming the northern coast of the Propontis to the east.

Thrinacia: Sicily. See Trinacia.

Thunderbolts: Mountains in the region of Illyria.

Thybris: In *Idyll* I this appears to be a mountain which is otherwise unknown.

Thyiades: Bacchants, ecstatic followers of the wine god Dionysus.

Thynia: The area around the European side of the Bosporus.

Thynias: An island off the coast of Bithynia.

Tibareni: A people of the southern shore of the Black Sea.

Timon: A famous Athenian misanthrope of the fifth century B.C.

Tiphys: An Argonaut, son of Hagnias; the Argonauts' helmsman.

Tisaean headland: A promontory in Thessaly in northern Greece.

Titanian goddess: The Moon.

Titans: Giants who warred against Zeus for supremacy in Heaven and were cast down into Hades. Prometheus was among them.

Titaresian: Of Titaresus, a river of Thessaly in northern Greece.

Tithys: Wife of Oceanus.

Titias: I. One of the Dactyls. 2. One of the Mariandyni.

Tityrus: In *Idyll* I may be the name of a real poet in disguise but probably not.

Tityos: I. A giant who insulted Leto and was therefore slain by Artemis and Apollo. He lies outstretched in Hades and a vulture feeds on his liver. 2. In *Argonautica* I the father of Europa.

Tmarus: A mountain near Dodona in Epirus, northwestern Greece.

Trachis: A town in Thessaly, scene of Heracles' funeral pyre.

Tricca: A town in Thessaly. A center of the cult of Asclepius.

Trinacia: Sicily. The Trinacrian or Thrinacrian Sea is another name for the Ionian Sea, the Mediterranean between Greece and Italy.

Triopas: Father of Erysichthon.

Triopidae: The sons of Triopas, that is, Erysichthon's family. They were of Thessaly, northern Greece.

Triopum: Triopium in Caria, Asia Minor.

Triptolemus: Son of Celeus, king of Eleusis, inventor of agriculture and a judge in the underworld.

Triton: I. A sea god, son of Poseidon; lord of Lake Triton in Libya. He is also called Eurypylus. 2. The river Nile, father of the nymph Thebe for whom Egyptian Thebes was named. 3. "Tritons" is also a general name for sea gods.

Tritonian: Epithet of Pallas, who according to one account was born on Lake Triton near the smaller Syrtis in North Africa.

Troy: The city on the Hellespont that the Greeks besieged for ten years and burned to the ground.

Turning Islands: The Strophades, islands in the Ionian Sea west of the Peloponnesus. Formerly called the Plotae, or Floating Islands.

Twelve Blessed: The twelve Olympian gods.

Tydeus: Father of Diomedes. Adrastus had once purified him after a murder and gave him his daughter as a bride.

Tymnes: Nothing is known of this poet. His name is Carian and he may well have worked in the third century B.C., since his epigrams resemble those of Anyte.

Tyndareus: The husband of Leda and father of Helen and Clytemnestra. The father in name of Castor and Polydeuces, whose real father was Zeus.

Typhaon: A dragonlike monster born from Earth as a challenge to Zeus, who killed it with his thunderbolt. Typhaon's rock is a rock in the Caucasus Mountains on the eastern end of the Black Sea where the dragon who guarded the golden fleece was born from Typhaon's blood.

Typhoeus: Another spelling of Typhaon.

Tyrrhenian: Etruscan. Of the people who lived north of Rome, Italy.

Upis: A name for Artemis, especially in Ephesus, Lydia, Asia Minor.

Uranus: The sky personified as a god. He was one of the primordial gods and with Gaia, or Earth, produced the Titans.

Virgin: The constellation Virgo.

Wandering Rocks: The Planctae, a hazard to ships in the strait between Italy and Sicily.

Xanthus: A river of Lycia in Asia Minor.

Xenea: Known only from *Idyll* VII.

Xynian lake: A lake in Thessaly in northern Greece.

Zelys: One of the Doliones.

Zetes: An Argonaut, son of Boreas, the North Wind. He and his brother Calais were equipped with wings.

Zethus: Son of Zeus and Antiope; with his brother Amphion rebuilt the city of Thebes in Boeotia, central Greece.

Zeus: The king of the gods. His weapon is the thunderbolt.

Zone: A town in Thrace, the area north of the Aegean Sea.

Wisconsin Studies in Classics

General Editors
Barbara Hughes Fowler and Warren G. Moon

E. A. Thompson
Romans and Barbarians: The Decline of the Western Empire

Jennifer Tolbert Roberts
Accountability in Athenian Government

H. I. Marrou
A History of Education in Antiquity

Erika Simon
Festivals of Attica: An Archaeological Commentary

G. Michael Woloch
Roman Cities: Les villes romaines by Pierre Grimal,
translated and edited by G. Michael Woloch,
together with A Descriptive Catalogue of Roman Cities by G. Michael Woloch

Warren G. Moon, *editor*
Ancient Greek Art and Iconography

Katherine Dohan Morrow
Greek Footwear and the Dating of Sculpture

John Kevin Newman
The Classical Epic Tradition

Jeanny Vorys Canby, Edith Porada, Brunilde Sismondo Ridgway, and
Tamara Stech, *editors*
Ancient Anatolia: Aspects of Change and Cultural Development

Ann Norris Michelini
Euripides and the Tragic Tradition

Wendy J. Raschke, *editor*
*The Archaeology of the Olympics: The Olympics and
Other Festivals in Antiquity*

Paul Plass
Wit and the Writing of History: The Rhetoric of Historiography in Imperial Rome

Barbara Hughes Fowler
The Hellenistic Aesthetic

F. M. Clover and R. S. Humphreys, *editors*
Tradition and Innovation in Late Antiquity

Brunilde Sismondo Ridgway
Hellenistic Sculpture I: The Styles of ca. 331–200 B.C.

Barbara Hughes Fowler, *editor and translator*
Hellenistic Poetry: An Anthology